PRAISE FOR LORRAINE

"*Gripping stories which illustrate the power of past life therapy. Where magical transformations can happen – and this sure ain't Kansas anymore....*"

URSULA JAMES

"*The clarity I have recently gained is fantastic and things are going from strength to strength. I have been blown away by the impact of the Past Life exploration – it's been immense, not only has it helped with my relationship but I am sure that it has brought me to this place of clarity.*"

ELIZABETH B.

"*The jigsaw puzzle of my life makes sense now. I can see where each piece fits and why it has to be there. The people, the events, even all the drama that I had as a child. I no longer feel fearful or that I am not good enough. I know for sure what I am supposed to be doing with my life, for the very first time. It is such a relief; thank you.*"

MARGARET C.

"*Hi, Lorraine, just wanted to say thank you for a very enlightening experience. I feel a sense of ease has come over me knowing which path to take...or to walk towards – a lot of the inner arguments; the 'should I or shouldn't I,' the 'whys' or 'what ifs' that have clouded my mind at times seem to have dissipated – the message that came across was crystal clear. Very best wishes to you – you are fantastic.*"

SALLY A.

"*Thanks to you, it really feels like I have made a breakthrough. I feel like I have loads of space in my head suddenly.*"

MICHELLE K.

Healing With Past Life Therapy

Transformational Journeys Through Time and Space

Lorraine Flaherty

FINDHORN PRESS

Published in 2013 by Findhorn Press, Scotland

ISBN 978-1-84409-634-3

Edited by Patricia Kot
Cover design by Richard Crookes
Interior design by Damian Keenan
Printed and bound in the EU

Published by
Findhorn Press
117-121 High Street,
Forres IV36 1AB,
Scotland, UK

t +44 (0)1309 690582
f +44 (0)131 777 2711
e info@findhornpress.com
www.findhornpress.com

Contents

Contents

Dedication

This book is dedicated to all the beings I have ever known and loved, to those I am yet to love, and all those that I will never know personally and yet love unconditionally anyway because they are all a part of the whole. I dedicate it to all the people who have ever lived and are yet to live; you are all amazing.

Especially Ursula James, who had an idea.

Introduction

Welcome. I would like to take this opportunity to introduce myself to you. My name – in this life – is Lorraine Flaherty. Although I feel compelled to say that I have had many other names and many other lives; some of which you will read about in the chapters of this book.

As I begin, I am very aware of the curious feeling that I always get when meeting new people for the first time, because you know how it goes: You get introduced and generally within a very short space of time the question that arises is "So, what do you do?" and usually I smile and say, "That is a very complicated question. How long have you got?" I do get a great deal of satisfaction when I say that I help people find their way to inner freedom, but I know from experience that this can generate some very strange looks. Telling people that I spend my day travelling through time and space does not seem to help matters either, and when I tell them that I spend a lot of time making people cry it really gets me in trouble. The work I do has developed into something really quite incredible over the years, and I feel very passionate about it; hence, the desire to share my discoveries, and the messages that these discoveries have revealed, in a book. The message that this book will deliver is both a spiritual and a practical one. It was born out of a huge sense of curiosity, because from a really early age I wanted to know why I was here, who I really was, and what I was meant to do with my life. As I looked around at other people who seemed really dissatisfied with their lives, who treated each other badly because of it, I couldn't help wonder if there wasn't some way to help them feel better. "Why can't people just be nice and be kind to one another?" I asked my father when I was about 7 years old. "Because life isn't like that," he said. "'Why not?" I asked. "It just isn't!" he replied. I don't think I ever stopped asking that question, and I still find myself asking it to this day when I see what is going on in the world around me. Thankfully, I do now have a much better understanding of what the answer to it really is. It was that question that led me on a quest, in search of something that would really make a difference to myself, the people around me, and even to the world as a whole. Eventually, after many years of study, and hands-on experience, I found it. I struck lucky and found a whole, magical set of tools that I could use to set myself and other people free.

Nowadays I get to take people on journeys into their subconscious world, to the place where all of their memories are stored, memories that can be good or bad, and then deal with them accordingly. They get to explore experiences from the past, present, future, and the space between lives to learn more about themselves and discover more about who they really are. This means that they no longer get distracted by unnecessary clutter in the back of their minds, and they are able to take more control and live more fully in the present. My goal in life is to help people to live their lives in a happier and more fulfilling way – free from all limitations. I feel very honoured and blessed that, every working day, I get to share incredible experiences with my clients. Their stories never cease to amaze me, and inspire me, and offer all kinds of invaluable insights into who people really are and why they live their lives in the way they do. I would like to share some of their amazing stories with you, here, in this book. But before I do that I would like to share with you a little of my own story and explain how I came to be having this transformational journey of my own, through this time and space.

I was one of those really annoying children that drove everyone around me crazy by asking the "Why" question all the time and from a very early age; much to the dismay of my parents, the priests, and the religion teachers at my *very* Catholic school, I questioned everything I was taught about the so called origins of mankind, particularly the stories they expected me to believe that stemmed from the Catholic doctrines. They insisted I believe that they were right and everyone else was wrong. They wanted me to believe that God built the world in six days and then on the seventh day he had a rest; that he was a loving God but if you misbehaved, didn't follow the rules or questioned them in any way, you were going to hell! This seemed a funny thing for a loving, and supposedly benevolent, God to be responsible for; but what did I know, I was just a child! When I was around 11 years old it became clear that the teachers and the priests had no rational, or satisfactory, answers for me, with regard to where we really came from and why we were here; and they had neither the means, nor the wherewithal, to prove their way *was* the right way. This led me to begin an extensive search into the roots of early religion and spiritual teachings. I studied the Mesopotamians, Essenes, Christian Gnostics, Jewish Kabbalists, Persian Mystics, and the Ancient Egyptians, to name but a few! I used to love bringing in proof that many of the teachings of the Catholic Church had origins that went back way before the time of Christ and the stories that were written about in the bible. I found that there were legends of great floods that predated Noah and even discovered that the dates of all the significant celebrations, such as Christmas and Easter, had been purloined from either the pagans or other ancient cultures. The priests really didn't like that one! My studies meant that I gained a much clearer understanding of all the world's religions and acquired a belief that essentially they are pretty much all the same – at a certain level, if you go back far enough. It seemed obvious to me, even back then, that it was the same God at the end of the road. The names, and the details, just changed depending on the country, or the culture people happened to be raised in. My studies taught me that God – higher power, Source, pure consciousness, the universe, the Eternal, the "I Am," the Oversoul, or whichever name you use – is not a man sat in the sky watching everything we do, so he can punish us if we do wrong, but an energy, an essence, something that we are all a part of. An essence that chose to know more of itself and did this by splitting into myriad parts, each part destined to experience the wonders that life has to offer, both good and bad; and then satiated and full of knowledge and wisdom and marvel that the experience of life can bring, to find the way back home, to itself. In my late teens I discovered the work of Jane Roberts, who channelled a multidimensional being who called himself Seth. In one of their communications he said, "You have lived before and you will live again, and when you are done with physical existence, you will still live."

This was a very different message to the one that I had been receiving from the majority of people in my world and it rang really true for me. It inspired me to know more and to connect with who I really was, to see if I could find some of that wisdom inside of myself. I also wanted to know why this information wasn't widely available, and I discovered that the real truth about life, the universe, and everything was hidden from view. It was hidden in the esoteric and more mystical sides of religion, in the secret corners of the world where truths, that were protected and guarded by certain elite groups, remained unchanged for millennia. I found that there were secret mystery schools holding this wisdom, which was only for the chosen few – for those who would dedicate their lives to a spiritual path, for those who would seek out a teacher, a master, and give up their everyday lives for the pursuit of this wisdom and the resulting enlightenment.

After making these discoveries I decided that I wanted to be one of *them;* I decided that I wanted to follow the path to greater enlightenment so I could discover who I was, why I was here, and what the meaning of life really was. I wasn't sure how I would do this, and no one around me seemed to have much of an idea either. So, bearing in mind that I came from an Irish Catholic background and had parents that still dragged me to church, unwillingly, each Sunday, I began a search for an enlightened master. Unfortunately, growing up in Streatham, South

West London, spiritually enlightened masters were a bit thin on the ground. I tried having discussions with some of the older and, seemingly, wiser priests but they just seemed to get upset with me. In fact, I upset one of them so badly that he had actually tried to strangle me. It all started at Mass on a Sunday. I had been really shocked when they had sent the collection plate round not once, as usual, or even twice, but three times. Once for the roof, once for the starving in Africa, and I cannot remember now what the third thing was. I left the church feeling strangely upset by it and to compound my discomfort, the following evening the priest who had conducted the Mass arrived at our house, uninvited. My parents were delighted that he had chosen to visit us and got out the best china for the tea and biscuits. They insisted that my little sister and I sit quietly and behave ourselves in front of our very important guest. It soon became obvious that, once again, he was asking for money; for the starving millions around the world!

Here he was, asking my parents – who were not at all well off – to provide it; my hardworking parents, who struggled to make ends meet. Something just didn't seem right about this. This priest had turned up in a brand new car, and I knew that he and all of the other priests had a housekeeper to look after them; they lived a very comfortable life, which I noticed included drinking and smoking and frequenting the Irish clubs in the same way that nonpriests did. I was pretty sure that some of them were not quite as innocent with regard to women as they were supposed to be either; I knew of at least one who was having an affair with the married mother of a friend of mine, and that had never seemed quite right to me. If they were going to be acting as the emissary of God, I thought that they should have been living pure, simple lives – like the ones they had us believe from the bible, the ones they went on about so much. We were expected to give up all our vices, to be pleasing to the lord, including even thinking of bad words; never mind saying them, a fact that had been drummed into me when attending my weekly confessions. So I surmised that their responsibility for being good citizens, and abiding by the ten commandments, should have been even greater than ours. Were they not supposed to be setting us a good example?

Now, don't get me wrong; I know that there must be some very good and holy priests out there doing great jobs – just not the ones that I met back then!

My young mind was boggled, and at that moment in time something became very clear to me.

As I opened my mouth and said "Father," in a questioning tone, I could see my parents holding their breath, praying that this time I would be good and make them proud.

It didn't happen.

"Father," I said smiling sweetly, "Doesn't the Vatican have a huge collection of amazing art?"

Nodding proudly he said, "Yes, my child, that is true; the Vatican houses one of the world's most impressive art collections."

"Then why doesn't the Vatican sell a few of the priceless paintings they own? That way they could stop having excessive amounts of collections at Mass, and they could feed the starving millions all around the world."

As a young girl the idea made complete sense to me, and in some ways it still does; not so to the priest, who got up, red faced, and loudly proclaimed that I must be a communist. When I dared to disagree with him, he went completely berserk and threw his hands around my neck. My father had to pull him off me, and I got sent out of the room in disgrace because I had upset the man.

I mean, really!

And they wondered why I rebelled.

As it became obvious that I was not going to find myself a guru, or a spiritual master, or someone who could answer my rapidly expanding questions satisfactorily, I had to be satisfied with my books. Luckily I loved reading, and I constantly had my head in books– not just about religion but secret societies, shamanism, the power of the mind, and all things esoteric.

Along the way, I admit, I sometimes got a little distracted from my spiritual path, and I had to give up on the idea of enlightenment for a while. As a teenager in the '70s and '80s, when the New Romantic era was at its peak, I decided that being a hair and make-up artist would be one way of helping people to feel better about themselves. What I discovered was that I could make them look better on the outside with my technical skills, which was great and very rewarding, but the real revelation for me was that by listening to people, and by being genuinely interested in them and their lives, they got to feel better on the inside.

I liked this – a lot.

After many years in the world of showbiz and glamour, I was prompted, quite forcibly, through a series of unusual events (one of them being a near-death experience) to make a change. And there really is nothing more conducive to getting your life back on track than coming face to face with your own mortality. I had decided I might like to be a therapist one day, and so I thought it might be a good idea to get some therapy myself. I spent several years working with a woman who practiced psycho-synthesis, a kind of spiritual psychotherapy. I got to see for myself how life could be improved by a process of "self-exploration." I learnt a huge amount about myself in that time; I learnt about the effects that my past had on me, I learnt more about who I was and who I really wanted to be. I gained the confidence I needed to step out of my old, familiar, and relatively "comfortable" life, which increasingly left me feeling dissatisfied and sure that there had to be something "more." I got fed up of reading about other people's adventures in the spiritual world and decided that it was time to experience them first hand; the sceptic in me wanted proof that the things that I had been reading about over the years were real. I joined the College of Psychic studies and tried out just about every course you could think of, testing to see whether psychic abilities were real, and whether you really could communicate with the dead. I learnt that they were and that you could. I was very blessed and got to work with some amazing teachers and had some really remarkable and transformational experiences. So many "wow" moments that I think should be a part of everyone's life – where the truth just hits you and there is no going back.

I couldn't go back but I wasn't sure where I was going, so one day I packed a bag and took myself off to Dahab and sat on a beach, alone, for a week. While I was there, pondering on my life, I did an exercise that I now share with many of my clients. I imagined floating all the way out to the end of my life and thought about what I would regret not doing or what I would regret not doing more of. There were many things on my "bucket list," and I am still working on some of them, but by far the most important thing on that list was that childhood desire to help people: to help them to be kinder to themselves and each other, to help them to understand who they were and why they were here. I really wanted to share with people some of the wonderful things that I had learnt, mainly that they were more powerful than they imagined and that their views of the world, and the beliefs that they held, could impact hugely on the life they lived.

At that point I had no idea how I would get to do that; none of the things that I had learnt so far had ticked the right boxes, so I looked to my list to see what else I had put there. As I child I had always wanted to act; I had recurring dreams of being on a stage, and I had spent a lot of time in various productions of one sort or another at school. I realised that acting was one way of delivering messages to people, so when I got back I signed up to the City Lit in Covent Garden for a two-year acting course. It was a great time in my life, and I learnt huge amounts about people and the way they related to the world. However my time in my drama classes and subsequent sojourns on the stage, and in the world of film and TV, taught me that I didn't want to pretend to be someone else – I didn't want to just play a part or speak someone else's words. Especially when most of what was considered to be entertainment, tended to be focused on gratuitous violence and people being really unpleasant to one another; I fell out with one agent quite badly when I told her that I would never be appearing on Eastenders; she couldn't see why I had a problem with it. I tried to explain that it was negative and full of people being abusive to one another and that as I wouldn't watch it, I certainly wasn't going to be in it; but all she could see was that it paid well and it was a fairly easy gig. I felt very frustrated by the whole thing. I wanted to inspire people, to motivate them into changing their lives and reclaiming their personal power and there just wasn't a lot of that kind of thing around. The one thing I did love about acting was being on stage, I loved the interaction with people and I think this is where the seeds were sown of me wanting to teach. I just wasn't sure what it was I would be teaching or who would want to listen. I needn't have worried as it all unfolded perfectly as it was supposed to.

I attended a course on presentation skills and there I met Stewart Pearce, who now runs the Alchemy of Voice, while we were on a break; he told me he could see my past lives and that I had many of them; I was intrigued. I booked an appointment to see him and he put me into a hypnotic trance, while I was there I saw myself in ancient Greece, in Rome and in what looked like Atlantis. It was amazing and I decided I needed to know more; especially to find out what I was meant to be doing with my life. I distinctly remember him, at the time, telling me the answer was right under my nose!!! And how very right he was, unfortunately it was going to be a few more years before I realised just how accurate his words had been.

I spent days meditating and asking my higher mind to show me something that would help me to get the clarity I needed; and I was not disappointed. As I was meditating I had the most amazing experience. I tapped into a lifetime in a very beautiful and very ancient civilisation. It seemed that I was in ancient Atlantis; it was beautiful and it felt very serene. In my "Atlantean" incarnation, I was a teacher, who used telepathy to communicate. I was privy to knowledge about crystals and energy that could help educate mankind and I was entrusted with showing them how to use these crystals and this energy to create a better way of life. There was a struggle, however, between the leaders of the time. The struggle centred round the knowledge that was to be imparted. Too much too soon and mankind would surely destroy themselves, too little and they might never evolve. The focus was on how that knowledge would best be given and what needed to happen to ensure mankind's future would be safe. As I remember that experience I can't help feeling the comparisons with our experiences on the planet right now, this time not crystal energy but nuclear; and we know what happened to the Atlanteans! I think this is one of the reasons why there are so many more evolved souls here at this time; to make sure that the people of planet earth wake up and do not allow the same mistakes to be made again.

Anyway, once I decided I wanted to focus on inspiring and motivating people to change their lives for the better; to be more positive and optimistic, I just had to work out how. I felt drawn to learn Counselling so signed up for a course but, not long into it, it didn't feel right so I left. I started a course on life coaching but that didn't work for me either. In the end I was starting to despair and so I asked the universe to give me a sign. I got more than one. Over a three week period, everything I read and, almost, everyone I spoke to mentioned NLP; Neuro Linguistic Programming. In the end I decided I had no choice but to learn more about it. I had no idea that it was going to be my route into hypnosis. The first time I put someone into a trance on my NLP practitioner course, it felt as though it was something I had done all my life, it came so easily to me and the results were astounding. I loved it and I really felt as if the people there spoke the same language as me; they too wanted to make sure that people were kinder and nicer, to themselves, and to each other. It felt like coming home.

Once my training was completed I was invited back to work as an assistant on all the different NLP training courses and I spent many years with Paul McKenna and Richard Bandler, the co-creator of NLP. Many of the exercises in this book were inspired by the amazing work they do. From that point on I wanted to learn as much about hypnosis as I could, because somehow, it seemed that it tied in with all of my earlier studies, particularly the meditation work I had been doing. In the state of hypnosis people really could access higher states of consciousness and find the answers they needed to solve their problems.

I studied Clinical Hypnosis for about three years with Ursula James at the LCCH and once my training was finished she became my mentor. Once I had gained sufficient experience and had developed a successful practice, she invited me to teach hypnosis to medical students, midwives and dentists all over the country; at various universities, including Oxford and Cambridge. I loved having the opportunity to demystify hypnosis and prove to those in the medical world that hypnosis really does have a place. The response from the students was always amazing with many of them greatly impressed by the results they achieved for themselves as well as the improvements they saw in others who experienced it. The students learnt how to alleviate their stress, to revise more effectively and, as a result, do considerably better in their exams than they had done previously. I became quite popular with the students, if not the faculties of the colleges, who were concerned that my teachings might have been a little "kooky". It was wonderful to have the opportunity to help the students in that way and know that future generations of doctors would be aware of the power of the mind and the undeniable connection between the mind and the body.

Even though it was not a big part of my clinical hypnosis training, my interest in the esoteric was still present and I wanted to be able to explore past lives with my clients. I set about reading everything I could about past life regression and I practised on anyone who would let me. The results were fascinating but I was aware that I still had some doubts, and a few fears, about whether the more esoteric work was right for me. It was strange as I could really see the huge benefits people got from doing this work and many of the people I worked with reported massive shifts in their lives. So I was really curious to see if there was anything from the past holding me back; stopping me from being able to really help people which, after all, seemed to be my life's purpose. I asked a colleague to help me and found myself revisiting a life where I was being burnt at the stake for being a witch. Something I had made many jokes about throughout my life; although it was not quite so funny when I went back there and lived through it again. It all started with me being talked through the hypnotic process. I was told to relax all the muscles in my body; I felt as though I was getting heavier and heavier. In fact at certain points I could not even feel my body; it was as if I had just floated away. It was a lovely relaxing feeling. I felt very safe and able to follow the instructions. I was asked to imagine myself in front of a very old door; a door that was to be the entrance into my past life. I was told I would find a lifetime that was relevant to this issue and as I stood in front of the door I had a distinct sense that something important was waiting for me on the other side.

I was right.

As I opened the door I found myself in a very strange and rather unsettling scene; I was tied to a burning stake and saw, what appeared to be, mediaeval villagers watching me burn. Some were watching with fear and hatred in their eyes and others were looking at me pityingly. However, I was aware of a great feeling of sadness and did not feel in the least bit wicked or witch like – something about this did not seem right to me.

As the physical body perished I imagined I was floating out of it. I was then able to observe the lifetime from a higher perspective and see what was really going on. As I floated above the scene I became aware that I was not a witch at all. I was a healer. I possessed the gift of hands on healing and was wise in the ways of herb-lore and child-birthing. My mother had the gift as well; it had been passed down the family line for many generations. I saw that we lived at the edge of this village and we were not accepted as part of the community. We were tolerated because we had the skills of child – birthing and could aid those that were sick and dying. So we remained at the edge of the village; not quite feared and not quite accepted either. As a young girl I had been confused as to why I could not go to the village and play as all the other children did, I could not understand why people looked at us suspiciously; never making full eye contact. I felt terribly lonely and frustrated at being separated in this way but eventually I got used to feeling like an outcast. My mother, in the past life, warned me to be careful, she told me we were lucky to have a home near the village and we should never do anything to draw attention to us or upset the others. I had no choice but to play by their rules. One day we were called to the village to attend to a woman who was with child. When we arrived she was in great pain and distress. My mother announced that it was too late and there was nothing we could do to save the child. She offered to stay with the woman and help soothe her loss, but she said she could do no more. I immediately jumped in; I felt sure I could help, that my gift of healing energy would save this woman's baby. I was eager to help and prove my skills and I sent her all the healing energy that I could muster. My mother yelled for me to stop but it was too late. The woman relaxed and smiled at me gratefully as her pain subsided. I knew she would be fine and her baby would live but it was a most unfortunate thing for me that her baby did live. The truth of the matter was that she had actually been having two babies; not one. And part of the information that had not been available to me in my quest to save her was that it wasn't just twins; the children were joined together.

They were Siamese twins!

Now in the course of history Siamese twins have caused somewhat of a furore. In mediaeval times they would have been a sure sign of being in league with the devil. A baby with two heads was not considered to be a good omen. Needless to say I was held responsible. My, supposed, witching ways were believed to have cursed both mother and baby; I was led off to be burnt. There was nothing else that could have been done; it was the way of the times and I had to accept it.

So there it was; proof that I had once been burnt to death for trying to help someone with my healing skills. At the end of the session I was guided through a symbolic healing process and was amazed to discover that my mother in that life was also my mother in this one. She had tried to protect me then and had returned to do it again in the here and now. In this life she has always been very protective of me, she used to worry a lot about the things I was interested in and she always wished that I would be a little more "normal" like most of my friends. She tells me how guilty she feels when she thinks about how much she complained about the way I was and the way I dressed in particular; especially my black, gothic phase. I was adamant that I wanted to be different to everyone else and she just kept insisting that I should try and fit in a bit more; but that was never going to happen. Thankfully she is very proud of me now and the work that I do. The session was wonderful as it allowed a release of all the negative feelings associated with the idea of doing healing work. I felt as though a huge weight had been lifted from me and as though a deeply rooted feeling of fear had gone. I was really grateful for the release and I felt that something had shifted. It was to mark the beginning of a new journey; one in which I could help others to change the same sort of limitations that were holding them back. That was many years ago and since then I have had many more adventures into the lifetimes I once lived; not surprisingly, in many of my lives I was a healer or teacher, of some sort. All the past lives I explored helped me to understand more about who I really am and what I came here to do. As a result of this work I have been able to let go of many of the blocks that were holding me back from achieving success in my own life, although of course, I am still a work in progress; there will always be tests and challenges that need to be overcome, and nowadays I embrace them all. I have no idea how many lives I have had, or how much I will learn from them, but I do know that I will keep exploring and searching for the information that my unconscious mind has buried away like undiscovered treasure.

Like so many who are on a spiritual path I have been a constant seeker of wisdom, and knowledge and my training continues to be updated, I have no doubt that I will go on learning until the very end of my life. I joined the Regression Academy in Dorset, several years ago and now have a diploma in Regression therapy and Life between Lives. It was here that I was introduced to the world of Spirit release therapy and this has since become a very important aspect of my work. I will be eternally grateful to the wonderful teachers there, both Andy and Hazel for all that they shared with me. And of course my adventures and my acquisition of knowledge will continue and it seems that I was always destined to share knowledge in one way or another. It will be no accident that, in my childhood this time around, I kissed the Blarney stone twice. For those of you that have never heard of it, it is a stone built into the side of an ancient castle just outside of Cork in the south of Ireland. It is said that upon kissing it you get the gift of the gab, which translates into the ability to talk the hind legs off a donkey! The gift has served me well and at last my voice is being heard; by my medical students and midwives; my private and corporate clients; my workshops participants; the people who come on retreats with me and you, the reader, with whom I will share both the clinical skills and the more esoteric processes. I have managed to maintain a sense of balance in my life with one foot in the world of Clinical Hypnotherapy; where I keep a more scientific view of the work I do and the other foot firmly ensconced in the world of the esoteric; where I get to travel through time and space and help my clients to enjoy the benefits that Inner Freedom Therapy can bring. I feel that it is invaluable for me to have this crossover as I view everything I do with an open minded perspective.

This book has been designed to help you understand just how powerful the exploration of past lives can be and show you how to access past life stories for yourself. You will find out how unfinished business and unresolved karma can be resolved, how it is possible to heal and release negativity that is stored away at the back of your mind and you will find stories of positive learning and achievement. My greatest wish is that you use these tools to get free from anything that has been having a negative influence on you, your thoughts and your actions. The most wonderful thing about clearing your mind this way is that once the negativity is cleared there is nothing to stop you from reconnecting to all of your inner resources, your personal power and your sense of inner freedom. Once you find true inner freedom your very best life will be right there waiting for you.

Many of my clients have made profound changes in their lives. The knowledge of who they were, and the challenges they endured, has given them a completely different insight into why they behave as they do, what drives them and what they can do to change their lives for the better. To change their lives they had to identify the beliefs that were holding them back first; because it is the beliefs that you hold about yourself – about what you deserve and what you are capable of – that determine the course of your life. If, for any reason; be it from a past life or from your current life, you harbour any self doubt, or have feelings of unworthiness, then you will not believe that you deserve to have great things happen in your life. And if you don't believe you deserve them then it becomes almost impossible for them to come to you. You will only ever achieve what you think you can, or believe you can, and no more. Many of the doubts you have about yourself and what you really deserve, or are capable of, can have a profound impact on your thinking, and on your life. Some of them may be from your childhood, they may have come from family, friends or your peers; some of them may have come from your relationships or work colleagues, some of them may have come from your ancestors and some of them may be from your past lives. And while it is certainly true that these doubts and negative beliefs can, and will, affect you and the life you are living; the only person who is responsible for the life you are living right now is you. Henry Ford once said, "If you think you can or you think you can't; either way you are right." Dealing with those doubts, and any unhelpful thinking that you have been engaging in, is the first step to inner freedom and the right way to go to achieve personal mastery. In this book are all the steps you need to show you how.

I once heard a great story about a man who, having lived a reasonably happy and successful life, died and went to heaven. Once there he was taken by the angels to have a review of his life. The angels took him into lots of different screening rooms, some contained one big screen on which he could watch significant scenes from his life play out and review the consequences of his actions and behaviours. Some had lots of smaller screens that showed the effects that his actions had had on the people that were close to him. Some had snippets of scenes from people that he had inadvertently had an impact on, whether a person he had paid a particular kindness to or in some way a grievance or a hurt that had affected the course of their life or how they felt about themselves. He was able to view all of this with no judgment from anyone else but himself and he experienced a certain sense of sadness when he realized just how much more of a difference he might have been able to make, often by very simple means.

At the end of the review the angels told him they were going to bring him to the place where all of his loved ones would be waiting and he felt very happy about this, but just as they were leaving he noticed another door with his name on it. He asked the angels what was contained within this room but they shook their heads and said that he would not wish to see what was inside. His curiosity was now piqued and he assured the angels that he really did want to know what the contents of this room might be. With obvious reticence one of the angels pulled out a key. The angel made one last attempt to persuade the man that he really had no need to look into the room but the man insisted. As the door opened the man was overwhelmed by the riches and the treasures that lay beyond. Inside were pictures of beautiful homes beyond his imagining, incredible art, jewels, and objects of great beauty. There were images on screens of incredible trips and adventures around the world and of life changing projects that brought great joy to all that were involved in them. There were images of moments of great love, tenderness and passion and of great joy and laughter.

The man was sad and confused as to why the angels had not wanted him to witness all of the glorious treasures in the room and asked if perhaps he had not been good enough or deserving enough in his life to enjoy them. But the angels turned to him sadly and told him that this was no punishment. This room, they said, showed him all that had been available to him during his time on earth, it had been provided for his pleasure and enjoyment and all he had needed to do was to acknowledge that he was worthy of it, to believe that he deserved it and it would all have been his.

Unfortunately he had never quite believed, while he was on earth, that he deserved such good things and so the doors had remained firmly closed, the treasures within locked away. He walked away with his head bowed low, sorry that within that lifetime such remarkable opportunities had been missed simply because of his lack of belief in himself and what he deserved. As he was led away he vowed that he would return in another life and dedicate his life to helping people unlock their treasure, to find the positive beliefs about themselves they needed to achieve success and to allow them to recognize, most importantly their own self worth, for without this they could never reach their dreams and live the wonderfully abundant life that was awaiting them.

My greatest dream is that this book can be a catalyst for your success. All that is required of you on this journey is a state of curiosity and a desire to learn more about who you really are.

As the information in the book unfolds you will get to realise why it is so important to clear out the unhelpful clutter from the past, both physically and mentally. You will begin to understand why you must plan your future very carefully; being very careful what you wish for and just how you wish for it…. and learn why it is so important to pay attention to the present because it is the only time that is real.

One of my favourite NLP sayings is that "*The best thing about the past is that it is over.*"

The best thing about the future is that it is in your hands. What you do with it is up to you. This book is really about you. Who you were, who you are – and who you have the potential to be. The choice is yours….

1

Are Past Lives Real and, if so, Why Explore Them?

For centuries people have enjoyed fairy tales and the metaphors and messages contained in books and movies, not only for entertainment, but also as a way to help them make sense of their lives. Even in the earliest times man liked to learn through stories. The bible was filled with parables, in Zen teachings there were Koans that got the students to see things through different eyes, and there have been many Sufi teaching tales that were designed to act directly on the unconscious mind. The idea of a hero with a quest has been around since the beginning of time, and this book has taken its inspiration from one of the greatest examples of this: *The Wizard of Oz*. People the world over have resonated with its timeless tales of adventure and challenge, overcoming adversity, determination to reach your heart's desire, tragedies and disappointments, faith and friendship, as well as its archetypal imagery of witches (both good and bad) and wizards. It many ways it parallels life and all its many weird and wonderful encounters and experiences. If you look back over your life so far, you will see that your life story unfolds just like a movie, or a book, with all kinds of opportunities, experiences, and characters coming in and out to help you to learn and grow. You may not have always recognised what you were learning at the time, and it is only when you take time out – to really explore what has happened to you – that you get to understand exactly what was going on. But it's not just what you learn from this lifetime that can be of benefit; exploring your past life experiences can teach you so much more about who you are and why you are the way you are, right now. As you delve deeper into your previous lives, you will see that the events and the people that seemed, at first glance, to be against you, were really there for your benefit. As a result, you will get to experience a state of curiosity for all the things that happen to you in your life and you will be able to generate a state of gratitude for everyone, and everything, that you experience in your life – no matter what happens. My favourite saying in life is this: "Life gives you everything you need"; but I felt the need to add this to it: "You may not know you need it, when you get it, but it will always become apparent later." This applies to all of the experiences in your life– good and bad.

I would like to take this opportunity to answer some of the questions that I am frequently asked about past lives.

Are past lives real?

Some believe that what happens in a past life session is just the result of a person having a very vivid imagination. They believe it is simply the unconscious mind being clever and creating vivid metaphors, or analogies, to explain what is going on in current life situations; and there usually is a real correlation to the person's current life. These experiences do allow people to view the events of their lives from a dissociated perspective, so that they *can* see the wood, not just the trees.

Now, I think it is very important for people to have their own ideas; I have always respected others' views and opinions, and I do know what it is like to be sceptical because I was for many years. But I can say with great certainty that I am not sceptical any more; the work I have been doing over the last ten years or so *has* convinced me that past lives do exist and that exploring them really can make a difference. I have witnessed all kinds of positive changes and profound healings, all of which have had a massive impact on people's lives.

When people experience a past life regression are they really gaining access to the memories of lifetimes they have lived before, their soul housed in a different body, and having a different experience?

The simplest answer is yes; it appears that they are. New discoveries in the field of quantum physics reveal that everything in the universe is made up of energy, billions of particles of energy all vibrating at different rates. When you die, your physical form, your body and the energy that it is made up of, returns back into the melting pot of the universe waiting to be recycled again and again in physical form. The cells that make up your body are holographic, meaning that each cell is imprinted with a genetic knowledge of all that you are. So, it stands to reason that some part of you, albeit on a deep cellular level, did once exist, at some other time, in some other form. In the state of hypnosis, where we get access to the sub-conscious realm, or the realm of infinite possibility as it is otherwise known, it is possible to get access to this information and find out exactly who you once were.

Is it possible that people are just recounting information that has been picked up throughout the years from books, television, or movies?

Investigators and sceptics often claim this to be the case. They claim that people are just rehashing information that has been stored in their memory banks, information that is out of their current, conscious memory recall. The technical term for this is cryptomnesia, which occurs when a forgotten memory returns and is not recognized by the person, so they think it is something new. However, in most cases the stories that are recounted in past life sessions will never have been reported anywhere as the people involved are simply too unknown, or unimportant, in the scheme of history.

Contrary to many beliefs, there are not that many people who explore their past lives in the right setting who claim to have been famous or historically known. In my experience, people who do discover they were someone well known are more likely to be embarrassed about it, and really feel afraid that they are making it up; they are not doing it for the prestige.

I am pleased to report that after all my years of working I have never once had a Cleopatra or a Napoleon, although I did once have a young male client who discovered that he had been a casual lover of Marilyn Monroe in his last life. He left with a big smile on his face and some very pleasant memories to keep him company. All the concerns that he had come to see me about, which involved a lack of confidence and a worry about whether or not he would be able to get and keep a girlfriend, were long gone.

Is it possible that people are being led by the therapist or just want to please them by creating an imaginative tale?

This theory is also widely used as a way to discredit past life stories, however, a good therapist will never, at any time, use leading language or be over-directive. The language used is always clean and open and involves questions such as "What are you experiencing?" and "What happens next?," leaving no room for conjecture or for planting ideas.

What else could be used to prove that past lives are real?

Occasionally, people speak fluently in a language they do not know. This is rare but it can happen; the technical term for it is xenoglossy, and it is a phenomenon in which a person is able to speak a language they have not learnt by natural means (for example, a person who speaks French fluently, whilst in hypnosis, but who has never studied French or had any kind of exposure to the French language). Psychologists generally do not accept its existence, however, Dr. Ian Stevenson, a professor in the Department of Psychiatry at the University of Virginia, who studied past lives, documented many cases that he considered to be authentic.

One of my clients returned to a life in ancient Egypt and had great difficulty in speaking to me in, what was clearly, a completely different language. I am not familiar with ancient Egyptian so couldn't say for sure if that is what it was but her accent was very guttural and she was really struggling to get the words out. In order for me to understand what she was saying, I asked her to translate the words into a form she could more easily express and with this, she relaxed and returned back to her normal voice. She then gave a very clear picture of what life was like as a high priest, at work in a temple, and the subsequent violent death at the hands of an enemy tribe who came to steal gold and other sacred treasures. Interestingly, in this life she had always avoided wearing gold and had an intense dislike for it, which up until this point had never made sense to her. Another client had a stutter in the past life, which remained for the entire time she was experiencing the past life. As soon as the exploration of the lifetime came to an end the stutter disappeared.

What other proof is there that past lives are real?

The three strongest factors in favour of the lives being more than just creations conjured up from the imagination are, first, the level of details that people provide once in the experience: names, dates, specific events, and descriptions of people and events. Often there is a change of accent, voice pitch, and tone as the person steps into their new persona. Second, the emotional and physical responses people have whilst in the session. Clients experience really powerful, deep emotions that are way beyond what they would experience if they were just remembering a story from a book or rehashing ideas they had picked up along the way. Whilst in the past life experience people will report changes in body temperature, they describe smells and sounds around them, and they will describe both physical and emotional sensations, sometimes in great detail. Afterwards they are shocked at how real the experience was for them and how easy it is for them to remember it afterwards, as if it really happened. And third, my clients report that, even if they wanted to, they could not change the details of the events they were experiencing; they could only describe exactly what was going on. If it was just a figment of their imagination they would be able to change it in any way that they wished.

Have you ever found hard evidence that these lives really happened?

In many cases I have found evidence that shows these lives did happen and these people really did exist. Over the years I have discovered all kinds of fascinating facts, and even photographs on the Internet and from other sources.

One fascinating case was a man who described a life as a Missionary priest who travelled from Southampton and landed in Fiji in the 1800s and was allowed by the local chief to build a church. He described the island as being volcanic and was very proud of his work there. After the session I did some research online and found a photograph of a church built at exactly the same date, on Levuku, one of the few Fijian islands with a volcano on it. I have to say it made the hairs on the back of my neck stand up.

Another fascinating case was of a woman who claimed to be the bodyguard of a Middle Eastern king called Darius, who reigned in the year 525; she was absolutely certain that she had never heard of such a man, and so memories or previous knowledge of historical data could not be blamed. Research showed the king in that area at that time had indeed been called Darius, and many other elements of her story fitted exactly as she had mentioned them.

If past lives are real and people have lived before, why don't they remember their past lives?

The experience of being born usually leads to complete amnesia for everything that happened before the current incarnation. As people awaken to a new body, in a different time and space, they also forget all the plans they made before they got here – ensuring that they are able to live their life free from any external influence.

However, many people do remember their previous lives, and children under the age of seven in particular often do this spontaneously. Some people have vivid dreams or flashbacks that are unrelated to any memories from this life. They may experience strong feelings of déjà vu, arriving at a new destination and instinctively knowing what will be around the next corner; I know this because it has happened to me on more than one occasion. Sometimes people get a sense that they have met someone before and feel as if they have known them all their lives, even though they know this is impossible.

Why can children remember their past lives more easily than adults?

One theory is that their memory banks are still sufficiently empty at a young age and this allows them access to these deeper memories. Many of the stories of children who vividly remember their past lives come from India and countries where there is little chance of watching television or having computer games filling the child's mind with external images and ideas.

In his research into past lives, Dr. Ian Stevenson discovered thousands of stories, from around the world, from children who had a very vivid recall of the lives they lived before. Often these were lives that were cut short for one reason or another before they reincarnated into another body, another life. He was able to officially validate over 1,000 of these cases and found much evidence, including birth marks that matched the cause of the previous person's death, such as scars where damage had been done to the body.

I had one client with a large birthmark on his back. He was very curious about it and in his past life he found that he had been a Samurai warrior who had been killed in a battle; a spear had gone into his back in the exact same spot where the birthmark was found. In his current life he was fascinated with martial arts, and it suddenly all made sense.

So what is reincarnation?

Reincarnation is referred to as a rebirth or the transmigration of the soul. The literal translation of the word in Latin is "entering the flesh again.' The Greeks referred to it as *palingenesis* which translates as "being born again." In the Bhagavad-Gita, an ancient Hindu text, reincarnation is described as a process that all mortals must follow. In it Krishna talks about the self advancing through childhood, youth, old age, death, and then another body. He described the process as being the same as casting off old clothes and putting on new ones, except that in this case it was the immortal self which cast off the body in order to enter into a new one. Pythagoras said that the soul survived physical death and returned to experience another life, in another body, with a new lesson to be learnt. He believed that when a soul achieved full mastery over its desires and completed all of its lessons, it became free from the cycle of life and no longer needed to return. This did not include the Bodhisattvas – souls who chose to return to earth to assist those still learning lessons, souls such as Jesus, Buddha, and Krishna.

What is a soul?

The Oxford Dictionary's definition of a soul is "the spiritual or immaterial part of a human being or animal, regarded as immortal; a person's moral or emotional nature or sense of identity." Your soul is the part of you that brings in life force; without it your body would just be an empty suit, an empty vessel, like a computer with no data and no hard drive to make it run. Your soul is your true nature, your true essence, and is just a drop that came from the infinite ocean that is the source. In the trance state, where you shut out all the external noise and the inner clutter of your mind, you can reconnect to this part of you. You will recognize it as the "I am" presence that sits still, and silent, within you – the part of you that is always connected to the realm of spirit and the knowledge and the wisdom that comes directly from the Source.

What influence does the soul have on the body?

When your soul arrives it brings in aspects of personality that get carried over from lifetime to lifetime, the qualities that make you uniquely you. It brings in the instinct to survive, the ability to experience emotions, and it brings in certain challenges and contracts with other souls that need to be fulfilled.

So why do souls choose to incarnate?

You came to earth because it is one of the only planets in the solar system where free will exists. You came to experience love and joy as well as suffering and pain. You came to learn and grow and experience "all that is"; and experiencing "all that is" requires many lifetimes. You came to earth as a representative of Source, so that you could experience all that life has to offer: poverty and wealth, health and sickness, kindness and cruelty, the love of power and the power of love. Your soul's mission is to experience love, to expand your awareness and your consciousness, and to remember the truth of who you, and all the other souls here with you, really are.

What is the truth?

The truth is that you are a divine, spiritual being of light having a human experience. The problem for most people is that they have completely forgotten this truth; they focus instead on their human limitations and get caught up in states of fear that prevent them from remembering who they really are.

Why do souls choose to reincarnate again and again?

Within each lifetime different lessons need to be learnt, and sometimes karmic issues arise which need to be resolved before the cycle of lives can come to an end. Each individual soul continues to evolve and grow throughout their lives, moving onwards and upwards in an ever expanding spiral, in just the same way that nature does; you can see these cycles in everything around you, including your own life, as that which goes around comes around again and again.

Does this idea of reincarnation explain the reports about life after death?

Yes, there are thousands of really well documented cases of people describing what their near-death experiences (NDEs) are all about. All of them describe very similar events: There is usually a tunnel of light and loved ones waiting to take them home, a review of the life that was lived so far, and a clear instruction that it was not yet their time to die. Almost all people who have experienced NDEs report that they no longer fear death because they know that when it happens they are merely going home, back to a place that is filled with peace and love.

In a fascinating movie that he directed, called *Hereafter,* Clint Eastwood gave people a glimpse into this. The movie followed the story of three very different people who were all affected by death in some way, and I can only applaud Eastwood for bringing the message it contained to the world.

One of the real explorers of the NDE experience was Dr. Raymond Moody. In 1975 he released a best-selling book called *Life After Life,* in it he compared the experiences of over 150 people who almost died and then recovered. In fact it was he that coined the phrase "near-death experience." All of his research corroborated all of these experiences.

So why do people choose to explore their past lives?

Many of my clients come to me with big questions about who they are and why they live the way they do. Often they find themselves repeating patterns, whether in their relationships, their weight, family issues, financial struggles, physical health, or work challenges. They come wanting answers, and they come because they are ready to change – to let go of the unhelpful behaviours and negative beliefs they hold about themselves. My job is to help them to find the answers, and the insights, which can set them free and allow them to live their life to the full.

Milton Erikson, a leading American psychiatrist and hypnotherapist, taught that the best place to find the information you need is already within your own subconscious realm. All I need to do is be the guide for people's journeys, "the spiritual Sat Nav," if you like, with a gentle voice, directing them to the memories stored within their subconscious minds, which, once explored, allow them to make sense of things and allow profound shifts to occur.

How can past life experiences affect people?

They can affect them in many different ways. People often find themselves repeating patterns in their lives, over and over again, in an attempt to resolve something that began many lifetimes ago, or they may experience "unexplainable" physical symptoms that do not respond to any kind of medical intervention. Memories of positive past lives tend to generate greater feelings of self-esteem and confidence, but some of the more negative experiences from the past can, if not properly dealt with, really undermine the way a person feels about themselves, and as a result can have a huge impact on what they achieve in the world.

Just how do these negative memories impact people's lives?

For a moment let me just ask you to imagine a picture of an iceberg. When you see an iceberg you only see the top of it protruding out of the water; the rest of it is submerged and out of view. This is a great analogy for the mind. The conscious part of your mind is above the water line: It is awake and aware and present; it is analytical, questioning, rational, and decides what information to accept, absorb, keep, and discard; it is the problem-solving part of the mind that deals with day-to-day thinking, often referred to as the logical mind; and it is connected to left-brain thinking.

The subconscious part of the mind is hidden, as though submerged under the water, but just because you can't see it, it doesn't mean it doesn't exist. This is the storage facility of the mind; it is the storehouse for all of your memories and all of your emotional responses. It is also the place where you can connect to your beliefs, instincts, creativity, and inner wisdom. It is more commonly referred to as the intuitive, emotive part of the mind as it is more associated with right-brain functioning.

Everything you have ever experienced from the moment you were born is stored here. Research has shown that you have memories that go all the way back to your time in the womb and even beyond… into the memories of other lives.

How are these memories stored?

Your memories are stored in a very particular way. If you think about it for a moment, your mind is picking up billions of bits of information, every moment of every day, through all of your senses, and this means there is a huge amount of information being processed and stored all of the time. The amount of information you store is constantly expanding and, in order to ensure you don't get overloaded, your mind has created a simple way to organize your memories.

It operates like a powerful computer, and your memories are stored like data files. Each one of these files has a different label, according to the event or the experience, and there are even files containing the beliefs you have about yourself and how you appear to the world. Each file has the memories organized in a way that, at first glance, appears to make sense; but making sense doesn't always mean it is the most helpful system.

Why is it not always helpful?

The memories in these files are stored in order of emotional importance, meaning that the more you reacted to something, or someone, and the more intense your emotions were at the time, the more important your mind will have decided the memory is. Highly charged memories are given a high position in the memory file, whether you want them there or not. This goes for current and past life memories.

How does this work?

The memory of what you had for breakfast three years ago on a Tuesday is probably not very important and therefore not a very big, or significant, piece of data in the filing system. However, if it had been a wedding day or a significant birthday, or the day you crashed your first car, it might be different.

What happens to the memories that are registered as significant or important?

If a memory is labelled as important, your mind will want to make sure you can get access to it again, quickly and easily, and it will be put at the top of the file; if it is seen as really important it will have a big, shiny flag attached to it.

Why is that?

When you find yourself in situations where you are not sure how to respond, your mind goes on a search for information; it wants to know how you responded to this kind of thing before. It is a bit like doing a Google search: You tap in the question and your mind pulls up a file. You don't have time to look at the whole file, so you just open the one that is at the top of the box, or the one with the biggest flag on it. This will determine how you respond, and it happens in an instant. It means that you are at the mercy of the events of your past.

It makes sense to recall the good memories, but why would you want to relive the bad memories all over again?

The protection, or defense mechanism, part of the mind wants you to have access to the bad memories to prevent you from making the same mistakes again. It will want to make sure you learnt from them and, just in case you put yourself in the same bad situation again, it will remind you of just how bad it really was. By allowing you to relive the event and the bad feelings all over again, you are likely to want to avoid that experience and as a result will be prevented from putting yourself at risk, making a fool of yourself, or being in a place of perceived danger – whether real or imaginary.

Your mind may make you revisit these memories again and again just to really make sure you don't go there. The plan is to keep you safe and out of danger. In theory this is a good idea, but the trouble with this system is often, all that happens, the recall of the memory makes you feel bad and when you feel bad you are much more likely to make mistakes and be at risk of doing the very thing that you were afraid of in the first place.

Is there any benefit to be had by revisiting certain negative memories?

Yes, if there is something left unfinished or unresolved from an event that needs to be dealt with or something that needs to be healed, but you want to be able to choose when you do that and not have it happen spontaneously.

So how could it happen spontaneously?

These memories at the top of the memory file are easily visible and ready to pop up again at any given moment. They can be inadvertently triggered by all kinds of things that go on around you, and if something does trigger a memory you will re-call it with the same intensity, and the same level of emotion, you felt at the time. These triggers can be very subtle, and you may not even be aware of them. How many times have you heard a piece of music and been transported back to a time in the past, or smelt a perfume or an aftershave and been reminded of someone you know?

Now, this is all very well if the memories that you recall and the emotions that you relive are positive, but unfortunately the filing system tends to place a higher value on the most highly charged negative emotions. It is as if these get to have really big, bright red, shiny flags on them and it makes it really easy for you to relive them – over and over again. This is what happens when people experience flash-backs of traumatic events and, in extreme cases, is known as post-traumatic stress disorder. Bad memories keep returning over and over again, re-traumatizing people and leaving them feeling out of control. It also means that many good memories and experiences get forgotten, as people tend to focus on the bad stuff that is stored first.

Why would people do that?

Your unconscious mind does not decide whether or not it is a good idea to store the memories like this, it just does. I think, perhaps, we are programmed from an early age to focus more on what is wrong. Think about what happened to your work at school: Everything you did wrong got a big red line through it or a cross next to it, and most of the stuff you did well tended to be ignored.

But let me give you an example of the way this works: Imagine for a moment that you have a favourite restaurant. It is near where you live. It is convenient and, for the purpose of my analogy, it is the only place where you can get food for a hundred miles. Now, you have been there 100 times. Ninety-seven times the food was great, the service was good, and the price was reasonable; you go two more times and it is really exceptional, everything from the service, to the quality, to the price was amazing. You go once more and you find maggots in your food. From that moment on, when people ask you about that restaurant, which memory comes up? Of course, it is the negative one, because the emotional charge attached to it is going to be huge.

What impact will this have on people?

It can have a very negative effect. Many of my clients have had terrible experiences in their past and are unable to let go of the memories. They torture themselves by reliving horrible memories again and again. I had one client whose father had died and instead of being able to remember him as the lovely man he was, she found herself reliving the most horrible and sad moments from the end of his life, making herself feel terrible. Of course, this prevented her from being able to remember any of the wonderful moments she had experienced with him, which was of no benefit to anyone. It can also happen when there has been a break up of a relationship; people will go over and over the bad times, reliving how hurt or wounded they felt, generating more and more bad feelings and damaging their sense of self-esteem and preventing them from being able to move forward. Now, going back to my analogy, in most circumstances, if this really happened, you would just never go back to this restaurant. But remember this is just an analogy, and in the analogy there is nowhere else to eat for 100 miles. This is important because sometimes you *have to* go back to places and situations you don't like. In order to get on with your life, you may have no choice.

Is it possible to change the impression that you have?

Yes, there are specific changes that can be made that can help you to overcome this problem and make it so you are not filled with horror every time you *think* about that restaurant and the bad thing that happened to you, never mind attempt to *go back there* and eat some food.

How can you "change" your mind?

Actually, it is fairly simple. All you have to do is to make alterations to your perception of the memory, to change the experience you have when you open up the file at the top of the box. You can't take the bad memory away, but you can change the emotional attachment to it in your mind. You can do this in a variety of ways.

One way is to alter the memory and the way it is stored, allowing your unconscious to see it as less important. You can do this by shrinking the image in your mind, draining the colour out of it, distorting it, turning the sound down, and even locking the memory away in a box so that you can no longer see it. This way it will no longer bother you so much. However, a more effective method would be to replace it with one of the good memories that already exists inside your memory bank or create a new memory that is even more highly charged, but this time with a positive emotional feeling. You would not even have to go to the restaurant to do this but could simply imagine you were there, and that it was incredible, and you were having the most fantastic experience. You could make the images bigger and brighter, the sounds clearer, and imagine the good feelings are even stronger.

Research has shown that your mind cannot tell the difference between a real experience and a very vividly imagined one. What this means is that the memory that sits at the top of the restaurant file, the one with the highest charge, is now good and whenever you think of the restaurant in the future the flag that pops up is a pleasant one; this allows you to go back there without any discomfort. Another way of dealing with it is to imagine going back to the original memory and see it play out differently, perhaps you imagine that you go back and choose a different dish, so that the bad experience doesn't happen; that way you can imagine having a wonderful experience instead. By changing the memory in this way you allow the new version to be superimposed over the old memory and the feelings you have towards it changes.

The important thing to be aware of, in all good analogies and in the significant events in your life, is that there will have been a purpose to it and something that you may have needed to learn; so perhaps, from that moment onwards, you would choose to be a little bit cautious about your food and would slow down and check that it is all good before leaping straight in.

How will this be of benefit in the long run?

In order for you to not be at the mercy of your negative memories, it is essential that you clear out, or deal with, anything that is stored there that no longer serves you. Whether the memories are from your current life, past life, or negative fears you may be holding about the future, or fears of things that haven't even happened yet, it is all the same. Mark Twain once said, "I have known a great many troubles in my life and most of them never happened." People can waste an awful lot of time worrying about things that never happen, and these worries clutter the mind up just as much as real-life memories do. So I like to think of this work as an inner clutter clearing – internal Feng Shui, if you like.

For a moment just think about your mind as being your internal home; you know that for your home to be a beautiful space you have to maintain it and keep it tidy and clean. It is not going to be experienced at its best if it is full up with all the debris and rubbish you have collected from the past. It would not matter how many beautiful things you put in it or how fabulously you tried to decorate it; if the space is full up with clutter, the space is full up. And if the place is full of garbage, and things you don't like or want to look at any more because you associate them with bad experiences, then your experience is going to be tainted and, undeniably, unpleasant. And no matter what you do or how much you try to stay positive, no matter how much you try to stay in the "now" or how many positive affirmations you make, no matter how often you meditate on it or visualize it as perfect, if the place is full of junk it will remain unpleasant. The only way to see the full potential of your inner space and enjoy it completely, in the "now," is to get it cleared out of all unhelpful rubbish first. Once you start to clear the space then you can decide what is important to you and what you want to keep. The new design of your inner space is completely up to you. It no longer needs to be made up from the ideas that were handed down to you over the years: the negative beliefs, fears, limitations, and negative ways of thinking that were passed down from your ancestors, your family, your friends, your peers, your work colleagues, and more importantly, your past lives. You get to take complete responsibility for it all.

Now, something for you to ponder on: Your outer world is a reflection of your inner world. Your environment is a mirror of what is going on within you. So, you may want to take a good look around at your life and see what, if anything, needs to change. You may want to see if you are holding on to things that you no longer need, things that you no longer have any use for but are afraid to let go; this can apply to jobs, people, things. As you assess what needs to stay, and what needs to go, you may want to think about what this is telling you about what requires healing inside of you. As you get ready to let go of the clutter from your inner world, you may want to commit to letting go of what is no longer needed from your outer world as well. The rule is if you haven't used something in five years, you are probably never going to, so it might be time to let go and let someone else have use of it.

Is it important to deal with current life memories as well as past life ones?

Yes, dealing with current life memories, especially traumas, is very important and these memories need to be dealt with accordingly. However, the triggers and powerful responses that you experience in this life, to people and events that cannot be rationally explained, often have their origin in your past lives anyway. The emotional charges that are attached to past lives can permeate into the subconscious realm and influence your thoughts, actions, and behaviours – sometimes causing you to act in ways that seem completely irrational and make no sense to anyone, least of all you. This is why it is essential to recognize, and deal with, any lifetimes where there has been unfinished business. When you go to the source of the issue and heal it there, the healing creates powerful shifts that occur in the current life as well.

How do you know which past life memory to explore?

The initial consultation ensures that the lifetime explored will provide some sort of therapeutic benefit, learning, or healing for the person experiencing it. This is quite different to a simple regression where people go back out of curiosity just to see who they once were – something I rarely, if ever, do. Most people, when questioned, will be aware of something in their life that is not working for them, or not working quite as well as they would like it to, and others are very clear on what their blocks are. The challenge is to find the origin, or the source of the problems, so they can be understood and resolved.

How many past lives do people usually have?

Everyone is different. You may have had very few lives or you may have had many, and a bit like breakfast on a Tuesday, many of them may not have been important. You may have been born, lived, did what you had to do, and no emotional charges were left; as a result, these lives do not need to be explored. But, in many of your lives, there will have been karmic missions to be completed or vows you made that might not have been completely fulfilled; perhaps the life got cut short too soon, perhaps you got distracted and didn't complete your mission, perhaps you just decided to ignore it and do something else. Either way, at the end of a life, where there is regret or anger or a real passion for something, any emotional charge, good or bad, is going to leave an impression. This impression, albeit deeply buried within the energy field of the soul, will nevertheless have an effect on you at a deep, unconscious level. This is why it is essential to understand what needs to be cleared and to take steps to deal with it.

What happens once a lifetime has been explored?

Once it has been explored, the charges de-fused, the healing complete, and the big life lessons learnt, it is then possible for you to relax for a while, get on with your life, and move to the next level – making it so much easier to live in the "now," which is what all of the greatest teachers, very wisely, advise us to do. Once the inner clutter has been removed you can get access to the positive resources that are waiting there for you: the good memories that are stored away and often forgotten, perhaps moments of pure, innocent joy from your current childhood, or memories of lives where you had specific talents and skills, skills that, perhaps, you can utilise again to help you in the here and now.

One of my clients, Carla, was really struggling with relationships, mainly because she had never seen any good role models. She went back to a lifetime where she was very happily married and raising a family. She experienced an overwhelming sense of being loved unconditionally and felt completely supported. This example allowed her to really believe that good relationships did exist, and she was able to let go of the fears holding her back from having someone special in her life.

Where do people go to access the past life information?

Jung believed that everyone has a "personal unconscious," a storage centre in the mind where experiences that are unique to the individual are held. He also believed in the "collective unconscious," which he said acted as a giant storehouse for the memories and experiences of everyone that has ever lived. This, he believed, was a place where you could go, whilst in a trance state, to review other lives and to learn lessons from those who have gone before you. His work was influenced by the American mystic Edgar Cayce, who claimed to be able to access what he called the Akashic records, a storage place for past and other life information.

Who was Edgar Cayce, and what are the Akashic records?

Edgar Cayce was a successful prophet and mystic who made many, very accurate predictions for people. He claimed that when he was in a trance he could get direct access to the collective unconscious, otherwise known as the hall of records or, as he called it, the Akashic records. He said that these records referred to a universal filing system, or giant library, that stores every single thought, word, and action of everyone who has ever lived. They were said to be held in a substance called *akasha,* a Sanskrit word meaning *sky, space,* or *ether.* Cayce believed that everyone would be held to account after their life and "confronted" with everything they had, or had not, done in their lifetime – and would then have to deal with the consequences of their own karma.

What is karma?

In many cultures the belief is that you reap what you sow – that your decisions and actions in the present may have serious consequences on the events of your life, or lives, in the future. However, it is important to note that the idea of karma is not necessarily based on punishment or retribution; the term simply means *deed* or *act* and is based on the principle of cause and effect or action and reaction. According to many ancient teachings, if you sow goodness, you will reap goodness; if you sow evil, you will reap evil. This simply means "what goes around comes around," a concept that most people are familiar with.

Can past life memories provide explanations for the unusual, or more challenging, events in life?

Yes, uncovering your past life experiences can make sense of fears and phobias, injuries and ailments, obsessions and great passions. When you recognize where these fears have come from, the resulting insights can lead to a release of old negative ways of thinking, fears, and limiting beliefs. Even unexplained aches and pains and physical ailments can be released.

Do all past life sessions have to deal with healing or resolving bad experiences?

No, in some cases people come because they wish to explore a particular passion, or skill, they have that cannot be easily explained. I always think of Mozart who, as a very small boy, began playing and composing music for large orchestras. Now it is extremely unusual for a child of such a young age to have those skills and abilities, but it is entirely possible that he had already learnt those skills in another lifetime. If the memory of that skill was already there, buried away in the back of his mind, it would have been possible for him to access the skill again. Most musicians are in a very focused state when they perform, and this focused state of attention enables people to get access to subconscious; as a result, they can get access to their past memories as well.

Were any more of the great geniuses of our time accessing the subconscious realm?

Many were known to have had their epiphanies in moments when they were in a trance-like state. Newton was sat under a tree, pondering, when an apple fell on his head and broke him out of his reverie with a cry of "Eureka"; Einstein was visualising himself and a friend travelling on a beam of light when he discovered the theory of relativity; and Mozart himself said that when he was composing he did not hear the parts of the music in his imagination successively, but he heard them all at once, as though in a pleasing and lively dream. All of them were able to get access to powerful resources, and information, by taking the time to allow their focus to go within. The trance state was the tool they used to help the information, already within them, to come to the surface so they could make productive use of it.

How can the memory of skills from another life help in the present life?

The discovery of information from a past life, or the memory of a talent that was once held, can allow that skill to re-emerge and can start to open up all kinds of new possibilities.

One of my clients found herself as a very successful opera singer in her past life. She died feeling fulfilled and very happy to have lived a life doing what she loved. In her current life singing was just a hobby for her, and she had seen it as something that was a bit of a waste of her time – a bit of an indulgence. She was caught up in a job that she despised but because she had been there for many years and was reliant on the money, she could not see any way out. Her joy and great passion for life and for singing, in the past life, reawakened something in her and she decided she would have some lessons. Almost straight away her teacher insisted that she join a singing group, and before she knew it she was the lead in one of their productions.

Her experience of life changed completely and even her boring day job was no longer so bad, because she had something else to look forward to, and that something else really made her feel alive and inspired. She was determined to make the move, once she was confident that she was ready, to make singing her livelihood. She assured me she had no doubts this would happen, and I believed her.

Is it difficult to recall past lives?

When you recall past life memories, it is very similar to the way you experience old memories from your current life. If for a moment you were to stop and think about your last holiday, you would probably find that you can remember some of the key details: the place where you stayed and some of the key people you met. You might remember some of the more interesting experiences you had, but you would not remember everything. If you were to close your eyes and imagine you were back there now, and see things as if you were really there, you would notice that you begin to remember more details.

As you recall one part of the story it opens up more details, and the more you connect to it the more comes up for you. You will not necessarily see the events as if you are watching a 3D colour movie; most of the time the images will be hazy or vague. You might have more of a feeling, or just a knowing, and some of the details, such as names, may just pop into your mind as if you are hearing them from somewhere else. It is different for everyone, but more often than not, the experience is usually a combination of all three: seeing, hearing, and just sensing or knowing. There is a misconception that you have to be very deeply in trance to experience this, and it is really not the case.

I will explain more about hypnosis and how it works later in the book, and the accompanying recording has a track that you can listen to that will guide you safely into the experience so you can enjoy it for yourself and begin to practice your visualization skills.

Do people have to believe in the idea of past lives for them to be effective?

The simplest answer is no. Beliefs about who you are, where you come from, and whether or not you really have lived before are going to be different for everyone – just as it was for the people whose stories are contained within these pages. The one thing they all had in common was that they were all curious to know more about themselves. They wanted to know more about the situations in their lives that seemed to make no sense to them, and all of them were open minded to whatever the truth might be. They were prepared to leave their logical, rational minds to one side for a short time and see what might emerge.

Are the stories in this book real?

All of the past life experiences in this book are written exactly as they were told at the time of the session; no details have been changed, with the exception of some of the real-life names. My hope is that you will not only be inspired and amazed by these stories but that you too will make use of the powerful processes and techniques described in the book in order to make more sense of your world, and so gain more control over your own destiny.

EXERCISE 1: *Possible Past Lives*

1. Is there something that you are passionate about that does not fit with your family background and upbringing?
2. Is there an era or a time in history that really appeals to you?
3. Is there a place or a country that you have felt an affinity to?
4. Have you ever had déjà vu in a place that you know you have never visited before?
5. Do you have any obsessions or fascinations with things, people, or places that you cannot understand?
6. Do you ever have recurring dreams? If so, what are they about?
7. Do you ever daydream about something that you know is not from this life on a regular basis?
8. Have you ever felt as though you had been here before and wondered why you were here? Do you ever have the feeling that you have something that you must do with your life, a feeling that there is a reason why you are here, a mission that you have to accomplish?

9. When you were a child did you ever tell stories about who you were before?
10. Have you ever experienced what seemed to be a past life, either in meditation or in trance or just in a dream?
11. Has anyone else ever told you who you were in another life and somehow it felt right, or have you ever been repeatedly called by another name?
12. Have you ever met someone and felt as though you had known them forever?
13. Have you ever taken an instant dislike to someone without knowing why?
14. Do you find yourself repeating patterns, getting into the same mistakes over and over again?
15. Have you ever felt as though you were born into the wrong family and that you just don't fit in with the people around you, and do you ever feel the need to go home but are unsure where home really is?

If you have answered yes to any of these questions, the chances are you are experiencing the residue of a past life.

2

How Do You Access Past Lives?

*T*he Wizard of Oz, a tale of one girl's journey into another realm where she gets to learn important lessons about herself, and about life, is therefore the perfect analogy for the journeys that my clients have taken. It greatly intrigued me to discover that Frank L. Baum, the author of *The Wizard of Oz,* was not just a children's storywriter. He had a great interest in theosophy, a philosophy that included aspects of Buddhism and Brahmanism, especially the belief in reincarnation and spiritual evolution. He didn't accept all the teachings, but he did believe in reincarnation and in the immortality of the soul. He believed he and his wife had been together in many past lives, and they would be together again in the future. He also believed in karma, that the good or evil deeds a person commits in their lifetime will affect their future lives. He was introduced to these ideas by his mother-in-law, Matilda Gage, an active figure in the American women's rights movement. She explained reincarnation to a grandchild, very simply, by saying that after people have been gone for a while, they come back and live in another body, in another family, and have another name.

His story of *The Wizard of Oz* really makes for a wonderful film. If you haven't seen it yet, then I recommend that you find a time and a space to do so. And whether you are watching it for the first time, or having seen it many times before, I suggest you really pay attention to the words that are said and the messages between the words. The magic begins when Dorothy, the heroine of the film, having gone through a difficult time, opens the front door of her old and familiar grey Kansas house and finds a whole new technicolour world outside – a world where anything was possible and dreams really did come true. But was the metaphor in the movie as far fetched as it may have seemed? Perhaps not! Because just as Dorothy was able to enter another realm and experience a transformational journey through time and space in the magical land of Oz, where she discovered much about herself and the means to achieving real happiness, people who experience past life regression are able to travel through time and space too, and experience adventures that are just as fascinating and transformational as her journey along the yellow brick road. Of course my clients' lifetimes do not involve fantasy characters: the people in their other lives are real; as a result, the stories and the learnings are even more powerful.

What is the best way to go on an inner journey?

The search for true inner power and potential has been undertaken by many through the centuries – by the early philosophers, mystics, alchemists, and spiritual seekers of wisdom. Over that time many paths have been discovered, but one that has really found a key – a key that unlocks all kinds of mysteries – is the state of trance or hypnosis. This key allows you to access all kinds of memories that are stored away, deep within your subconscious mind. It is as though, whilst in this state, you can unlock the doors and windows of your mind to allow deeply buried treasures to be revealed – treasures that can be dark, mysterious, and sometimes unpleasant to witness, which inevitably would benefit from release and clearance, as well as uplifting, heart-warming and illuminating, which can be of huge benefit to your sense of self and of what you believe you can achieve. Whether you are exploring your past lives, early experiences from your current life, or just getting access to the information that has been stored in the subconscious realm, hypnosis is the key. It is the key that enables you to make sense of your life in the present.

So how do people access their past lives?

Some people have spontaneous experiences of past lives, when they find themselves in a new and unfamiliar setting, or sometimes they will have very vivid and recurring dreams. These experiences are sometimes put down to déjà vu, although it rarely explains what is really going on.

What is the most effective way to deliberately access past lives?

The most effective way is to use hypnosis, a term that can conjure up all kinds of weird and wonderful ideas, from mind control, dancing like a chicken, barking like a dog, impersonating Elvis, and being in a very deep sleep where you have no recall of anything that happens.

Isn't hypnosis a type of mystical or "otherworldly" state?

Contrary to beliefs that many hold about hypnosis, it is a naturally occurring state that you will experience many times in your life. In fact, you drift in and out of hypnotic states many times in a day. As you drift off to sleep at night you enter what is known as the hypnogogic state; many experience this if they fall asleep in front of the television or on the train – the mind has drifted off and yet they are not fully asleep and they know at a certain point they will have to get up. This state is very pleasant and enjoyable, and often you can have wonderful dreams and visions. You also experience it first thing in the morning as you slowly awaken; this is called the hypnopompic state. This is where you will often have very vivid dreams that you recall upon fully awakening. This state is often accompanied by sensations of floating or a feeling of heaviness in the body.

So, what is hypnosis?

It is simply a state of focused attention, where the mind is focused on one thought or idea to the exclusion of anything else. Milton Erickson described it as being "the loss of the multiplicity of the foci of attention," which puts you into a trance state just thinking about it. It often leads to physical relaxation, where the body relaxes and outside distractions fade away so that the mind can focus clearly on one thing at a time.

Whenever you are deeply engrossed in a task where you lose track of time, you are in hypnosis. When you drive on autopilot, not needing to think about changing gears or even the details of the journey because your mind is somewhere else; when you are lost in thought, drifting into the realms of daydreams and reveries; and when you lose yourself in a good book or a good movie, you are in a state of hypnotic trance. Athletes and sports people, musicians, and artists regularly enter this state whenever they perform. They usually refer to it as being in the "flow" or being in the "zone."

What difference does being in the state of hypnosis make?

In the hypnotic or trance state, access to the subconscious mind is easy, the recall of memories is heightened, and the ability to imagine the future is enhanced. In this state you are better able to absorb what is put into your mind, you are more open to suggestions, and you are better able to gain access to both positive and negative memories.

This allows you to deal with the "not so good stuff" of life, those memories with the big red flags on, with a clearer mindset and a better sense of perspective and make the adjustments to them that you need to. It also enables you to reconnect to "the good stuff" so that you can remember your strengths and talents; as you enhance your sense of belief in yourself you can begin to imagine a more empowered future.

Are there any negative side effects to being in hypnosis?

No, absolutely not. The state itself is very beneficial and is very similar to the state experienced when people meditate. Most people recognize the benefits of meditation, whilst at the same time struggle to find the time to fit it in; even if they do find the time, they will often struggle to keep the mind still or their thoughts at bay.

Over the years I became well aware of the benefits of meditating, but like so many people in the West who live busy lives and are constantly on the go, I kept finding excuses not to do it. As soon as I sat down I felt almost guilty and kept thinking of all the other things I should be doing; it seemed indulgent and almost a waste of my time. I think many people have this battle with themselves. It was so empowering for me when I learnt just how similar hypnosis was to meditation and how it was just as beneficial. The state you go into is very similar; in fact, it is almost identical and has all the same benefits for mind and body. I see the two processes being akin to the Yin Yang model, with both elements equally as important as each other.

Meditation is the passive, restful state where the aim is to allow the mind to be focused on a thought, a mantra, the breath, or an image in order to achieve an inner stillness – where thoughts can just come and go and eventually a sense of peace emerges, often followed by powerful insights.

Hypnosis, on the other hand, is the active use of the state, where the aim is to be focused, calm, and deeply relaxed, and then take action of some sort, guiding the mind through a process that enables information to emerge and answers to problems to be found. In the hypnotic process you have an aim, a purpose, something that you want to discover, or something that you want to achieve – whether that is giving yourself positive suggestions, doing mental rehearsals of something that is important to you, dealing with unpleasant memories, or just recalling a previous positive event to remember the good feelings you had back then.

Are there any dangers in accessing the hypnotic state?

The only time it is dangerous to access a hypnotic state is if you are handling any sort of machinery or driving. Many people do end up doing this, particularly when driving late at night on the motorway; all of a sudden they find themselves jolted back to awareness as they drift into another lane or the hard shoulder. They call this highway hypnosis. It is important for you to know that you cannot get lost, or stuck, in hypnosis and you are always in control, whether you are practicing self-hypnosis or being guided by someone else. You can bring yourself out of it easily by bringing your focus of attention back to external events. If you were very tired and went a little too deeply into the hypnosis you might just fall asleep and would just wake up as normal, feeling refreshed and rested. In reality all hypnosis is self-hypnosis as no one can ever force you into the state: You have to be willing to listen and to focus on what is being said or to what is happening in front of you.

What if someone can't be hypnotized?

All hypnosis is really self-hypnosis and everyone experiences this daydream type of state many times in a day so, pretty much, everyone can be hypnotized. The exceptions will be those people who are unable to follow instructions or those who find it difficult to concentrate. Interestingly, it seemed to motivate my medical students, especially the ones at Oxford, into wanting to experience hypnosis when I let them know that the more intelligent you are and the more willpower you have, the better you will be at going into the hypnotic state. The only thing to take into consideration is that not everyone can be hypnotized by the same methods or by the same people.

One of the most important things in the hypnotic process is trust. If there is any level of doubt in your mind then you are very unlikely to follow the instructions and allow yourself to relax completely. If you are not sure about what is going to happen and are waiting for some "other worldly" state to occur, then you are also going to be disappointed and, as you question what is happening, your inner voice will keep you from being able to relax. You know the one I mean, it is the one that goes: "I can still hear her, I am still sitting here, nothing has happened yet, I don't think it is working, I am not relaxing… it is not working." And on and on. This is the surest way to *not* experience hypnosis.

How do you prevent this from happening?

I always make sure that my clients know exactly what to expect and tell them to just be curious about what is happening. I let them know that the most important thing for them to do is just relax and enjoy themselves, whatever the outcome may be. Once the trust is there it is very, very rare for someone not to access the hypnotic state; and once they are there, it is very rare that they will not get access to the memories they want, or need, to explore.

What are the benefits of experiencing hypnosis?

Medical research and the advent of electroencephalography machines (EEG) have shown that there are four key patterns of brain wave activity. It has been proven that when you are in the state of hypnosis there is a major, and very beneficial, change to the way the brain functions.

BETA: This is the state of normal waking consciousness, a state of full alertness often connected to physical activity and even excitement. The logical and critical reasoning parts of the mind are active here. Unfortunately in this state, the reasoning part of the mind can sometimes slip into being the inner critic. This can lead to the experience of stress and anxiety.

ALPHA: This is experienced with the onset of physical and mental relaxation. The mind is alert but relaxed; there is a sense of passive awareness like being in a pleasant daydream. It is experienced in light meditation and hypnosis. In this state you get to experience a greater sense of well-being, pleasure, and tranquillity; the imagination is heightened, visualisation is easier, and there is a greater ability to learn and remember things. Whilst in this state you are able to tune in to the voice of your intuition.

THETA: This is the state that is present during deep meditation and light sleep and includes the REM dream state. It is the realm of the subconscious and is experienced whilst in hypnosis or as you drift into the hypnogogic state, on your way into sleep, or the hypnopompic state, as you wake from a deeper sleep. In this state you can connect to the spiritual realms and the collective unconscious, you are capable of accelerated learning, healing of psychosomatic illness, increased creativity and insight, more vivid visualisations, and memory improvement. It is here that you experience the still silent space and the connection to the "I am" awareness.

DELTA: This is where the brain waves are the slowest in frequency. You experience this state when you are in deep, dreamless sleep or very deep, transcendental meditation where the awareness is fully detached. The body goes into what is known as the rest and digest phase, where the para-sympathetic nervous system is activated. This is the complete opposite to the "stress" state, which is often called fight or flight – when the body is primed for danger. It is here that deep healing and regeneration occurs, which is why not getting enough of the proper kind of rest can be damaging to the health. It is the gateway to the universal mind, where deeper wisdom can be accessed.

GAMMA: Recently it was discovered that there is another brain state, which is running at a very high frequency. Little is currently known about it but the research shows that it is associated with flashes of insight and high-level processing. A study was done with Tibetan monks who experienced this state whilst in very deep meditation; it is said to lead to greater feelings of bliss, longer life expectancy, and greater cognitive functioning.

In a normal waking state you have a combination of beta and alpha brain waves. As you drift into deeper relaxation, and the state of hypnosis, you access the alpha and sometimes theta waves. When you are very deeply in the hypnosis state it is possible to access delta waves as well and, of course, it is while you are in the delta state that the body is able to repair and heal itself. This explains why the state of hypnosis itself has so many benefits, beyond what you can learn while you are there. Just being in the hypnotic state allows you to gain a greater sense of mental clarity and inner peace; it allows the body to recover from stresses and strains, and frees up more energy for you to utilize in your future.

Why is hypnosis not recognised fully within the medical world?

In 1892 the British Medical Association endorsed hypnosis and in 1955 approved its use for childbirth and pain control and the area of psychoneuroses. At this time they recommended that hypnosis be taught to all physicians and medical students.

Unfortunately, the medical schools were a bit slow on the uptake. In the last ten years or so it has been offered as an optional module to students, but it is a long way off from being part of the curriculum. It is more widely taught in many European countries, and there are more and more people in the medical field who are starting to see it as a hugely beneficial tool. Unfortunately, due to many different factors over the years hypnosis has been given a lot of bad press, and it has not been taken seriously and there are still many misconceptions about what hypnosis really is.

Why does hypnosis have such a bad name?

In my role as a lecturer I often come across scepticism about hypnosis, due mainly to the negative connotations brought about by stage hypnosis and the characters throughout history that have used it, such as Svengali types and people like Rasputin and even some of the more modern-day entertainers who would have people believe that they can control people's minds and make them do things that they would not ordinarily do. Some people still think that it is dangerous and all about mind control, and others just think it is a joke and that it doesn't work. Generally this is because of this misunderstanding about what the state really is, and what can be achieved when they are there. Once people discover that it is something that they experience everyday anyway, and that they really are fully in control all the way through the experience, they can relax and allow the experience to unfold.

Can you really make people bark like a dog or cluck like a chicken in hypnosis?

This is a questions that my students, and often my clients, will ask; what they really mean is can I control them when they are in hypnosis? Can I get them to do things that they would not ordinarily do and the answer is always no – not unless they have a great desire to do these things, in which case I can help them to do it very well.

The key difference between stage hypnosis and therapeutic hypnosis is the fact that in the first instance, the volunteer, by going up on stage has handed over temporary control to the hypnotist. They have joined, what they already know will be, a situation where they are asked to do things out of the norm. Usually the people that volunteer are with friends, and this is an opportunity for them to get their fifteen minutes of fame; the buzz they get from the audience applause and laughter; and the praise from the hypnotist, egging them on to greater and greater feats.

In the therapeutic session it is very different; not at any point is control handed over – in fact, in this case the client gains more control over themselves and how they behave. It is always a partnership; the therapist is just the guide in the process, the navigator, who has the map of the journey and knows where to go. However, the client is driving the car and can decide how fast they want to go, if they want to stop at any point, and if they want to go in a different direction – although I do point out that it makes sense to go the way I suggest, as I know where to take them.

Do people blurt out their secrets in hypnosis?

This is another myth, perpetrated by the media and movies about hypnosis being like mind control, and it simply is not true. People can lie whilst under hypnosis or choose not to tell you anything. I had one client who had several past life sessions, and we did the whole thing content free. I communicated with his unconscious mind, using what we call "ideomotor" responses, signals from the unconscious; he got all the answers he needed, which was the only important thing.

Do people need to be very deeply in hypnosis to get access to past life memories?

I like to explain to my clients that their awareness is a little bit like a submarine. While they are in the conscious, waking state the submarine is floating on the surface of the water and they are able to decide what to take on board and what to reject. In order to get them into the subconscious realm I need them to go just below the surface of the water, into a space of inner peace and into the space where all their memories have been stored. Very deep trance is not really necessary; what is important is that their awareness drifts to just below the water line.

How do people do this?

All they have to do is to get into a comfortable space, preferably not lying down completely, as this is too reminiscent of sleeping – just reclining. I then ask them to close their eyes and focus their attention on their breathing. I am able to use my voice, the words that I say, and the timing of my words to get them into a state of physical relaxation and mental focus. By focusing on the breath and on the sensations in their body they move their awareness more and more inwards and are able to leave external distractions behind. They are then given easy instructions to follow that can take them safely into the state of hypnosis.

How do they know if they are hypnotised?

Sometimes people will report that they heard every word that I said. Other times it is as if my voice drifts away and they miss parts of it; sometimes it feels as if they have nodded off for a short while or they find themselves thinking of dinner that night or what they did at the weekend. I reassure them beforehand that all of this is fine and perfectly natural. All I need them to do is remain curious about what they will experience. After the session most people report that they have lost all track of time and even though they were in the trance state for an hour or so it may feel that only a few minutes have gone by; or if they had a very long and detailed past life experience, especially the ones where they explore more than one life in a session, it might feel as if hours and hours have passed. Time distortion is very much part of the hypnotic process.

Will they remember it all?

Generally once people have reconnected to past life stories they do remember it all, in the same way that they can recall their real-life holiday memories. The events are now stored in the memory bank in the same way. Occasionally people will have amnesia for the events that occurred, but the sessions are always recorded and so they can go back and get a reminder later.

What if the past life is very traumatic?

As the process is designed to release any negativity attached to the past life, and to allow a deep healing to occur, the memories are always emotionally neutral at the end. The insights and understandings remain but the negative charges are gone. Sometimes it may take a little while for the person to process what they have learnt, but they always feel a sense of relief afterwards.

What happens once they are in the state of hypnosis?

Once they are physically relaxed, and mentally focused, they will be asked to visualise certain things and I always reassure people that they are not expected to "see things" clearly but merely get a sense of the things I am describing. I will often ask them to tell me what colour their front door is and whether the key goes in high or low. In order to tell me this they have to make a picture of the door in their "mind's eye." I get them to imagine going through the door and tell me what colour the walls are and what is on the floor. Once they have done this they realise that they *are* able to visualise, and they are then able to relax and let the experience flow. They are then given instructions to visualise a staircase, and to imagine going down the stairs; this is done in time to their breathing, one step down for each breath that they release. This helps them to relax more deeply and is a metaphorical indicator that they are going deeper into their own inner world; all of this is reinforced by what I am saying as they go down the stairs. Once they have reached the bottom of the stairs they create a safe place within their imagination. This can be the image of somewhere that they know in real life or just somewhere they would like to be, like a beautiful beach or a garden. I always set this up so that if at any point throughout the process they were unhappy or did not like what they were experiencing they could just visualise this safe place and they would float straight to it.

Although I have to say in all the years that I have done this work, very rarely has anyone ever gone there before the session was over, as the past life experience is far too interesting and they are usually far too absorbed in what is going on around them.

How can you make sure that they will only go somewhere that is safe for them to explore?

In order to ensure that I am not taking them anywhere that would not be safe, I always communicate with their unconscious mind directly. I can do this once they are in the trance state by using what we call "finger signals" or ideomotor responses; this is simply a means by which I can speak direct to their unconscious, bypassing the conscious mind. The unconscious mind is asked to lift one finger as a *yes* signal and one for a *no*. I ask them to signal to me whether it is okay for them to explore their past lives, and I will only proceed once I have received a signal that is affirmative.

How else can the unconscious signal help?

Once I have permission I ask the unconscious mind, or the higher mind, to guide us to the lifetime that will show us the origin, or the root cause, of any problems they might be experiencing. Alternatively they can be guided to the lifetime where major talents and skills originated. Specifically speaking, I want them to be directed to the lifetime that will provide the greatest insight, or healing, for them in the session, and their unconscious mind knows better than either of us where that will be; I am always led by them and, more importantly, their higher mind.

If there are many past lives, how will they know which life to choose?

I ask them to visualise a pathway or a corridor leading off from their safe place; this is their imaginative realm and so they can usually do this quite easily. I tell them they will find many doors or entrances.

I have learnt over the years to be ambiguous at this point as sometimes people decide that they would like to climb trees, go through portholes, float on clouds, or simply travel into light or mist to get to their other lives. What usually happens is that one of the entrances will stand out in some way – it might be a different shape or colour to the others, or they might just sense that it is the right entrance.

Do people always need to experience the hypnosis or see the corridor or pathway?

If the past life memory is quite close to the surface already and they have some thoughts or feelings about it they can easily identify, they may not even need very formal hypnosis. It is possible that they can get access to the past life via what we call bridging – focussing on the feelings or the particular phrase that goes with their problem.

For instance, one client who was struggling to see anything had been very clear that whenever she found herself near water she would start to feel panicky and breathless and a voice in her head would say "It's not safe, it's not safe." When she was relaxed she focussed on this feeling and repeated the words to herself; she soon found herself as a small child, floating in a very cold sea, a large liner sinking in front of her. She was very keen to reassure me that it was not the Titanic but a much smaller vessel. She was freezing and desperate to find her younger brother and parents. She found her brother clinging to some debris and held on to him as best she could, but there were no signs of her parents. In the distance she could see several smaller boats with people on board but she could not get them to see or hear her. Each time she tried to cry out her mouth filled with water. As she sank for the last time her last thoughts about the water were "It's not safe, it's not safe." Sadly, both she and her brother had drowned.

It was an emotional discovery but after the session was finished, and we had re-leased the emotional charge, she reported feeling so much lighter, as if a weight had been lifted. She saw that she did not need to be so afraid of the water and that the sea, albeit something to be cautious of, was not a real threat to her in her current life. She was able to let the irrational, and life limiting, belief that had held her back and prevented her from any activities connected to the sea, be released for good.

Is there anything that might prevent someone from getting access to their past life memories?

Generally there is nothing to prevent people from getting access to the unconscious realms and getting the information they need; however, in some cases there may well be issues that need to be resolved in the current life first. If there are big, red-flag memories in the way that need to be dealt with, then they may emerge first.

Are there any other ways that you can be sidetracked?

Sometimes sudden intense emotions may surface, either as tears or uncontrollable laughter; this is because once they are in the safe place, within their subconscious realm, memories with flags on can, and often will, take the opportunity to come straight to the surface so that they can be dealt with. The release that occurs is always of huge benefit, and it is always important to reassure the client that this is a very good thing. "Better out than in" as I always say. At other times a person might need to pop into a safe and pleasant memory first, from either their current life or a past life, just to see what the experience is like. Once they are reassured, and know that they can control where they go and what they do when they are there, they are then easily able to slip into the more challenging past life experiences.

Is there anything else that can get in the way?

From time to time people will report that there are other energies, spirit attachments, thought forms, or even beings that claim to be demons, in the way. If this is the case then they need to be cleared before you can proceed; more on this in a later chapter.

Once they do have access to the past life experience, how do you know what they are experiencing?

Once they have found the lifetime they need to explore, I tell them that they will be able to speak to me and share with me what is happening to them. I reassure them that the sound of their voice will help them to stay relaxed and focused and that they can share whatever they are experiencing, even if it feels a little strange.

What if they feel as if they are making it up?

Before the process begins I always let people know that at this point a funny thing will happen because they *will* feel as if they are making it up. Going back to my submarine analogy, they are now below the surface of the water; in the subconscious realm, once I ask them to speak to me, it is as if a part of their conscious mind has to re-engage – a little like putting a periscope up. As a result, the questioning and analytical part of their mind is now present, and this part of them is going to feel as though everything that they experience is being made up. It will wonder how on earth, they can possibly be seeing what they are seeing, or knowing what they appear to know. By warning them in advance that this will happen, it diffuses the effect and allows them to stay open and curious about what comes up. I also reassure them that it is very much like when they recall an old holiday memory: the more they connect to it the more information begins to emerge. By sharing everything that comes up, no matter how trivial it may seem, the more the story starts to unfold and the more sense it begins to make.

What happens once they have accessed the life?

This can be different for everyone; for some people it is as if it all unfolds like a movie. They experience the story as if they are really there, fully present within it. The story emerges bit by bit, jumping from key scene to key scene. Some people see nothing at all but when they are questioned about who they are, where they are, and what they are doing the answers just pop into their minds. Other people just sense what is going on and the answers just come to them. Often it may be a combination of all three. The idea is to get as much information as possible.

What is the first thing that they are aware of?

The first thing I do is get them to become aware of their feet. This really helps them to identify with the person they have become, and to get grounded into the character. Often they are shocked to discover that they are the opposite sex, from a very different cultural group, or just very different to who they are now.

One of my clients was quite sceptical about past lives and after I had taken him into his safe place and given instructions for him to enter into the past life, he insisted that he could see nothing, that it was all just dark. It was only when I asked him to tell me what he was wearing on his feet that things changed; immediately he laughed and told me he was wearing sandals that had straps and were made of leather, was wearing a toga, and had a sword tied over one shoulder. He found it strange that such a weapon would be worn over a toga, but having identified more with his character he soon allowed himself to have the experience, which was, in the end, of great value and very healing.

What do you need to find out next?

We establish where they are and get as much detail as possible about them: what they are wearing, what year it is, what they are doing, and most importantly what is significant about that moment in time – for them. We need to find out why they have found themselves in this particular experience.

Then what happens?

Once we have exhausted the first scene, and found out everything we can, I move them on to the next significant moment in time. It is possible that at this point they may slip into another life. This usually happens if there is a theme to be explored in several lives. In my experience there is usually one profound life that needs to be addressed or a series of lesser lives with a theme that has continued throughout.

One of my clients had been having trouble with her weight and it did not seem to matter what she tried, it would not shift. She had some strange habits with regard to her eating and would often torture herself by buying indulgent foods, such as cake and chocolate, but not allow herself to eat it. Her husband would eventually dive into it, not wanting it to go to waste, and could not understand why she would keep doing this. She wanted to know if it was a problem from a past life and was somewhat stunned by what she learnt. She discovered not one but five lives, all of which were relevant.

In the first she found she had been a Roman slave girl serving decadent Romans with tables laden with fine foods – none of which she was ever allowed to eat. She had been angry that she was not one of them and had felt deeply deprived and hungry throughout the whole experience. In the next life she returned to the early 1800s where she had led a very sheltered life; her younger sister had died at an early age of consumption and this had left her feeling bereft. The cook, in that lifetime, had prepared all sorts of delicious foods to comfort her and make up for her feelings of sadness. She ate her way through her problems and ended up incredibly large. Then we learnt of another life where she and her husband had been wrongly accused of a crime and had been sent, as criminals, to Australia. She had been pregnant and the voyage had proven to be incredibly distressing; they had been separated and sent to different sides of the ship and she nearly starved. Her baby hadn't survived the trip and this loss was extremely distressing for her.

Her next life was in the late 1800s, in England, a fairly simple life where food was still her main source of comfort. She married at a very young age and when she gave birth to her first baby she had not been strong enough; she lost a lot of blood, and died very young, feeling as though it had all been a waste. All of this had left her with very intense emotions around food, and so we set out to heal all the negative responses and the feelings of loss – to allow her to acquire a sense of normality in her eating habits. After the session she reported that she no longer had the old compulsion to eat all the time; she found that she could trust herself to eat when she wanted to and no longer had to torture herself with the chocolates and the over-indulgent foods. As a result she experienced a great sense of relief and was able to actually enjoy her relationship with food and with herself; her husband was happier too and ended up a few stone lighter himself. So whether there is one life or several it doesn't matter; all are equally as valid in the healing work that is to be done.

What is the most important part of the session?

The key part of the work, which always sounds a bit morbid, but it isn't, is the point at which the life comes to an end: the death scene. Some clients are fearful that this will be traumatic and upsetting but it very rarely is. This moment in the session is vital because what we are looking for is the last conscious thought a person has before they leave the life and the emotion that the thought carries. This is the "emotional hook" that affects them, in the present, and this is the bit that needs to be addressed. This is where the powerful healing can begin.

What happens after the death scene?

At the point at which the life comes to an end I ask them to float up and out of the body and find a safe place above it where they can safely view the life they have just left. This is a place in the spirit realms where they get to see through their "spiritual eyes" with a much greater sense of perspective. This is the place where they can review the life and begin to understand what the lessons were all about. First we look at the Karmic lesson they had chosen to learn in that lifetime and see if it had been accomplished. If not, it gives them a powerful sense of what they may be working through in this life; if it was completed, they can relax knowing that the work for that particular lesson is done.

What happens next?

The next part of the session involves healing any physical damage that has happened to the body that has just been left. The body is repaired in whatever way is needed and is restored to wholeness. One of my clients had been fatally stabbed in his past life and in the transformational part of the session he needed to remove the knife and allow the wound to mend; he imagined stitching the wound up and then sent healing energy to the area. After the session he reported that a dull ache that he had felt in that area for most of his life, which had been unexplained, had gone.

Memories of physical events that have been stored in the body's energy field need to be dealt with and healed too and sometimes people are returned to replay the significant events, helping them to break free, fight back, or release any physical ties or restrictions. This is immensely empowering and the catharsis that often accompanies this process is immensely beneficial. Sometimes clients need a little help to break free, or to get away from people, and if this is the case then they are invited to bring in a spirit guide to help them, or perhaps a power animal, that has the qualities they need.

One client who wanted to escape and run free brought in the energy of a gazelle. This animal was chosen because it had long legs, first to kick her attacker out of the way and second so that she could reach great speeds, run away, and never be caught. Negative emotions and feelings that have been held in the body also need to be released.

How are they released?

Once the client has identified where the stuck emotions, or blockages of energy, are in the body, they can either bring in healing white light energy or remove the energy by more practical means.

What do you mean by this?

Energy held in the body may take many forms, such as a gas, a liquid, or a solid, and it can be cleared in whichever way makes sense to the client. One of my clients had what she described as "a heaviness" around her heart and she saw it as a heavy grey gas. When I asked her what she needed to remove it she said, "I need a Dyson to suck it out," so that's what she did; apparently modern gadgets have their place in this work too. Once she had visualised it being drawn away she then filled the space with healing white light; afterwards she reported feeling a lot lighter. Other times the energy has had a solid quality and clients have required hammers or chisels to move it away. I always allow the client to choose the tools they need and never impose my ideas upon them; in the past when I have offered suggestions they have usually been rejected.

It is amazing how much clarity clients have about what type of healing they need when they are in this focused state. Sometimes they need to verbalise their pain or let the emotion out in a vocal way. This is not always so good when you have another client, or someone that knows them, waiting in the next room. When I used to rent rooms I would often have to reassure them that I was not beating my clients with sticks when they had been yelling at the top of their voices in the middle of a session. What was reassuring for the centre, where I rented the rooms, was that my clients always left smiling and reported feeling hugely liberated afterwards. They often left tired but very, very satisfied. It is a little standing joke that I have with my clients that when asked what I do for a living I should say that I make people cry – but only in the best possible way.

What else is important in the healing part of the session?

One of the key elements of the transformational work is the clients meetings with the significant people from the lifetime. It is important that they meet with, and talk to, all of the key characters in order to understand the roles that they have played and bring meaning to their experiences. I will talk more about the dialogues that occur in the next chapter.

Is there anything else that can happen to ensure the healing is complete?

If there had been huge disappointments, or the life had not gone the way they would have wanted, it may be that the person needs to go back and relive the life, and this time have it go the way they would have liked it to happen; this "reframing" can be profoundly healing.

I had one client who was a sailor on board a ship in the 1700s; the man was about 27 years old and had come ashore at an English port. Whilst walking through the port a fight had broken out and he was arrested and wrongly accused of murder. Within days he had been tried, found guilty, and was hung in front of a baying mob. He did not speak the language, was alone, had no one to vouch for him, and was desolate. My client released huge sobs throughout the whole ordeal, incredibly upset by the unfairness of it all.

Strangely, it turned out that she had felt compelled to travel from her native home in Italy, at the age of 25, and settle down to live in the UK. Shortly after her arrival she began to suffer from an immune disorder that had no known cause. It had started when she was 27, at just the time before her hanging in the other life. You have to wonder if she had been drawn back to the UK as a result of that memory and whether the imprint of the fear, and the frustration at being wrongly accused, had affected her health.

Can that happen?

Anything is possible. In the past life session she got to go back and reconnect with the sailor; when we checked what he needed for his healing to be complete he said he wanted the chance to have more adventures. So we rewound the memory and instead of him going to the port that night he stayed on the ship. He then got to imagine having all kinds of adventures and dying of old age, content, satisfied, and at peace with himself and the world: a very different energy at the end. After the session my client reported that she felt as if the weight of the world had been lifted from her and she felt really liberated. She was very curious to see if her immune system would now be restored; the last I heard from her there had been great improvements and she was well on the road to recovery.

What else needs to be addressed?

Unhelpful vows or promises that may have been made in other lives need to be identified and replaced with something more helpful, creating powerful new mantras for the person to utilise in the future. One of my clients, who had been single for many years, had been betrayed, in her past life, by her husband and had vowed that she would "never love again." In the session she discovered that she had a contract with him. She had chosen this experience in order to learn about suffering and when she realised he was just doing what he had promised to do, before they arrived, she was able to forgive him and let go of the pain. Her new affirmation was that she was free to love again and to be loved. She left the session with a renewed optimism and a belief that, perhaps, she could now explore a relationship.

Once all of the transformational work has been done, what happens to the past life body that was previously lived in?

There is a powerful release that comes at the end of the session, because once the lifetime has been fully explored and all of the healing is complete, it is time to release the connection to the past life body. This means the past life body, which has been healed and newly restored – the body that had housed the soul energy, and was still energetically trapped in the experience because of the unresolved issues – is free to return back to loved ones in the spirit realms, back to the light, and back home to reunite with source. The releasing of ties, or cords that make up the connections to that body, is always done with a sense of gratitude and love. The part that returns to the light is able to collect up any lost fragments of their soul energy that may have been scattered, and lost, along the way and is able to collect up any other lost souls that may have been floating around and help them to find their way back to the light.

Then what happens?

The person is then guided back to their safe place for a period of rest and recuperation. Sometimes a spirit guide, a loved one, or even an angelic presence will be there to greet them, to thank them for the healing work they have done in the session, and to offer them unconditional love and support. Their spirit guide may appear in human form or just as an energy, and these guides will often provide additional insights and explanations with regard to what has just happened.

Sometimes the messages are cryptic, and are for the client to ponder on, and sometimes they are very clear, concise, and to the point. It is different for everyone. The great thing is that, once the connection has been made, it is easy for the person to communicate with their guides again whenever they need to. They can also just go to their safe place again whenever they need to, to rest and to heal their minds and bodies.

What is the last step in the session?

Within the safe place there is usually a gift for the person. The gift is symbolic of the work they have done. It might be a shape, an object, a colour, or just a feeling, but whatever it is, they always know what it represents for them. My sailor client was given a basket of beautiful shiny apples, which represented nature and freedom and health. Another client received a shiny red heart to represent love and blessings; another found a pure white crystal to represent purity and greater clarity of thought. I usually recommend that my clients find something that will remind them of this symbol so that whenever they look at it they remember the healing that has occurred and can remember to feel better as a result.

How do people feel when they wake up, do they remember it all clearly?

The general response when people wake up is "Wow." That goes for me and them. They will often say it is not at all what they expected, and they are hugely surprised at the experience they have just been through. It is important to identify the parallels the past life has to their life in the present and in the many, many sessions I have experienced, the parallels are always there. It can take some time for all of the learnings to sink in fully and I generally advise my clients to go home and write up the story in as much detail as they can remember, because, just like those holiday memories, the more they focus on it, the more information can emerge and the more connections they can make.

Is it usual to record the sessions?

Yes. So much can happen in a session that it is sometimes difficult to remember everything and often there are very profound insights and messages that can be helpful to the person later. I always record the sessions on a Dictaphone, and over the years I have discovered that I am able to write at exactly the same speed as the person is speaking; so I always write down every thing they say. That way there is always a permanent record of the session should they need to review it in more detail later.

So is it safe to explore past lives with no one to guide you?

Yes, because you are always in control and can choose to leave, or change things, if you are not happy with what you are experiencing. The recording that comes with the book has two tracks. The first will guide you safely into your very own comfortable state of hypnosis or deep relaxation. Once you are comfortable with this process you can move on to the second track. This has been designed to take you safely into a past life experience of your own, to a lifetime where you experienced something positive, and will allow you to gain access to resources and skills that you may be unaware that you possess. When I listened to it the first time I found myself in a life as a teacher in Austria who loved his job, just as I do, and had a large and very happy family (that bit I don't have). I also saw a life as a sheep herder in Norway; now this may not seem very insightful or profound, but it was a life of real peace and connection to nature. I loved being outside and having no responsibilities, other than to tend to my sheep, and lived very contentedly, dying alone but having experienced no stress in my life at all. As someone who teaches people how to live without stress this was quite an important experience to have. I remember it quite fondly.

What if you want to deal with negative patterns or deal with difficult challenges?

I would strongly recommend that if you are seeking to explore negative patterns and find the root of difficulties, or challenges you may be having in your life, that you seek a reputable practitioner to guide you safely through the process, ensuring you clear away any unwanted beliefs and negative emotions safely and completely. Information on how to find a good practitioner in your area is listed at the end of this book. A written version of the relaxation track is also included at the end of the book, should you wish to make a recording of it for yourself.

EXERCISE 2: *Changing the Pictures*

To change the way negative memories are stored:
1. Ensure that you are fully dissociated; imagine stepping out and watching the event as though you are watching a movie.
2. Freeze the images until they just look like still photographs.
3. Drain all the colour out.
4. Make them blurry.
5. Turn the sound off; silence them completely.
6. Shrink them down until they are tiny and send them into a sealed trash can in your mind.
7. Lock with a big padlock, or a big bow, so that the memories can only come out when you make a conscious and deliberate effort to find them.

Recalling good memories:

1. Imagine you are back at that moment in time.
2. Recall in as much detail, as you can, what was going on around you.
3. Make this image bigger and brighter.
4. Make the sounds louder.
5. Let the good feelings get stronger.
6. Leave this memory big and bright.
7. Float out of it and place this memory somewhere where you can see it clearly and can find it easily when you need it.

Recognize that you can now control what you focus on and, as a result, feel much stronger and more in control.

DOROTHY:
"Someday I'll wish upon a star ... "

3

Coincidence or Not?

In the movie *The Wizard of Oz,* Dorothy Gale, the young girl from Kansas, is forced to ask important questions about her life. She wonders, out loud, in her song "Somewhere Over the Rainbow" whether or not there is a better place where she could go, where life was easier, and where her troubles would simply "melt like lemon drops." She wondered if it was possible to "wish" her way into a better place. The saying "Be careful what you wish for" comes to mind because the universe does work in mysterious ways and strange circumstances then followed. First she nearly lost her beloved dog, Toto, to the wicked Miss Gulch who wanted to have him put down after he bit her; this led her to run away. She then ran into a travelling magician who persuaded her to go home but a tornado was about to hit her home, and she was too late to get to the shelter.

Once she got into her room she was knocked unconscious, and this meant she was able to get just what she wished for. For when she woke up she found herself in a strange and magical world in which she was about to have a very transformational journey. When her house, which had been caught up in the spinning tornado, landed in Oz it happened to land on the very spot where the Wicked Witch of the West was standing; she was a very powerful witch who had been terrorizing the local people, who were very small and known as Munchkins. The wicked witch had worn a pair of ruby slippers, which were very powerful and only the person who killed the witch could claim their power. They ended up magically appearing on Dorothy's feet. This was to be both a blessing – as eventually the shoes were to be her ticket home – and a curse, because before that could happen they were to become the source of her greatest distress, as the Wicked Witch of the West hunted her down in a desperate attempt to take ownership of the shoes and their power for herself. So was it just by chance that she landed on exactly that spot, or was it some strange synchronicity that brought her to that place – at that very moment? Was it a coincidence that Glinda the Good Witch of the South arrived just at the right moment, in a beautiful pink bubble, to inform her of the yellow brick road that would lead her to a wizard and his, apparent, ability to send her home to Kansas?

Was it a coincidence that the characters she met along the way had just the right attributes to help her, and all of them were prepared to fight to the death to save her – when the time came? And was it a coincidence that the quest the wizard set them (the kind of quest traditionally set to all heroes since the beginning of time: to test their courage and commitment) and all of the difficult situations they got into as a result of that quest, taught all of them just what they needed to know? I don't think so.

In the process Dorothy got to learn many important lessons, but the most important thing she learnt was that it didn't matter *where* you were geographically, it was what was in your heart and mind that mattered. She learnt that everyone and everything she needed was already in her life; in fact, they were already in her own back yard and all she needed to change was the way she behaved and the way she looked at her life. She got to see the value, and as a result, got to appreciate the key people in her life; this knowledge was to bring her all the happiness and joy she could ever need.

How can you ensure you learn all the lessons you need to?

Thankfully, in order for you to learn important lessons about your life, you do not need to have your home thrown into the heart of a tornado or be hit over the head and knocked into a dream-like state. Many people sail through life in a dream-like state anyway, taking things that happen around them for granted. But when things take a turn for the unusual, or seem a little strange, they are forced to open their eyes and really look at what life is trying to tell them. And when they really open their eyes and look around them they often see that there are all kinds of messages and signs – in all kinds of places. All kinds of strange coincidences that can't be explained.

Does coincidence really exist?

I have to say that I have never really believed in the word *coincidence*. I think it is just a word created to explain something that is clearly unexplainable. But it depends entirely on your belief system. Some believe that coincidences are merely random events, which are linked, but happen by chance; but Charles Fort, an investigator into paranormal phenomena, and Carl Jung believed that there was more to it than that. They spent years investigating people's accounts of coincidences and found they usually did have a deeper meaning. Jung believed in the idea of synchronicity, that events happen as a result of a predetermined plan, leading to a series of events that were inevitable.

In his book *Synchronicity,* Jung tells a story about a client who was struggling to deal with her emotional life and her ability to believe in herself. She was very good at intellectualizing the events of her life, but she could see no meaning to things. Whilst in the session she was recounting a dream in which she was given a substantial piece of jewellery, a golden scarab. As she recounted the dream he heard a noise at the window, a gentle tapping sound. When he turned he saw a beetle knocking against the window. He opened it and the beetle flew in. It was a scarabaeid beetle, which is golden-green in colour and very rare in those parts; it was also the closest thing you could get to her dream symbol. He handed her the beetle and said, "Here is your scarab." After the incident she could no longer deny that there was more to the nature of life than she had once supposed; she could not deny this "meaningful coincidence" and as a result she was able to let go of her limited thinking and get to the root of her problems. She then made real progress in her journey toward wholeness. Jung firmly believed synchronicity could be linked to the "intervention of grace" and that these events were linked to something outside of everyday occurrences, putting them into the realm of the paranormal. Even Albert Einstein, with whom he regularly debated these ideas, believed not all coincidence could be rationalized away when he said "Coincidence is God's way of remaining anonymous."

What does it mean, then, when these synchronistic events occur?

These "coincidences," or synchronistic events, are simply signposts to guide you along the right path, which you can choose to acknowledge or ignore as you wish; some may be messages from the divine, or from the higher spiritual realms, sent to help you see which way to go at critical times in your life, which you might otherwise have missed. Some may have been pre-arranged by you and some are just there to let you see the interconnectedness of everything around you.

What kinds of signposts appear for people?

Signposts can appear in a multitude of different ways and often most unexpectedly. Have you ever heard a piece of music, a snippet of a conversation, or read something in a book, newspaper, or even something on the side of a bus that just happened to answer a question you were asking in your head? It happens to me all the time.

When I got married, many years ago, it was in Las Vegas. I was very clear in my mind about what I wanted, and I spent a whole day looking for the right chapel; it was very important to me to have a proper chapel and just the right amount of shiny neon lights. Once I found the right chapel I just needed a decent Elvis impersonator to finish the whole thing off. "Where are we going to find a good Elvis?" I asked my groom-to-be while we sat on the bus back to our hotel. "Excuse me," said the man sitting next to me, "but my best friend is a fantastic Elvis and he is singing at a hotel which is two stops away; if you ask him, I am sure he would love to join you." We got off the bus, and there he was, all white jumpsuit and sparkling rhinestones – a perfect Elvis. What were the chances? The day we were getting married just happened to be his day off and he was delighted to sing for us.

That night in our hotel, which had about 3,000 rooms, we bumped into an old friend who was a musician and a bit of a Buddy Holly look-alike; we had attended his rock-and-roll wedding in London a few years earlier. "What are you doing here?" we asked. "My band is playing in San Diego and my wife insisted that we come to Vegas because she wanted to see a Vegas wedding." They were only staying for two days and our wedding was the next day. What were the chances? Now obviously you will have deduced that I am a bit of an Elvis fan, so when the car that came to pick us up turned out to be a burgundy limo that had once belonged to Elvis, and was given to the driver for all his years of service driving him around in Hollywood, we were even more blown away. I mean really, out of all the thousands of limos in Vegas, what were the chances?

On a slightly more spiritual note, I got an email from someone in Scotland, asking me if I thought that past life work would be helpful for a problem she was experiencing. I agreed and when she asked if I could recommend someone to help her, I found myself volunteering. She had children and didn't have the time to come to London so I asked her to find out if there was anyone else she knew who might like a session and that way I could justify the trip up there; I do love Scotland, and I hadn't been there for a while. Very shortly she came back and said that a friend would also like a session; she had a therapy room that I could use and a spare room that I could stay in if I wanted it. They lived on the outskirts of Edinburgh, and even though it was a bit impractical, with my very busy schedule, the next thing I knew I was on a plane.

As I arrived I remember thinking that I had no way of identifying the woman that would pick me up, but I needn't have worried. As soon as I stepped into the airport hall I knew her straight away. It was an odd feeling, as if we had met many times before. When we arrived at her friend's place it was a similar thing. We had tea and chatted and then got down to some work. It was an amazing few days but what was really astounding was that in the course of the past life exploration, not only did we resolve the problem she had, but we found out that all three of us were part of the same soul group. Clearly we were supposed to meet; we were told that there was work that the three of us were meant to do together. So I am now scheduled to run workshops there and continue the work that my soul group obviously set up in advance. I believe that there are messages, signposts, and incredible synchronicities all around you if you take the time to look.

If these signposts are there to prompt people through life, are they ever really free to choose the life they want to live or are there circumstances, relationships, or careers that are "just meant to be," no matter what other ideas they may have had?

A common phrase is "You can choose your friends but you can't choose your family!" It is one that I used to use a lot. I also spent a lot of my childhood telling my mother that I had not asked to be born. I now feel very embarrassed by that idea, knowing what I now know. Because I believe, with absolute certainty, that you do choose your parents, and the family, and the circumstances that you are born into before you get here. In the inter-life space, where you go when one life ends, you get to choose the kind of life that you want to live next. In this space you get to review the life just lived, and based on what you did or didn't achieve, generate a plan for the next one. This is when you choose the family and, as a result, the body you are going to move into. This process of choice requires an awareness of the character traits, and the qualities, that will be required to help you to fulfill your chosen mission. This will include the astrological star sign that will best suit your needs, providing you with the specific qualities and attributes that you will need.

If you are going to be a fine artist, a Virgo need for attention to detail may be required and if you are planning to be on the stage, or teach, you may need a little of the Leo's ability to show off – obviously no coincidence that I was born in the middle of August. You also get to choose the body type, whether strong or weak, healthy or poorly, sporty or not, musical or not, artistic or not…you get the picture. Then you choose the key players in your life, or wait for souls to volunteer to play different parts. You choose the environment that will serve you the best. Key events are decided upon and provisions are set up in advance to make sure they come to pass. These include signposts and agreements with these volunteers for them to turn up when you need them. These are planned to appear along the way to prompt you, and remind you of your mission, just in case you veer off track.

However, as I have said before, when you arrive on earth you have free will and are not tied to any of the choices that you may have made. There is also the small issue of the complete amnesia that happens at birth, for all the decisions you made, just to make it a little more challenging. Apparently this was not always the case. The souls who first came to the earth plane to have these learning experiences remembered what they were supposed to be doing while they were here and thought that the challenges were too easy. So amnesia was created as well as having complete free will, which means that you do not have to follow the preset path exactly as it was set out; however, if you do fail to make the choices, as they were preplanned, your karmic lessons may never get the chance to be worked out properly and that means that you will have to keep finding ways to work through the lessons until you get them right.

Some of you may have found that you have experienced something similar to this in your current life: you get presented with a lesson, or a test, and if you fail to pass it the first time round the universe has a very compelling way of ensuring that you get another chance. The first time you were tested you may have experienced the equivalent of a slight tap, which you may or may not have acknowledged. If you chose to ignore it, next time round you were likely to get a push; and if you still insisted on ignoring the obvious, the lesson, or test, usually arrives like a very large kick to the behind. This is just to make absolutely sure that you do what you need to do because if you still don't get it, and your lifetime ends with the problem unresolved, you will have to return again and again until it is. So, even though the tests that appear in your life may seem hard sometimes, it is really important for you to be brave and face them head on so you are free to move to the next level. There is no escape from the lessons which, clearly, are predestined.

Is this why so many people are keen to discover what their destiny is?

The word *destiny* comes from the word *destinare* in Latin, which means "to determine, to make firm, or to establish." The word *destination* has the same root. So when you talk about destiny you are talking about the plan, or cosmic blueprint, for your life, that which has been firmly established and set in advance. This is the path you are "destined" to follow because there is a goal for your life, an outcome that needs to be achieved and a place at the end of the road that you need to get to. However, how you get there is up to you.

How can you find out what your destiny, or mission, in life is?

Many people who find themselves on a spiritual path, or on a voyage of personal discovery, have a vague sense that there is something they are supposed to be doing with their life. This is often accompanied by a feeling that they don't belong "here" and want to go home to their real family; they just don't know where that family is. In order to remember what the mission is you have to pay attention to the clues life presents to you. You have to take time to still your mind and ask your intuition to be your guide. That way you don't ignore the signs when they appear – signs that, to the uninitiated, are just misconstrued as coincidence. You recognize that synchronicity is at work.

What can you do to encourage synchronicity in your life?

It is a really good idea to keep a journal so that you can remember the weird and wonderful things that happen to you. You can put down any unusual events, or significant dreams, and really think about what they may be trying to tell you. Keep in mind that when you dream, all the components of that dream represent you in some way, with the exception of prophetic dreams or ones where, perhaps, you have been astral travelling.

Is there something you can do to bring more synchronistic events your way, to help you achieve your goals, or a particular way to get the universe to help you?

You can ask for help if you need it, but there is a saying that goes "be careful what you wish for as one day it might come true," and it is one to be very aware of.

Why is this?

Often what you ask for is not really what you need, and when you get it you may decide you don't want it after all or it may arrive in a form that you really hadn't expected, especially if you are not very specific.

What about cosmic ordering? Can you not just order what you want?

Much has been written about cosmic ordering and the law of attraction, teaching you how to ask the universe for what you want. The teachings say that when you feel good about yourself on the inside, are clear about what you want, and visualize having it already, then you will get the help you need to reach your desired goal; these goals will be met through a series of synchronistically related occurrences or with help from external sources that are beyond our control, such as our guides or our guardian angels.

Do you think there are other forces at work?

I like to think so, and over the years have been provided with enough evidence to believe that it is true; I do feel a strong connection to my guides and the angels and regularly communicate with them. I tune in to the spirit realms before I start my work everyday, and I will call on them when I need help – and even sometimes when I don't; sometimes I just want to express gratitude for what I already have.

So is that all you have to do?

No, asking for help is not enough. If you really want something badly enough you still have to take action and make it happen for yourself. Guides and angels can lead you to the right place at the right time but none of them can do the practical work for you. The most important thing for you to do is to learn how to read the "signs" in your life, and when a sign does appear, to make sure you follow the path you are taken to. You then have to take action to make things happen; as my very wise therapist once said, "Trust in God, but tie up your camel." The one thing I do know for sure is that, whether you are receiving any kind of spiritual intervention or not, you will get more of what you focus on. If you look for things that are wrong and not working you will find them and continue to find them, and if you look for what is right and what does work for you, you will find more of that. Life just works that way.

So be very careful to focus on what you want, not on what you don't want, because the universe and your brain does not quantify the negatives that you say or think. "Don't think of a Blue Elephant" being the classic example; you cannot *not* think of the elephant, don't forget your keys, don't get stressed, I don't want to be fat or lonely or unhappy – guess what will happen? Whenever you are setting goals for yourself it is imperative that you set them in the affirmative and set them in the present moment, not at some distant time in the future. "I am happy" is much stronger than "I want to be happy."

How can you make sure you do not miss the signs that are there for you?

As long as you remain in a state of openness, and curiosity, you will see these signs around you. You will see meaning in the events of your life and you will be able to join up the dots.

When you access the calm, still place within your mind and tune in to your higher self, your soul's wisdom, you get to move into the "flow" of life and then magic can happen. The energy within you flows, you get to experience more and more synchronicity, and then you get to live the life you always dreamed of.

Is there anything that can block this flow of energy in your body?

If there are any blockages within the body's chakra system, it can prevent energy from flowing freely, and then it can become stagnated and trapped, causing problems.

What are chakras?

The word *chakra* is a Sanskrit word meaning *wheel* or *disk*; there are seven main Chakra centres in the body that are all dedicated to different body parts and different emotional centres. If they are out of alignment it can affect your general well-being. This can be checked using a simple body scan or with a pendulum. Each one is represented by a different colour, and they all vibrate at different rates, getting faster as they move up through the body. Some people can actually see them spinning. They start at the base of the spine and continue up the top of the head. The chakra names are: root chakra, sacral chakra, solar plexus chakra, heart chakra, throat chakra, third eye chakra, and crown chakra. They are all associated with different colours, starting with red, orange, yellow, green, blue, indigo, and violet. They can be rebalanced, if necessary, using visualizations, energy healing, and crystals.

Steve

So what strange coincidences have happened in your life and what might they really mean?

One of my clients has been asking himself the same questions. In August 2007 Steve and his partner of six years decided to tie the knot. They rode to, and from, the beautiful ceremony on white horses and he had never felt so happy in his entire life. He felt that he had met his soulmate and, at the ceremony, they vowed to love one another forever. A short while after the wedding his wife came home from work looking exhausted. She complained that her leg was sore, her muscles were tense and hard, and she had developed a bad cough. They both assumed that she had been overdoing it in the aftermath of the wedding, but the pain in her leg did not go away and she began to notice that the area was inflamed. The doctor diagnosed haematomas – blood that was collecting outside of the blood vessels. Further investigation revealed dreadful news: The lumps were cancerous and she would be lucky if she had a few months left to live. Even with a huge determination to survive and fight the cancer, three months later she passed away. Steve was totally overwhelmed with grief and unable to understand how fate could be so cruel.

A long while later, having been forced by his friends to leave the house, he attended a dinner party and was sat next to a woman who, it transpired, had the exact same birth-date as his wife. He could not believe the coincidence and was sure that the meeting had happened for a reason. This woman was my sister, and she told him a little bit about what I do. Up to that point he had never even heard of the idea of past life regression. He wanted to know why, if his wife had really been his soul-mate, she had been taken so suddenly from him and why was it that their connection had felt so strong. Stronger than anything else he had ever known. He booked an appointment the following day.

The journey began:

ME: I want you to drift back in time and see if there have been any other lifetimes that you shared with your wife.

Steve nods.

S: I am in a long corridor, with my family portraits either side of it, dark pan-elled walls. It is very elegant, and there are beautifully carved tables against the walls.

ME: What are you doing here?

S: I am walking down the corridor and I am dressed in very fine clothes.

ME: What is your name?

S: Henry.

ME: And your title or surname?

S: Beaufort. I am in a very grand house.

He smiles at this.

ME: What are you doing now?

S: I am opening one of the doors in the corridor and stepping into a room; on the floor is a very ornate rug, I move closer to the fireplace where a wood fire is burning on the hearth.

He strokes his face and smiles.

S: I have a beard. I am solid in stature, and I feel very strong.

ME: Is there anyone else with you?

S: There is a lady sitting in a chair reading a book; she is my wife, her name is Emily. All of the furniture is very regal.

ME: What room are you in?

S: I am in the bedroom and there is a large four-poster bed. Some children come in, two girls, Georgiana and Charlotte; they are running around, playing.

ME: Tell me about your wife.

S: She is very beautiful; she is wearing a big dress, it is very ornate with lots of embroidery all over it; she is pregnant, and we are very happy about this.

ME: Tell me, what do you do for a living?

S: In my working life I have a significant amount of power – it is a parliamentary role; I have lots of papers to sign and people coming to see me for guidance.

ME: Can you tell me what is of the most importance to you in your life right now?

S: For all my importance within my working life the thing that really matters to me is my wife; she smiles at me and the whole room lights up; I love her very much.

At first he smiles and then his face drops a little and he sighs.

ME: What are you concerned about?

S: Sometimes I feel afraid, afraid that I might fail her and the people who rely on me to protect them.

ME: How would you fail them?

S: By not doing the right thing by them.

ME: What do you mean?

S: Well, inasmuch as I am working for the government, I am on the side of the people. I have a lot of responsibility on my shoulders and I always endeavour to do my best.

At this he sighs deeply again and I ask him to move forward to the end of this lifetime.

ME: What are you aware of now?

S: I am in bed, in my large four-poster bed; it is a big room and to my right there are huge leaded windows; there are big double doors and lots of wood.

ME: How old are you now?

S: I am around 60 years old.

ME: What are you aware of?

S: I feel tired. My wife, Emily, is at the side of the bed; she is smiling at me. I am finding it hard to breathe and I have tears in my eyes; I feel very sad.

ME: Is anyone else there with you?

S: My children are here, they are holding their heads in their hands and resting their elbows on the end of the bed, looking at me; they are crying too. Emily has tears falling onto her face and there is nothing that I can do to make them better.

ME: What else are you aware of?

S: I can see the guards at the door and notice that they are looking at me sadly; even my dog, my Labrador, is lying close by with his head on his paws. All I can think of is how much I love my family, especially my beautiful wife. The thoughts of my love for her make me smile. I have been a very lucky man – I have done my best to help as many people as I could, I have many wonderful children and a wife that I adore. I am just so tired, my body feels weak and I cannot get my breath fully.

ME: Tell me what is happening now.

S: I am not worried, I feel at peace... as I take my dying breath I look into the eyes of my beloved wife and I tell her that I will love her forever.

He sighs.

S: I'm drifting now... just drifting....

ME: Can you tell me what you had chosen to learn in this life?

S: My karmic lesson was all about finding ways to make people happy. I think I was able to achieve a degree of that, so I feel okay, although I feel that I could have done so much more if I'd had more time.

ME: Is there anyone that you recognise from that lifetime? They may not look the same but something about them lets you know who they are.

S: Oh, wow, I see now that Emily, my beloved wife then, was my wife in this life; that explains my powerful connection to her, and the feeling that I had always known her, even from the first moment that we met.

At this point in the session we did some transformational work, helping him to release the emotions of regret and sadness at leaving his family and his wife behind. As the session came to an end, I invited Steve to look for some insights

ME: What have you learnt from this experience?

S: I was left with a feeling that I didn't achieve enough, which reminds me of how I have always felt in this life; I have always pushed myself hard to get on and make things happen. This is a reminder to me of how important it is to live life fully and not waste a single moment; because you just never know what will happen.

When Steve woke from his trance, he was quite emotional and had tears streaming down his face, but they were not tears of sadness – rather tears of relief. It made sense to him now why his connection to his wife had been so strong, as it appeared that not only had they loved one another before, but they had sworn to love each other forever. It was hugely comforting for him to know that death was not the end and he felt very strongly that he would see her again, perhaps in another life, and perhaps with another chance to enjoy the love they both had for each other. He had also received insights into why they had only had such a short time together; apparently they had agreed to it in advance: His test or lesson in this life was to learn that he could survive without her and that their love would stand the test of time.

One of the greatest surprises came when Steve decided to investigate the lifetime of Henry, Duke of Beaufort, who it turned out, lived from 1792 until 1853. His research showed that he had been an aristocrat and a member of Parliament. He had two daughters from his first marriage, Charlotte and Georgiana, and after the death of his first wife, he had married her half-sister Emily; they had produced another seven children. What really interested him was that in this life, even though his fitness levels were incredibly high and he had never smoked, he had mild problems in his left lung; it meant that he often had difficulties breathing. Henry Beaufort died of a lung disorder.

After this discovery Steve decided that he wanted to explore more of his past lives, partly because he was curious about his life purpose, and the patterns that kept appearing in his work, but he had a big question regarding a shoulder problem that had very unexpectedly struck him down at the age of 26. His shoulder had become paralysed for a short period and then somehow, what appeared to be, a miraculous recovery happened. It appeared as miraculous because no medical intervention had occurred; in fact, the investigations into what caused it ended up leaving him with a huge scar and provided no answers whatsoever. Once his shoulder got better he was able to use it again, however, he was left with a permanent dull ache that nothing, including pain killers, seemed to help. In the first part of the session he saw himself as a monk called Peter, living in a monastery in Britain in 1520. He wasn't happy as a monk. As a child, in that life, he had wanted to be an explorer and he thought that life as a monk would allow him to travel and teach and meet many people. But it was not to be and he ended up in the one place for his whole life. It was very frustrating for him especially as he didn't, actually, have a very strong belief in God.

He also saw a life in which he was a gangster called Simon Peterson, in 1928 in Boston. He was involved in some shady dealings and was amazed at the details he could remember: the old cars and the outfits that people were wearing, including his own shoes, which were black and white spats. As a member of a gangster family he had killed a man, but he said that he was just doing what he needed to do to survive – the man he killed had hurt a lot of people so his death seemed justified. He wasn't happy with the path that he was following and longed to be free of the fighting and the pressure to do what he was told. Unfortunately his life came to an end before he was able to resolve this issue, and when I asked him to move to the next significant lifetime he found himself in a lifetime as an American soldier, who, co-incidentally (or was it?), was also called Peterson.

The journey began:

ME: What are you aware of?

S: I am in an aeroplane; there is a lot of noise. My name is Sergeant George Peterson, I am American.

ME: What are you doing on the plane?

S: I am with my men, and we are wearing our fatigues.

ME: What year is it?

S: It is March and the year is 1945. I feel very apprehensive; we are getting ready to jump.

ME: Where are you going to land?

S: We are jumping into Germany.

Suddenly he gasps.

ME: What happened?

S: I have jumped, and I am going through the cloud cover; I can see the ground below me, my parachute is already open, it is floating above me...I am drifting...we are about to land on German soil.

He takes a deep breath in.

ME: What happens next?

S: We have landed in a field with big trees behind us; I am running towards the trees and I can hear gunfire – we have been spotted. I have made it to the shelter of the trees and my men are following behind me. The man on my right fires his Bazooka; he fires at the German truck that has followed us... it explodes and suddenly there are body parts flying everywhere. We head off through the trees, down a slope and towards a stream; we head into the stream so that we can cover our tracks – there are Germans with Alsatian dogs just behind us; I am firing at them and my men are firing too. There is a lot of noise and confusion.

Suddenly he jumps up in his seat and cries out.

ME: What has happened?

S: Aghh, I have been shot; I have been shot in the shoulder.

ME: What happens next?

S: My men take over and manage to kill off all the Germans; there is no threat now, but I am hurt and we still have to go on. One of the men wraps a bandage around my shoulder and they give me some morphine for the pain, and it hurts, I can feel it burning...I am looking at a map, oh god, there is blood running down my arm, it keeps dripping on the map, I can't see anything...I am so frustrated...am in so much pain.

His voice changes, and he starts to slur, as though the effects of the morphine are beginning to kick in.

ME: What happens next?

S: We are walking down a road with dykes down either side; it is a dirt road with raised fences and fields beyond. Our mission is to meet up with company B; we have to go 10 clicks west. I am low in ammunition now but I have my men behind me, we need to keep cover – damn it, I can see a plane, they have seen us and they are coming straight at us, firing bullets. Two of my men are hit, we have no cover! It doesn't come back though; I think it was just a random passing opportunist...my shoulder hurts, it is really aching.

ME: And then?

S: We come off the road, cross the fields...I have to keep telling the men to shut up, they are making far too much noise. I grab one of them and give him a right good telling off; right in his face.

ME: What do you say to him?

S: I tell him that if he wants to die he should die somewhere else...he is not going to kill my men by making noise!

ME: Then what happens?

S: He shuts up; the men have respect for me because I have been in lots of battles.

ME: How do you feel about all of those battles?

S: I am really fed up of people dying around me!

He sighs.

S: We have now reached the top of a hill; I hit the deck and check out the immediate area with my binoculars. In the distance I can see some tracks; there are Germans troops in trucks and there are way too many of them for us to deal with. There is a town to my right; we need to get though it and get to the other side. There are a lot of Germans in the town, and I need to get Smith into the clock tower, for sniper cover. Oh no, there are four Panzer tanks – this is not good! We are going to have to go in at night, it is too busy during the day. I tell the men to rest up and make no noise.

ME: What happens next?

S: I am on the radio to HQ; Seadog is my code name. I am telling them our position, telling them what I am going to do.

He sighs with irritation.

ME: What is bothering you?

S: I have to tell the men not to smoke; I know we are a long way off but there is a chance that the cigarette smoke might be seen or even smelt. They give me lots of hassle because they want to smoke. I have a tin in my pocket; I open it up, inside is food, biscuits, chocolate. I need some more morphine for my shoulder, the pain is killing me and giving me a headache. We have four more hours before we can move out. I tell my men to move closer to the town, and we move into the shelter of a gulley where no one can see us. There are lots of reeds; we place our guns above our heads and we wait – we rest –thinking of home…the realisation hits me that I don't want to be here no more, I've had enough.

Steve suddenly jumps out of his seat.

ME: What happened?

S: Big explosion…I look over the gulley, there are big explosions all round, it's artillery fire. I radio in "Seadog, artillery fire" and we move into the outskirts of the town; we have to move earlier than we want to, it's not yet night; I can see the confusion in the town, we are running towards it, the fires that are burning are our cover. We are half a click from the town and we are still in an elevated position; we need to get the sniper into the town, there is lots of noise. We are up against a wall now, on the outskirts of the town.

ME: What happens next?

S: The artillery fire has stopped. We need to take this town. We need to meet with B Company, who are coming in from the west side. We are early and so the B Company is not there yet. We are sneaking into the town; Johnson needs to take the right flank, machine gunner Smith needs to deal with sniper cover. We need to take out the tanks!

ME: How will you do that?

S: We use sticky bombs – they are the only things that ever work. The tanks are in the centre now...I can hear gun shots, more confusion...tank turrets moving...we need to run… need to disable the tanks...

He jumps again and is shouting.

S: Aghh, big explosion, my legs, something has hit my legs, have to keep going, the clock tower is gone, the tanks are firing, there is no sniper cover, just machine guns and dust, dust everywhere. We need to move, need to take out these tanks – bazooka fire – it does nothing, just bounces off the armour. We manage to get the sticky bomb on the tank tracks...need to take cover...the tanks are moving...tracks are coming off...I can see the men who are firing at us. I fire in a grenade – that stops them. I can see planes coming; they are dropping bombs – the bombs are coming thick and fast – they are ours, they are "wild cats"; they are dropping bombs on the tanks – yahoo! Go on boys... fantastic, the wild cats are dropping bombs on the tanks, although it is a bit close for my liking – eugh...

He slumps in the chair, and it goes quiet for a long time.

Once again Steve was in a life taking orders from others and feeling frustrated and dissatisfied with his lot, and once again the life had come to an end without him being able to resolve or change anything. We checked to see if this had been his most recent previous life and the answer was yes; this meant that the pattern of taking orders was still intact; it was clearly time to get rid of it.

In the session he was able to heal his legs and his badly damaged shoulder and forgive those who had hurt him. He saw that they were all innocent victims of war; each man just following orders and doing what they thought was right in that moment in time. He saw that following orders blindly – with no thought for the consequences of the actions – was never a good idea, and he was able to identify and destroy the contract he signed committing his life to "following the orders of others blindly." He changed the contract to a new one saying that from now on he would be in charge of making the decisions in his life, and he vowed to use his skills to make a difference in the world.

Since the sessions, Steve has reported that the dull ache in his shoulder has completely gone and he has had no more issues with his breathing. Although he still misses his wife, he knows that one day he will see her again and so he is able to focus on gratitude for all of the wonderful times that they had together, rather than being constantly sad and just mourning her loss. He says that even though he is looking forward to their next adventure together he feels as though he is now free to get on with, and make the most of, his time in this life.

Interestingly, since his sessions, one of his business ideas has been taken up by a company that has links all over Europe, and he is soon to be reaching a far greater audience than before. He will be getting the chance to help people to get healthier, and happier, and will use his skills and talents as a trainer, and a communicator, to take people to a much higher level physically and mentally – finally allowing him to achieve his new life purpose: one where he calls the shots.

So was it a coincidence that at this critical time in his life he met a woman with the same birthday as his wife who guided him to the space where he could learn all of this? Was it a co-incidence that his shoulder ceased to work at the same time as the sergeant was shot, and was it a coincidence that the ache in his shoulder went away after healing it in the session, or that his breathing improved? Was it a coincidence that his business went from strength to strength when he released himself from a contract that called for him to follow the orders of others and not put his best interests first? Or was there something more powerful at work? I will let you decide.

EXERCISE 3: *Synchronicities*

Make a list of all the strange coincidences or synchronicities that have happened in your life.

For example:

1. Has the phone ever rung and you knew exactly who was on the other end?
2. Have you ever been thinking about someone and suddenly they appeared or called?
3. Have you ever been trying to call someone and they were calling you at the same time or they sent you a text at exactly the same time?
4. Have you ever bumped into someone that you know in a very unlikely place?
5. Have you ever met someone, by chance, who had the exact bit of information, or the very thing that you needed, just when you needed it?
6. Have you ever had something really "lucky" happen to you?

7. Have you ever found yourself to be in the right place at the right time or, in what seemed to be, the wrong place at the wrong time?
8. Have you ever met just the person that you needed to – at just the right time?
9. Did you ever make a mistake, or get something wrong, only to find out afterwards that the outcome was perfect?
10. Have you ever had a really strong feeling that you shouldn't do something, which you ignored, and then later regretted?
11. Have you ever trusted your gut instinct, your intuition, and been proven right?
12. Have you ever picked up a book, or read an article, and found that it gave you answers to important questions?
13. Have you ever met someone who was to prove to be very important in your life, or fallen in love, in very random circumstances?

4

What Are Soul Groups?

In Dorothy's adventure she was to meet many of the key people in her everyday world, once again, in Oz. This time they appeared in very different guises, but they were still somehow recognizable as the people she knew back home; some remnant of their character and looks remained, but she was to have a very different experience with them when she stepped into the more magical realm of Oz. Miss Gulch's transformation into the Wicked Witch of the West left no doubts as to the nature of her character, and her three travelling companions – the scarecrow, tin man, and the cowardly lion – bore very close resemblance to the three workers back on her farm. Mr Marvel, the travelling magician, played his part perfectly as the slightly misguided wizard, who was really just a good-hearted old man, who was trying to help her get home.

Shortly upon arrival in the land of Oz, Dorothy is met by Glinda the Good Witch of the South. Glinda is not a living character from her life but represents her higher self, her intuition and inner wisdom; she acts as her guide throughout the journey, only appearing when she is really needed. In times of trouble she was there to help, but she never gave Dorothy all the answers to all of her questions. She would only share as much information as Dorothy needed each time, so that Dorothy could learn her lessons for herself.

Dorothy was to learn many lessons whilst in her "dreamlike world" of Oz, particularly with regard to the people in her life; this meant that she could live her life in Kansas with a greater sense of understanding, and a better appreciation, of those she loved. Glinda instructed Dorothy to start her journey at the very beginning of the yellow brick road, which began with a tightly curled spiral – a spiral that is replicated throughout nature and throughout your ever evolving lives. She told her to follow the yellow brick road, that it would lead her all the way to the Wizard. Just as Dorothy tried to ask what she should do if she came to a crossroads the good witch was gone – leaving Dorothy and Toto, her little dog, who all through this story represented her instincts, to find the answer to that question all by themselves. Except that they wouldn't be alone for long. The yellow brick road was to provide them with everyone they needed to fulfill the mission, or the quest, that they had embarked upon.

When you meet someone, and immediately feel as though you have known them forever, or you feel a very strong connection to them, can this be indicative of a past life connection?

Yes, many of my clients are amazed to discover that this is not the only life that they have had with someone. What can be especially surprising is the discovery of exactly what they had agreed to learn from one another or how they had decided to challenge each other this time around.

Can exploring past lives help to make sense of these connections?

Yes, the stories that emerge can help you to identify the souls who have shared lives with you – sometimes in the same roles, but often in very contrasting ones. Sometimes they are there to support you, lovingly, and other times they are there to play out bitter power struggles and battles. These will often be members of your soul group.

Why is this?

Soul group members usually play the more important or significant roles in your life – the ones that you get to learn from.

What happens once you discover these connections?

When you begin to unravel these past life connections, many things can begin to make sense for you, and you have the opportunity to respond to the people in your life in different ways. It really gives you a chance to take personal responsibility for the events, and relationships, in your life and you no longer feel like the "innocent victim" of your life so far; it's a much more powerful place to be in, for sure. This puts you, very firmly, back in the driver's seat and back in control of your life.

So, what does a soul group consist of?

Allow me to give you an analogy that may explain, very simply, how a soul group works. A soul group is a bit like a tree. A tree is made up of many different parts: the roots, the trunk, the branches, and the leaves. There are many different branches on each tree, and each branch will be made up of many smaller branches.

At the end of the smaller branches will be twigs that have clusters of leaves, and at the very tip of some branches there will be twigs that have just a few leaves that are very tightly grouped together. In some cases there may be several leaves that emerge from the same pod, a leaf that has split into two parts, or sometimes more.

Let me explain the comparison. The roots are what connect it to the earth, to the cosmos. The trunk of the tree represents the soul group as a whole. The larger branches represent the wide network of souls that are connected and working on the same theme. The smaller branches represent the closer soul group members; who often play the parts of family, friends and close working colleagues. The clusters of leaves at the end of the branches will represent the key people in your lives; lovers, partners, parents and children. The leaves that are closely entwined and from the same twigs are the ones that are often referred to as soulmates – indicating a very close soul connection, and the leaves that have come from the same pod but have split into more than one leaf are what some refer to as a twin soul. The number of times the souls splits will be dependent on how much learning the soul chooses to experience in any one time frame; the number increasing as the soul gains confidence in its ability to learn more than one lesson at a time and decreasing as more and more lessons are learnt and less karma is left to be resolved. This "twin" or "split" soul connection is one of the strongest and can often create a powerful pull for the people concerned – the sense that part of them is missing, leading them to search for this missing part.

This is not, however, always a romantic connection, which some mistakenly believe. So, even though it is quite rare, there may be a "twin" soul out there, perhaps many. In the further explorations of his past lives, Steve found out that he had more than one life at the same time. While one part of him was parachuting into Germany another part was living life as a pilot in the British Air Force. Both lives were similar in many ways, but the ends of the lives were very different. In the U.S. life, he won a posthumous medal for bravery in combat. In the British life he had carried out several dangerous missions but he had retired to the country shortly after completing his military service, living out the rest of his life with his family.

What was startling was that Steve was able to verify a huge amount of information about both men. Their names, their birthdates, the specific dates when significant things happened, the names of their family members, even where they lived, and we were able to find details of both of these men, who were not famous or in the public eye in any way, on the Internet and all of the details matched. In his British life he had made agreements with his family, who were all part of his soul group, to be there and take care of them, which he had done. The biggest surprise, however, was his discovery that this man had only died a few years previously, meaning that a part of his soul energy had been living another life, in another part of the country, totally unaware that he existed. He was struck by the idea that the members of this man's family were part of his soul group. There was a temptation to contact them, but on reflection he thought it wiser not to; he decided that if they were meant to meet it would happen somehow. He sensed that any contracts he had set with them would make sure of that.

Do people always set up agreements, and contracts, with members of their soul group before they arrive?

Not with every soul, but you will have done with the key players in your planned life experience. It may be that some members of your soul group chose to come into your life to impart a lesson and then leave, swiftly, once the lesson is done. It may be that they chose to be around to help you in some way and share part of the journey, or perhaps they chose to be with you right to the end. It may be that they made a vow or a promise to you, or you to them, and you have to complete this mission before you can move on. This is why it is possible to feel such strong connections with people around you, and even the people that you have met, even fleetingly, at different times in your life. If there is a soul group connection you may have played out many lifetimes with them, playing many different parts.

Are all the people that we interact with closely in our lives members of our soul group?

Not necessarily; the people in your soul group all tend to be working on the same lesson, and there will be an ongoing theme that is being worked through. These souls tend to have the same vibrational frequency and, at the spirit realm level, can be identified as having the same colour energy and the same sound frequency as you. That said, often members of other soul groups, who are working on different lessons, will volunteer to help you. It may be that you have something they can learn from, or vice versa, and agreements get set up with regard to what will happen when you meet on the earth plane.

How do we know if people are part of our soul group?

In a transformational part of a past life session it is possible to identify people that you recognize from your current life. They do not necessarily look the same, in the past life, but you know exactly who they are; it may be something about their personality or something about the way they look – often the eyes are the giveaway. If you are having more than one life with them they may well be part of your soul group.

How can you be sure?

To discover for certain if someone is part of your soul group, or to establish why they have chosen to be with you in your life, a dialogue with the person has to happen. Then you can find out exactly how many lives you may have had together, what the theme of the lives has been, what the lessons are that you have chosen to work through, and what contracts or agreements may have been set up. Once you understand all of this, the right healing can take place; unhelpful contracts can be changed and more beneficial ones put in their place. The healing that happens in the session doesn't just apply to the lifetime that is being worked on either but will have an impact on all the lifetimes that are connected, giving people the chance to let go of negative ties and unhealthy emotions that span the entire network of lives that have been lived – and are yet to be lived.

One of my clients, a man called Brian, who I will discuss more fully later in the book, had a difficult relationship with his father, who had been very enthusiastic about him training to be a boxer. Even though he showed a real aptitude for it, he never had the "killer instinct" that was required to "finish people off" and he lost many of his matches because of it. This drove his father crazy, because he knew that he was more than capable of winning. He found himself in a past life where he and his son fought all the time. He had been a very peace-loving man and his son had been furious with him for not defending his people by fighting with their enemies. Their town was attacked and, because he was not prepared to fight, they lost every-thing. His son never forgave him. Imagine his surprise when he discovered that his son, in that lifetime, was his father in this one. He was running the same program all over again, with the same soul, in order to find a way to heal it. The healing that occurred in the session did change the dynamic of their relationship and, instead of always being at loggerheads, they were finally able to enjoy spending quality time with each other.

What can be done about unhelpful contracts?

Once you understand the contracts, commitments, or vows that have been set in place, you can make sure that you deal with them appropriately, which usually means identifying them, making sure the lessons have been learnt, then getting rid of them – in whichever is the most appropriate way. This often involves seeing the contracts written on an old-fashioned parchment scroll, which can be torn up and set on fire, to ensure that all of the energy connected to it is completely gone. Once they have been destroyed, new and much better ones are created to put in their place. These new contracts, commitments, or vows can be used as daily af-firmations – people repeating them regularly until they really sink in.

These affirmations can be things like "I am worthy," "I do deserve love and abundance," and "I am enough." This reinforces positive new beliefs and provides people with the confidence and strength they need to succeed. It is a great opportunity to change the old, negative thinking habits that may have been with them for a lifetime. I usually get people to shrink the new contracts down and store them in a place within their heart centres so they know exactly where they are, and as a result, are always aware of the new message they are giving to themselves. This new message brings positive energy into their energy field, whether they are aware of it consciously or not.

How does the dialogue part of the session work?

Significant people from the past life are called to the inter-life space. My clients are then invited to speak out and tell these people all the things that they were unable to tell them whilst they were alive. This is very powerful work, and it is important for them to deal with the people who were responsible for generating good and bad feelings within that life. Often just the true understanding of what the other person's role really was allows powerful shifts to occur.

Does just knowing that you have a soul group help in some way?

Yes, it can. Once people acknowledge they are part of a soul group, they realise that they are not alone; they become aware of the support of their soul group and feel the encouragement they need to keep going. This can be hugely empowering, especially for people who do feel lost, and as if they don't belong anywhere, which is something that many who are called to a spiritual path experience at some point in their lives.

What is the main benefit of talking to people from the past life?

One of the most important components of this work is forgiveness, because this enables people to let go of the negative emotions that have been weighing them, and their vibrational energy, down. Huge healing occurs when the weight of anger or guilt, or any other negative emotion, has been released; this affects not just the individual but the entire planet because ultimately we are all one, and what affects one affects the whole. People need to let go of any negative emotions that have been held onto from their past lives, and they especially need to find forgiveness for the souls who have done them wrong in the past. There are times, however, when people struggle with this, particularly if someone behaved very badly towards them in another life.

One of my clients, Janice, who was a very successful and wealthy merchant in a past life, lost everything and had been imprisoned and tortured because of the orders of a pope. When the time came to forgive this man, in the past life session, she refused point blank. When I asked her what she wanted to happen she said she wanted him to suffer as she had. I asked her to let him see, and feel, the suffering that she had experienced in that life. She was able to do this by projecting the feelings and memories onto him, giving him a taste of what he had done to her and so many others. At first he had been very arrogant and stated that because he had been working for the Church it was all for a higher cause and therefore completely justified; but once she had projected her feelings onto him and he saw the truth of what he had done, he broke down, he cried, and he begged for forgiveness. But she still didn't want to give it to him; she felt that he had behaved too badly in that life and didn't deserve to be forgiven. I asked her to find out if there had been an agreement between them, before they came into the life, and she was stunned to discover that, not only had she agreed to this, but this man was a part of her soul group. They had an agreement that they would test and challenge one another, and this power struggle had continued through many lifetimes and had taken many different forms. She had not always been the victim either.

When soul contracts like this are identified the insights that occur are huge. Realising that she had agreed to this, she saw that she was the one responsible for it; the thought left her reeling. When she understood that what had happened to her was not the fault of this soul, this volunteer in her life experience, the forgiveness occurred. The contract was destroyed and a new agreement was put in place that said that they were both free to live their lives, without struggle, and free from the need to dominate each other. Then she realised that this man was the same soul as her ex-partner, who had been responsible for a very difficult break-up and, who had continued to make her life difficult even though they were no longer together. She knew then why it had been so hard to let him go from her life. The anger she felt towards him cleared and eventually she was able to move on and get on with her life.

Can the dialogue help in any other ways?

Yes, it not only gives the person the chance to say things that were left unsaid, but it also allows them to get their questions answered. One client, called Sarah, had been having real difficulties with her boss and couldn't understand why. Nothing she did seemed right and she felt really afraid of him; she was starting to experience a great deal of stress as a result and was taking time off work sick, which was just compounding the issue as her boss was getting frustrated at her for being absent. She went back to a life as a woman in the Middle Ages; she had suffered greatly at the hands of a man who had been a priest: he had tortured her and had her disemboweled and finally hung in public because she would not obey him and because she refused to bow down to the rules of the church; her only other crime was that she liked to take long walks at night-time. She preferred the quiet of night and the fact that there was no one around to watch what she was doing, although she was wrong in this thinking, as someone was watching. The local priest had her followed and then branded as a witch for her nocturnal abilities. Friends, family, and other townsfolk all turned against her for fear of reprisals – such was his power.

In the session she was able to confront him and ask him why he had done this, and he admitted that he had been afraid of her; she had shown no fear and no respect for his position. He relied on fear to keep the people under control, and she was jeopardizing his position, so he had no choice but to get rid of her. When she asked why he had felt the need to make her death quite so unpleasant, he visibly squirmed and was very apologetic. It was, he said, just a sign of the times. That was what they did to "witches" at the time and he had paid no heed to what that might mean to her; he was just carrying out the orders of the Church and for that he was very sorry. His heartfelt apology allowed her to forgive him and let the negative emotions go, which was just as well, as she recognized him as her current boss. After the session she felt as though something had shifted, she no longer felt afraid of him and found that by standing up to him and being more assertive she gained his respect. Her work life changed quite considerably for the better.

What happens when people have learnt what they need to, from another person, in the past life but feel they are still tied to them in some way?

Once an issue has been resolved with this person there may still be an energetic connection to them in the form of "etheric cords." In order to release the ties they have to a person they need to visualize removing these cords in some way; they can do this by cutting them, dissolving them, or just unhooking them. Healing energy is then sent to both parties to heal the space where the cords used to be.

What impact does cutting the ties, or cords, have for people?

Cutting away the unhelpful ties, or cords, to people means that they can reclaim their own power and are no longer at the mercy of others; they are no longer being drained in any way. This is very healing and often changes the dynamics of the relationships in this life quite dramatically.

One of my clients, Amy, was amazed because after her session, where she cleared away some very deep-rooted cords, a long-running family business dispute was resolved without any effort on her part. In her previous life she identified her current life father as a business rival with whom there had been a duel that was fought to the death. She had killed him and had lived with shame and guilt for the rest of her life. She had vowed never to challenge anyone in that way ever again. In the session she received forgiveness for what happened and there was an understanding that they had always challenged each other. The contract was changed to be one of support for each other instead. The cords were unhooked and both parties received healing white light where the cords had previously been. In a gesture of thanks, unconditional love was sent to the other person, from heart centre to heart centre. This illuminated a spark of light within them both and they saw that there had been access to an inner power source within them all along; it had not been necessary to take power from each other. After the session she reported that she felt a great sense of inner peace and strength. She had no desire to get into conflict with her father so she decided to accept him for who he was with no recriminations or blame; she would just continue to do her best for the company. At a family lunch a few days later she was amazed as, for the first time in many years, she had not been tied up in knots emotionally.

A few days after that her father called a meeting and, without any prompting, accepted the new ideas she had for the company to move forward. He even praised her on her innovative plans. He told her that he felt it was time for him to take a step back and that he wanted her to take more control. This was totally out of the blue, and she was amazed at the shift that had occurred for them all.

Do all ties need to be cut?

It is a good idea to let go of anything that ties people to a past life experience, but sometimes people want to hold on to loving bonds they have, with certain people, and these may not need to be released completely; it is up to the individual.

Why would other souls choose to challenges us in our lives?

Neale Donald Walsh, author of the *Conversations With God* books, has written a lovely book called *The Little Soul and the Sun* that illustrates this point very nicely, where a soul volunteers to help another soul with issues of forgiveness, meaning that it will have to play the role of the bad guy once on earth. As all souls are intrinsically love based this is quite a challenging role to play and is often only taken on board by souls who have a great affection or love for the other. Remember that it is not just your friends and the people that appear to love you the most that help you in life; you learn and grow the most from the challenges you experience, and the people who seem to be your worst enemy will often be the ones that have taught you the most.

How can you get more information about your soul group?

Dr. Michael Newton, an American hypnotherapist who spent 40 years in the area of regression therapy, pioneered a set of techniques that enabled people to go deeper into the inter-life space, which he called the Life Between Lives. Tens of thousands of these LBL sessions have since been carried out and the experiences that people have are uncannily similar. Here people can meet their guides, their higher selves, and even ascended masters who provide them with important insights and deeper levels of wisdom as well as meeting with, and really getting the information they need, from their entire soul group. I have worked with these techniques for several years now and the results are always incredibly profound.

Once you are part of a soul group do you stay with them forever?

Not necessarily. Each soul group will be working on a particular theme, and if your soul has learnt everything it needs about that particular lesson, that particular theme, then it may be time to move on, and up to a different level and a different theme. Your spirit guide may help with the transition into the new group, or you may find that you get a new spirit guide too.

So how do you know if a lesson with a member of your soul group has been learnt or not?

If you are still having troubles in your life with a particular person, then there is clearly something that still needs to be learnt; it is not always easy to see it when you are in it, and this is why exploring at the unconscious level makes so much sense.

Lynda

Lynda came for a session because she had been having problems with her ex-boyfriend. The relationship hadn't worked out and when she ended things he had become very bitter and had made things difficult for her. He refused to take *no* for an answer, called her relentlessly, put letters and photos through her letterbox, and harassed her friends and family. It had all been very upsetting, and she was really worried about why she was attracting someone like this into her life. It was starting to have a real negative impact on her thinking as she was constantly distracted and unable to pursue the ideas she had for her future. She wondered if there was something from the past she needed to clear in order to break free.

The journey began:

ME: What are you experiencing?

L: I am a woman, 25 years old. I am staring out to sea, thinking about my life, about where it is all going; particularly my relationship with my husband, Edward.

ME: How did you meet?

L: We grew up together in a small village in South America.

ME: What year is this?

L: It is 1856.

ME: Tell me about your life.

L: We have one child; her name is Pearl, and she is 5 years old.

ME: Tell me how you spend your time.

L: We work a lot, preparing food, so Pearl spends a lot of time with her grandmother. We are, kind of, happily married, but I am thinking that there are so many things to see and people to meet. I don't talk much to Edward.

ME: Why is that?

L: It always was that way.

ME: How are you feeling right now?

L: I feel anxious, and I have a deep sense that I just want to be free but I don't have a plan. I am just a little bit confused.

ME: I want you to go to the root of your confusion and anxiety.

With this she moved on to another life.

L: My name is Karla, I am 35 years old. I am in the countryside, and I am looking up at the stars. I have two children, they are 9 and 10, Dana and Eos.

ME: What year is this?

L: The year is 1978 and I am living in a big house in the countryside in America. I was married to a man called David Clayton but we split up.

ME: What caused you to break up?

L: I wanted to be free. Splitting up from him gave me the freedom I craved and now I am very connected to my children and to nature. Life is just peaceful and magical.

ME: What are you doing right now?

L: I am sitting with my legs crossed stroking Dana's hair and Eos is sitting silently with me. They are good children; they love their mum.

ME: Can you describe your life?

L: In order to take care of myself and the children I have a shop selling natural herbs and remedies. The shop is quiet and in order to survive my husband still sends me money.

ME: How do you feel about that?

L: It feels okay that he does that but I would like my business to be more of a success. I need to live my dream and really focus on my success.

ME: Where is this shop?

L: It is a very old shop in the town of Pittsburgh. A friend of mine, Sophia, works there with me.

ME: Is the shop well received?

L: Most people are open to the things that we sell, but some people don't understand and have a problem with us. My wish is that my daughter will take over from me in the future, to keep it going. I am very proud that I have made it work; it doesn't make a lot of money but it's enough.

ME: Tell me about your relationships.

L: I don't bother with men anymore; I have never found "the one."

ME: How can you be sure of that?

L: If I had I would have felt it.

ME: Is it important to you to have love in your life?

L: It has always been more important to me to have my freedom.

ME: Why is that?

L: I don't want to get attached to anyone because it ties you down and you forget your dreams.

I realised that there was a real pattern emerging regarding freedom so I guided her to find the root cause of that feeling.

ME: Tell me what you are experiencing now.

L: I am living in America, the year is 1696; I am in Mississippi, and I am a maid. My name is Mary, I am 43 years old, I have four children, and I come from a very big family.

ME: Who do you work for?

L: I work for a very rich woman called Pauletta.

ME: How long have you been there?

L: I have worked there for about 10 years.

ME: Are you happy with your life?

L: No, I don't get to see my family much.

ME: Tell me about your family

L: The youngest is 21 and the oldest is 29.

ME: Why do you see so little of them?

L: My husband died, and since then I have lived here in Pauletta's house. He was very ill and only 39 when he died.

ME: That must have been hard for you.

L: It was, but I am mainly used to it now. Sometimes, though, I feel like I just want to go home.

ME: What stops you?

L: Only the lack of money stops me.

ME: What has happened to your children?

L: All of my children work; they are all in similar positions. One of them works here with the horses, and we get treated okay. But I know where I stand.

ME: Tell me about you and your life.

L: I am a slave, and I am a big lady; I am wearing a grey dress with an apron. My family came from Africa originally. In my own time I like to play music, I like to sing. I think I have quite a good voice.

ME: Who do you sing for?

L: I just sing to myself. I like soulful music, the music that comes from my roots, my heritage. I know that I am a slave, but I am one that is better off than most. I think I get it good although I don't live in the big house.

ME: Where do you live?

L: I live in a very small cottage, in the grounds, with one of my daughters. She has a small baby.

She sighs deeply

L: I just wish I didn't feel so tired all the time. I have a cough and my feet hurt. I get no time to myself at all. It is hard because I love my children so much and I just wish I could be with them more. The circumstances just do not allow for it, and it makes me sad.

ME: I want you to move on to the next significant event in this life.

The scene moves on and she finds herself at the end of the lifetime.

L: I am lying in bed, I am now 56. I am very ill and sweating profusely. I have a flannel on my head. All of my children are there, but I feel so tired and sick. I am finding it hard to breathe, as if someone is sitting on my chest. But I am okay because all of the people that I love are here with me. I feel like I am ready to go as I am in so much pain.

ME: What is the last conscious thought that you have before you leave this lifetime?

L: It is that my heart was full of love but I wish that things could have been better and that I could have been free to live my life in the way that I wanted, not tied to someone else and constantly at their beck and call.

ME: What else needs to be healed?

L: I suffered from being overweight in that life as I cooked so much and ate anything that was left over; this didn't help my joints and caused a lot of my aches and pains as I got older; the stress meant that I had eczema on my elbows too.

We sent healing energy to the body to repair all the damage that had been done to it.

ME: Tell me about the emotions that need to be released.

L: I left that life feeling that I was a failure because I never really got to do anything for myself or to do any of the things that I wanted to do for my family. I was also very sad to lose my husband when I did; it was too soon and it was hard to raise my children without him.

ME: What have you learnt from this?

L: I guess the most important thing is being able to accept that was just the way things were and not be so hard on myself.

ME: Are you aware of what your karmic lesson was in that life, what had you chosen to experience?

L: It was to be strong, to follow my dreams, and to listen to the inner voice within me.

ME: How much of that did you manage to achieve?

L: Unfortunately, I didn't get to accomplish any of my personal goals; I had no choices in that life and was at the mercy of the circumstances.

ME: Why was it important that you experience this?

L: The thing I really have to learn from this is that I must now focus on what I believe in and go for what I want in life.

ME: How can you make sure this happens?

L: I just really have to believe in me.

ME: Is there anyone there that you recognize from your current life?

L: I recognize my grandmother from my South American lifestyle as my mother in this life; she was a real support for me then and she still is to this day. She was really there for me in the difficult times with my husband, Edward.

ME: Did you have any agreement made with her before this life?

L: Yes, she agreed to assist me in finding my strength, in learning that I do have the strength I need to succeed and to be my own person, not reliant on anyone else. She is telling me that she is part of my soul group and has been with me for many lives, each one with a theme of finding strength and freedom.

ME: What has prevented you from having this sense of belief in yourself so far?

L: It was the sense of slavery, of being owned, shackled and forced to submit to the will of another.

ME: What do you need to do to help you to be free of all of this?

L: I would like to remove the shackles that have been holding me back.

ME: What do you need to do to make this happen?

L: I want to break free and throw the shackles away.

ME: Do you need any additional strength to help you break free from the shackles?

L: No, I am ready to get rid of them now; I know I don't need them any more.

ME: Good, I would like you to do this now so that you can set yourself free. At this point she vigorously shook her hands to release the shackles, the ties that represented her enslavement; she then smiled widely and breathed a deep sigh of relief.

ME: How are you feeling now?

L: Oh, it feels so good to now be able to release all of that negativity and be free of everything that contained me in all of those lives.

ME: What are you experiencing as a result of letting it go?

L: I feel a much greater sense of love and freedom and joy.

ME: I want you to see if there have been any contracts or vows put in place with regard to your relationships.

L: Oh, yes, before I left I vowed that I would resist people that wanted to control me, and if that meant avoiding all relationships, then so be it.

ME: Does this vow serve you now?

L: I can see now that it might have been a little extreme.

ME: What could you change this to so that it is of more benefit to you?

L: I can promise to honour myself and my dreams at all times and to be open to a love that will be supporting and safe.

ME: Shall we bring in the spirit of Edward and see what he has to say?

L: Yes, he is here; he is laughing and telling me that he too is a member of my soul group and that he was there to help me learn this lesson. He says that it was hard to play the part of someone so distant in that life but that it was a part he had agreed upon in advance and so he had no choice. He says that he has been with me for many lives too, and I now recognise that my ex-partner in the American life and my ex in my current life is the same soul.

Apparently he was going to have to keep coming back and challenging me until I got it, and he is now very relieved that I understand as we can move on to something else, something that will require less frustration for us both. He is asking me to forgive him for the parts that he has played, and I can easily do that now. I feel a huge sense of gratitude and love towards him and feel ready to move on. I can now rip up the contract and set myself free.

With this powerful insight the session came to an end. Lynda was really surprised that the feelings had been so powerful throughout the session and was greatly relieved that she now felt a real release from all of the negativity. She felt certain that her pattern of meeting people who tried to control her came from those lives and was determined to make better choices in the future; now that she knew what to look out for she felt it would be easy. She was also pleasantly surprised to learn that her mother had returned to be with her again; it made sense of their very close bond and the real feelings of safety that she had when her mother was around. She was especially delighted to have learnt of her successful business in Pittsburgh, as one of her dreams was to study herbs and healing. She felt sure that this was what she should be doing with her life, and a short time later she reported to me that she had enrolled on a healing course that she loved and she felt completely certain that this was the right path for her. She took a position in a store that enabled her to use her new skills and was really looking forward to a fresh, new start as far as relationships were concerned, certain that things would be very different for her this time around.

Maggy

Another client, Maggy, came with questions regarding her son, who was mentally handicapped. He lived away from home but did come back regularly; he was a real blessing to their family, and she felt that the connection between them was very strong but she had questions over his fate and worried whether she was in some way responsible for his disabilities.

The journey began:

M: I am in a castle. I am very cold. The year is 1712, and my name is Catherine Argyll.

ME: Where is the castle?

M: The castle is in Lancashire, and it is my home.

ME: What are you wearing?

M: I am wearing a red dress in heavy velvet, to try to keep out the cold.

ME: Is anyone else there with you?

M: My two children, Bertie and George, who are aged 10 and 8, and my maid.

ME: What are you doing here?

M: I feel like a prisoner here, in my own home; we are not allowed out.

ME: Why are you not allowed out?

M: We are in hiding for safety's sake; the boys do not understand and are desperate to go out and play, but they cannot for fear of attack.

ME: What do you do all day?

M: I am forced to keep them as quiet as possible so that no one will suspect that they are still here in the house, but the boys keep giggling and laughing and I am so afraid that we will be discovered.

ME: Who are you hiding from?

M: We are hiding from the Roundheads. (When checked later, the dates fitted right in!)

ME: I want you to move to the next significant event and tell me what is happening.

M: The castle is being attacked. I can hear the sound of shouting and screaming; the children are terrified – I am holding them and just willing the soldiers to leave and not find us…but they are coming closer and closer and I feel so afraid, not for me but for my boys. I am their mother, it is my job to protect them and keep them safe…

She lets out a cry.

ME: What is happening now?

M: No, they are here in the room, they are lashing out with their swords, they are pulling the boys from me and I am forced to watch them die…nothing could be worse for me…I just want to die, I have no desire to live now…one man comes at me with his sword and he waves it at my head.

SUDDENLY SHE SIGHS DEEPLY.

ME: What are you aware of now?

M: It is over, I am dead. I feel so sad and so desperate at the loss of my boys – so tragic and such a waste of young life!

ME: Can you get a sense of what the karmic theme was?

M: It was to deal with loss and to accept that I am not responsible for everyone around me.

ME: What else are you aware of?

M: Oh, I see that my son in this life is one of the boys who died with me in the castle. I have been carrying the guilt of their deaths with me, and I think that perhaps I have been trying to make it up to him in this life by taking care of him.

ME: Bring him in; what would you like to say to him that you couldn't back then?

M: I want to tell him how sorry I am that I was not able to save him. I wish I could have done more.

ME: What does he say?

M: He tells me that it is not my fault, there was nothing I could have done. He also says that it was planned that way. He had not planned on being around for long in that life; and, anyway, it was too cold in that castle.

ME: Does he have a message for you?

M: Yes, the message is that I do not need to feel that guilt; he found me again and all I need to do is love him the best that I can. He is telling me that his disabilities in this life have helped him to get a completely different perspective on life, and he is enjoying this lesson. He wants me to stop worrying about him.

ME: How does it feel to know that?

M: It feels very good to know that – a huge sense of relief.

ME: I want you to find out if he is part of your soul group.

M: He is smiling and saying *yes*, that we have been together in many lives. Apparently in our last life together I was his brother. That seems strange.

ME: What has been the theme of these lives?

M: Dealing with loss.

ME: Was there a contract set between you?

M: Yes, and it has been running for many lifetimes.

ME: It is time to get rid of it now; let's bring in the contract and destroy it. She sets fire to it.

M: That feels good.

ME: What contract would you like to put in its place?

M: One that gives me permission to focus on bringing more love into my life and keeping it there.

ME: Good, let's write that one on a new scroll and store it safely in your heart centre.

She smiled and sighed; for Maggy, realizing that her son had chosen to come back to her again, even after the tragic circumstances of the last life, was very heartwarming. She was really happy to find out that he was part of her soul group too; it meant that their connection and their bond now made total sense. She felt very blessed that she had been given another chance to be his mother and let go of any worries that she had that she had done something wrong.

EXERCISE 4: *Significant People*

Make a list of the key people who have appeared in your life:

1. Family
2. Friends
3. Teachers
4. Professors
5. Work colleagues
6. Managers
7. Business partners

Make a note of the emotional impact they had on you:

1. Who inspired you?

2. Who hurt you?
3. Who loved you?
4. Who did you love?
5. Who challenged you the most?
6. Who taught you the most?
7. Is there anyone that you have been unable to forgive?
8. Is there anyone that you have been unable to forgive yourself over?
9. How old were you when they appeared?
10. How old were you when significant events happened with them?
11. What were the qualities they had – good or bad?
12. Do they remind you of anyone else in your life?
13. What, if any, patterns can you see?

WIZARD OF OZ:
"Hearts will never be practical until
they are made unbreakable."

5

Soulmate Connections

Dorothy found herself on a quest, a transformational journey, and like all quests it had to begin with a challenge. Back in Kansas Dorothy had relied upon her Aunt Em and Uncle Henry to take care of her after her parents died. They were hard-working farming people, struggling to survive in difficult times, and they didn't really have a lot of time for a child, especially one with a dog, who got herself into all sorts of trouble. But they did their best and even though at times they seemed emotionally distant, they tried to keep her safe and away from harm, as did the workers that helped out on the farm. They had all warned her to keep away from a certain Miss Gulch, who was notoriously bad tempered and mean. "Avoid her house; just find a new way to walk home everyday," they said, but Dorothy didn't listen.

One fateful day Miss Gulch arrived with an order from the sheriff to take Toto away and have him destroyed because she said he tried to bite her. Dorothy turned to her Aunt Em, the woman she depended on for her and Toto's survival, only to find that she was unable to save him. Feeling powerless and devastated by her loss, Dorothy ran to her room in tears, but it wasn't long before the canny Toto escaped from the clutches of the evil Miss Gulch and found his way back home. Dorothy knew she would be back, and in that moment the decision was made to run away and find a better life – a place where she and Toto would be safe. It was a travelling magician she met along the way who pointed out that by running away she would break her auntie's heart. This thought made her turn on her heels to go back, but by the time she decided to go back home, it was too late and before she knew it she was in Oz. And as marvelous and as colourful, and as magical as it was in Oz, there was only one place she wanted to go and that was home. She wanted to go back to

Kansas and the farm where her family and her friends all lived; she wanted to get back to her Auntie Em, the woman she loved the most. Her journey, along the yellow brick road, was an archetypal journey leading her to a place of self-knowledge and self-awareness. It was a journey into the complete unknown, and all journeys into the unknown have an element of risk; but in her desire to get back home Dorothy did not consider any of this. She just knew she had to get back to the farm; back home to Auntie Em, where she was safe and where she felt loved.

What drives people to look for love?

Love is one of the most powerful emotions you can experience whilst on the earth plane; and it has many forms. From an early age you are bombarded with messages about love, particularly romantic love. It is right there in all the stories and fairly tales and in the books, movies, and programmes that you see.

How many forms does love have?

When I was 15 I had an Italian boyfriend who sent me a card saying that the Ancient Greeks had four words for love and the one he would give to me was Eros. It was probably one of the most romantic things I was ever sent. Unfortunately at that age I wasn't really worldly enough to appreciate it. I do now.
The four words for love that the Ancient Greeks used were:

AGAPE: This refers to unconditional love or holding someone in high regard.
PHILIA: This refers to friendship. It is a virtuous and loyal love.
STORGE: This refers to the affection that parents feel for their offspring and their family. And then there is…
EROS: This refers to passionate, romantic love, with sensual desire and longing. Apparently this didn't always have to be sexual in nature, or so said Plato; hence, the use of the word *platonic* for friendships that are nonphysical.

I'm sure my mother would have been very relieved if she had known about the platonic version of the message in the card when I was 15. As it was I didn't see him again after that anyway; all that romance stuff was a bit too much for my liking back then, and I had too many books to be getting on with. Anyway, when eros or "erotic love" as it became known, was of the passionate kind, it was said to resemble a kind of "madness from the gods." Cupid (another name for Eros) and his arrows were blamed for "love at first sight" – the complete enchantment of another – although I have to say that this was far more likely to be a signal that there was a recognition from a past life going on and these souls were just remembering a time when they had loved each other before. Still, the myth was that if his arrows pierced your heart and you found yourself suddenly besotted and deeply in love, you would end up feeling dizzy with desire and as high as a kite. Now whether this was to do with a past life connection or the fault of a stray arrow, biological research seems to be able to explain this phenomenon because, apparently, when people fall in love, the brain releases a set of chemicals including dopamine, pheromones, and serotonin, which act as amphetamines, stimulating the brain's pleasure centre and leading to side effects such as increased heart rate, loss of appetite, inability to sleep, and intense feelings of excitement. It is no wonder the desire to fall in love can be addictive.

Unfortunately, it is said that these chemicals are only produced for the first year and a half to three years, covering what is commonly known as the honeymoon period. So romantic love is a constantly changeable thing and moves through many stages; it leads to many different outcomes – good and bad depending on how you look at it. If you can survive the loss of the "madness"- inducing chemicals, and the need for the "highs" that the initial stages of love can bring and move to the next stage, which is more to do with attachment and security, you are likely to be in it for the long haul. Not everyone manages to do this though, and the disappointment they feel when the buzz wears off often leads them to start looking elsewhere to get their fix.

How would you describe romantic love then?

It is many things: caring, kind, nurturing, supportive; it can bring great feelings of bliss, joy, and ecstasy, but it can also be cruel, harsh, painful, tragic, and bring feelings of suffering, sorrow, and despair especially when it is unrequited or if someone is betrayed – and yet no matter how much people suffer, how much pain they go through in the name of love, the desire to love is still strong.

Why is the desire to feel love so strong?

Nat King Cole put it so beautifully in his song "Nature Boy," which was used to great effect in the movie *Moulin Rouge*. "The greatest thing that you will ever learn is to love and be loved in return." The desire to love and be loved is an instinctual need that everyone experiences from the moment they are born. Freud believed that all people, at the deepest essence of their human nature, were seeking the satisfaction of certain needs: self-preservation, aggression, the impulse to attain pleasure and avoid pain, and a need for love. Unfortunately in the early years, which is the time when the need to experience love is the most important, not everyone gets the love they need. This can lead to all sorts of troubles later in life.

What sort of troubles?

It can lead to people being unable to love and value themselves fully. This lack of self-love leaves people feeling empty and in need; it can lead people to search for love outside of themselves. They look for someone else to validate them and prove that they are worthy of love. They may wait longingly for their soulmate, the prince or princess, who will save them from their emptiness, isolation, and loneliness. The only problem is that when they are unable to love themselves fully, it is almost impossible for anyone else to love them fully either. This nagging feeling that something is missing may lead them to look for love in all the wrong places or may lead them to shut themselves down and avoid love completely.

What causes this to happen?

If someone grows up in a world where they are loved and cared for and treated as though they are special, they will treat themselves and others that way too. If they felt, as they were growing up, that they were loved enough, supported enough, and were given the praise they needed to believe in themselves, they would never have to look outside for reassurance or proof that they are okay. Only trouble with that is that a large number of caregivers didn't know this was important.

Once upon a time, and unfortunately not that long ago, it was believed that children should be "seen and not heard," meaning many young children were not given all the love, nurturing, and attention they needed; particularly at the crucial early stages, many children found themselves left alone for long periods of time and left to cry. This was done so the children would not become needy or spoilt. Some were even beaten to toughen them up: "Spare the rod, spoil the child" once a popular phrase. This was not done because people were deliberately trying to sabotage, neglect, or damage their children in any way, but because people just did what their parents did to them and their parents before that and so, at the unconscious level, it seemed normal. Even those who may have disagreed with this idea in principle, and attempted to offer love and kindness, simply didn't have the time or the energy to be fully present for their children all the time, especially when life got busy and parents found themselves forced out to work instead of being at home.

What this ended up generating was a whole society of people who, unconsciously, felt unloved, unworthy, and in need of attention. This they sought from others, who were equally in need and for a short while, at the beginning, it may have seemed that they were able to provide what was needed for one another. But it would not be possible to maintain the level of attention required, especially when the first rush of the endorphins started to wear off and then, in a panic, because their needs were no longer being met, their hearts become closed and many rush off in search of another fix, another lover to fill the emptiness they feel inside. This unhealthy cycle continues until love of self is discovered and then, and only then, can wholesome and open-hearted relationships commence.

What causes people to avoid opening their hearts?

The biggest thing is fear – fear of being hurt, of being rejected, or of being abandoned. One of my clients, James, had big fears around falling in love and making a commitment. On one level he wanted to get married and have a family, but the reality of it was not so easy. He was in his late forties and had been through a string of relationships that lasted for about two years. Each time they began to talk about love and commitment he would find some excuse, some complaint about the woman, some reason why he could not stay, and he would leave. Upon reflection he realized that there hadn't been anything wrong with any of these women, so he decided to see if there was a deeper reason behind this pattern so that it could be resolved before it was too late.

Instead of going to a past life he found himself as a very young child, alone in a pram, in his back garden. He could hear his mother vacuuming inside. Suddenly a big black crow landed in the pram; to an adult a crow is not that pleasant a creature, just imagine the response of a vulnerable infant! Absolutely terrified and fearing for his life, he screamed and he screamed, desperately wanting to be rescued by the woman who was his protector – the one that he relied upon 100% for his survival – and she never came. She just carried on with her vacuuming, oblivious to the scene of devastation that was happening in her own back yard. Now this was not fully her fault as she had no idea what was going on, but in his young mind, at that moment, he made a decision that the people that were supposed to love you, and take care of you, would not be there for you when you really needed them, and he vowed that he would never trust anyone again. It was this vow that was preventing him from trusting that the woman he loved would be there for him in a time of need, and it was just easier for him to walk away when the risk of being hurt got too great.

I have to say he was a little disappointed that the cause of his problem was such a "seemingly" trivial event, until I pointed out that to a young child this would have been much more than trivial. I got him to go back to the memory, as an adult, who knew better, and placate the inner child who was still trapped in the pram. He held his hand and shooed away the crow, telling him that everything would be okay. He told him that he was safe and that he was loved unconditionally and that from now on *he* would take care of him. He explained what crows were and that they generally never hurt humans and that this one was just very nosy. This made him

107

laugh and the child, he once was, stopped crying and instead was able to see the world through very different eyes. They hugged and all of the inner fear and pain was released. He was also able to float back along his mother's time line, to view her childhood, and see that his mother wasn't being deliberately mean, she was just doing what her mother had done to her as a child, which she thought was for the best.

He discovered that for many generations of his family, children had been treated this way – left for long periods to cry and expected to be self-sufficient as a result. He also saw that it didn't work, that all of his ancestors had been fearful of being hurt and had avoided close contact with people as a result. He went to the very first time this happened and saw that one of his ancestors in 1575 had been orphaned. He had struggled to survive and had never been able to trust anyone; even though he had married and raised a child, he had been distant and afraid to get too close. He saw that this descendent needed to understand how it felt to be loved and so he sent love to him; he forgave him for all that had happened, and this set him free from the weight of his fear. As he did this he released the fear throughout his whole family line and a wave of love and gratitude swept over him. As he floated back along the family line to view the memory with the pram again he saw his mother in a completely different light. She was smiling and happy and delighted to be free of that fear; she picked the small boy up in her arms and vowed never to leave him alone like that ever again. The healing of this memory meant he was free to let his vow go. He did go on to be married and is now the proud father of a young boy; he is very careful not to ever leave him outside on his own.

Can events from past lives create fears about commitment?

Yes, they can have a huge effect and because the memories are buried so deep there is very little chance of understanding where the fear comes from, and the only way to find out is by exploring at the unconscious level.

One of my clients, Peter, had been experiencing similar issues with commitment. We had already explored his childhood and as his parents had divorced when he was fairly young there were some very rational reasons why he should have concerns over getting married; but nothing could explain the panic attacks and the night sweats that he experienced, particularly when the subject of having a family was raised. His long-term girlfriend was now threatening to leave him over it, and he really didn't want to lose her. He really felt that she was the person he was meant to spend his life with, because from the first moment they met he had felt a very strong connection to her; he said it felt as though they had known each other forever. He didn't know if he believed in the idea of soulmates "but if they did exist" he said "she might be mine." He knew he needed to take care of it – and fast. In his session he found himself at the mouth of a cave, wearing nothing but an animal skin around his shoulders and waist. In the cave were his family and several others, who were a part of his tribe. It was winter and the people had built a small fire that was keeping them warm. Outside of the cave was a very large, hungry bear and a pack of hungry wolves; his job was to keep them away. He had nothing but a very basic spear in his hands, and he soon discovered that this was not enough to keep the animals at bay. The bear lunged at him, and he landed on his back in the middle of the fire. With the bear on top of him, the wolves seized the opportunity, and they dived in too. The last thing he remembered were the screams of his family who were now all under attack. He died feeling like a failure and disgusted with himself that he had not been able to keep his family safe.

In the inter-life space, he discovered that his family had not thought of him as a failure or felt let down by him in any way. They held him in the highest regard, and they had been really proud of him. He noticed that his arm was badly damaged and was told that this was not the first time he had battled with wild animals to protect them. He had been afraid of nothing in that life and this was why he had been the one at the mouth of the cave and not any of the other larger, stronger men.

His perspective changed and he was able to let go of the idea that he was a failure and a coward. His family, from that life, embraced him and told him that he had been a wonderful husband and father and that they had been very lucky to have had him. He was amazed to discover that his wife from that life and his girlfriend in this were the same soul. She had been with him for many lifetimes and they had been partners many times. She confirmed that she was a soulmate and that she had returned this time to help him overcome this fear, and belief, that he was not good enough. That life was designed to test his bravery and he had passed the test; all he had to do now was believe in himself and let go of his fear. After the session his fear and anxiety were, pretty much, gone; he did have one more session, but I will talk about it later in the book. As a result of the work he did he was able to get married and really enjoy his second chance to be with his "soulmate" again.

If you meet someone and instantly feel as though you already know them, as if you have known them all your life but you can't explain it, could it be a soulmate connection?

It could just be that they remind you of someone you once knew a long time ago and have forgotten about, but it is more likely that they are from your soul group and have come along to help you. If they are part of your core soul group they may well have volunteered for the role of a soulmate, there to provide you with some of the biggest challenges you are going to have to face in your life.

Do you always know when you meet a soulmate?

In the course of your lifetime, you may meet thousands of people, some you will connect with and some you won't. Some people will really leave a mark, really make an impression, and these people often have a profound impact on your life – be it good or bad. These are usually your soulmates, souls sent to make a difference and keep you on the path of learning and growth.

What effect can meeting a soulmate have on you?

In each of your lifetimes you will be playing out dramas with souls that you already know. The residue of those experiences remains in your subconscious, within your energy field, and will be felt or sensed when you meet these people in your current life. You may have no conscious awareness of the events that occurred but as time goes on it is possible that this residue can emerge – shaping the relationships that you create around you. A powerful soulmate connection can explain why sometimes people experience powerful feelings, inexplicable desires, and even strange obsessions with the people they meet.

I had one client who explored over six different lives and she recognised her husband as the same soul in every one of them. In each life they had survived different tests and challenges, with regard to being together, but they had overcome all of the adversities and their deep love for each other was clear. It was no surprise for her to discover they were soulmates, but I felt sure that her husband would be sceptical; however, when we mentioned it to him, he just smiled at me and said, "Of course we're soulmates. She's not getting rid of me; whatever happens I'll just keep coming back and finding her." They have just celebrated their 50th wedding anniversary, in this life, so they must be doing something right.

Interestingly in Hindu wedding ceremonies, there is a very interesting ritual that occurs. The couple are made to circle around a fire together seven times, each time around represents a life that they promise to have together. Now this is all well and good if the marriage turns out to be a happy and loving one, not so good if they find that they cannot stand the sight of each other early into the marriage, left with the knowledge that they will have to do it again and again and again. Makes you wonder if in one of their lives my couple had signed a Hindu contract and still had more lives to go.

Thankfully they would have had no complaints as their connection was clearly based on love and support. Unfortunately that is not always the case and there are no guarantees that a soulmate connection will provide you with love.

Aren't soulmate connections always romantically linked?

No, soulmates can appear in many guises and although many do have romantic connections, often they appear in ways that you would least expect.

Does this explain why you sometimes meet people and instantly, for no apparent reason, dislike them immensely; when something about them just seems to set you on edge, with no real rational explanation?

This is something I do hear from people and, strangely enough, even though it comes as a surprise to many, this can also be attributed to a very close soulmate connection. One of my clients, Alice, started a new job and was really looking forward to the new opportunity; what she hadn't counted on was that the person they assigned to train her was someone that she would take an instant dislike to. There was no reason that she could see logically to explain her dislike, but it was tangible; she described the feeling very clearly. She said that each time this man walked into the room it was if her "flesh crawled."

In the session she discovered a lifetime where she was part of a religious community in the United States many hundreds of years ago; in the lifetime she was a young, pretty woman. This man had been one of the elders and had taken a liking to her. The men had believed that they had a divine right to do what ever they wished with the women of the group, and women were not valued very highly at that time. As a punishment for not doing her chores correctly this man would beat and rape her. Now in his mind he was doing the Lord's will, punishing her for her slovenly ways; in her mind he was just an abuser. In the session she got to communicate with her abuser and let him know that his behaviour had been unacceptable; she received a heartfelt apology and was able to forgive him, especially when she saw that he was not really a bad man, he had just been indoctrinated by his peers and held no malice towards her. In fact, quite the contrary, he had been in love with her and thought that this was the only way he could have her. His insecurity, in that life, meant he was afraid to ask for her love, certain that he would be rejected.

Further exploration revealed that they were indeed members of the same soul group. Not only that but he was one of her soulmates. They had been through many lives together in attempt to learn about, and experience, unconditional love for one another. In our searching we discovered that there had been a life in the 1930s, where as an up and coming film starlet, she had rejected him and had broken his heart, leaving him a shadow of his former self. Another lifetime saw them as brother and sister, who were caught up in a battle with Vikings; this time she was the brother who was unable to save his sister from being raped and murdered at the hands of their attackers. My client was amazed. She released the contract they had written for this life, which was about him testing her to see if she could still hold unconditional love for him in a difficult situation. She replaced the contract with one of support for each other and she was then able to let go of all the anger and guilt that she had been carrying from those lives. When she returned to work she found that her feelings towards him had changed. The anger and the intense dislike was gone, in its place came a sense of gratitude for all they had been through together. Their working relationship changed considerably and the man became a great support to her and a good friend to her family.

Can this knowledge help you make sense of why you choose the partners you choose – in business and in pleasure?

Yes, because soulmate connections are very powerful and there is a reason why you are brought together, you will usually have set an agreement to achieve something and the link will not be fully broken until the lesson has been learnt. So it can make sense of some of the good, and the not so good, situations you may have found yourself in. As you look back over your life you may see that there were some situations from which you were unable to get away, even though you knew something was wrong; something kept you there until one day a penny dropped and you got what you were supposed to learn. At that moment you become free instantly, as if a set of shackles have been dropped. My own experience of this was quite profound.

When I was 19 I began dating someone who had been in the year above me at school. From the start we felt certain that we were soulmates and that we had experienced many lives together. We made jokes about me being his mother as I was prone to taking care of things and him. We were together for 12 years and in that time many things happened that made me question whether we were right for each other, but as we were both certain that we were soulmates, I thought that I had no choice but to stay with him. We even decided to get married, after 10 years of being together, in attempt to make things work. And for a short while, with the fun of a wedding in Vegas to plan, things were okay but in the long term it didn't really help. It was really hard for me as I had always felt that people should only be together if they make each other happy, and it became increasingly obvious even after we got married that we were no longer able to do that. After a particularly frustrating and unhappy time, I asked a girlfriend to come away with me on a meditation holiday in Greece. I needed some time to breathe and think about my life. We booked a ticket for the next day, packed a bag, and set off. I have a little ritual each time I travel and that is to buy a book at the airport; I leave it to chance and read whatever comes my way. The book that fell into my hands was a book entitled *Soulmates*; it was that synchronicity thing at work again. It told me lots of things that I felt I already knew until I got to the chapter that said that we only needed to stay with our soulmates until we learnt the lessons that we needed from them. I felt that I had really learnt that being like someone's mother did not make for a good marriage. It was the answer that I had been looking for. I understood that I no longer needed to play the part of his mother; it was a role that I had already played – in this life and in several others it turns out. I knew then that I had to let him go so that he could grow up and stand on his own two feet. I felt overjoyed, but my happiness was very nearly short lived. The next thing I knew there was a loud bang and the plane began to hurtle downwards. People were yelling and screaming and even some of the cabin crew were hysterical. It was like a scene from a very bad B movie, with lots of people shouting that we were all going to die. Including the cabin crew!

Not a good sign!

My life did flash before me but I decided there and then that I did *not* want to die as I had just been given permission to move on with my life. I also decided that if I was going to die I was not going to go in a state of panic and stress, so I took some deep breaths, said a few prayers, and carried on reading my book. After a very dodgy landing in a deserted airfield in Italy, my friend and I found ourselves feeling very grateful to be alive and extremely grateful for the chance to live the rest of our lives. A very long wait in a deserted aircraft hanger waiting for another plane to take us on the rest of our journey gave me plenty of time to think and for the sense of gratitude to really sink in. I knew that I had been neglecting my own journey, by focusing so much of my time and attention on a relationship that wasn't really working, and I really wanted to do something more with my life. On that trip I felt a real call to serve in some way, to find a way to help others get free of the limiting beliefs that were holding them back and it was a real turning point in my life. That state of gratitude has stayed with me and to this day I always make the effort to say thank you for everything in my life.

On return from the trip I was able to let go of my relationship, and although it was hard at first, we both knew it was the right thing to do. The divorce was incredibly amicable, and we remained good friends afterwards. I am delighted to say that he did get to stand on his own two feet and now has a great job, is happily married with two children, and is doing very well. I'm happy because it set me free to find my role as a therapist and a healer, and I know for certain that letting him go was the best thing for us both. The knowledge that he was just one of my soulmates made me very grateful to him for the lessons I learnt and freed me up to have other people in my life who have taught me more and more valuable lessons. I am grateful to them all, without exception, even the ones that have challenged me the most – in fact, especially the ones who have challenged me the most.

Do many people, in relationships, come for a past life because they want to know if the person they are with is their soulmate?

Yes, and in a lot of cases, the answer they get is the one they want to hear: that they *have* had other lives with this person, sometimes many, and they get the reassurance they need that this person is who they are meant to be with; they get permission to stop looking elsewhere, relax, and enjoy their relationship – for as long as it is meant to last.

I have to say I find the idea of being together forever a bit tricky; being together for as long as you make each other happy seems a much better promise to make. Of course, there are times when they are very surprised when they find out what the connection to this person really is and the truth can be something they may never have imagined.

So how many soulmates can you have in your life?

This will be different for everyone; you may have many soulmates, and some of the connections may be stronger than others, especially if there have been vows or promises made to each other that have been carried over. Ultimately a soulmate is someone who volunteered to help you with the bigger life lessons; as you have free will there is no guarantee that the lessons will get learnt and if they don't, well, they may not be the only soul to have volunteered.

If one soulmate fails to help you learn your lesson there may be another waiting in the wings to test you again. This is a very important idea to remember as you choose your partners for life.

Will meeting your soulmate really make you happy?

Some people get a bit caught up thinking that they have to find "The One" and are never satisfied until they think they have found them. They may reject people who don't perfectly fit the criteria they have in mind or the qualities they think their soulmate "should" have. They are constantly on the lookout for someone who ticks all their boxes, waiting to feel a magical spark and signs to tell them that this person really is the one. Then they wait to be convinced that the relationship is meant to be.

These people tend to dive headlong into relationships with great gusto, thinking that they will live happily ever after. And when problems arise, which is inevitable in any relationship, no matter how perfect it may seem at the beginning, instead of working through it, they decide they must have got it wrong. Then they leave believing that their soulmate, "The One," the person that is perfect for them, is going to be right around the next corner.

Is there ever a perfect one?

One of the biggest misconceptions about soulmates that many people still believe is that you only have one of them. Once you understand that there may be many people destined to help you on your journey of life and play the role of a soulmate you can relax and take the pressure off people to be perfect or "The One." They can just be the perfect one for right now to help you learn what you need to learn.

The reality is that you can have many soulmates, and just because you connect with a soulmate on the earth plane doesn't mean that you have to be with them forever; you need to be with them for as long as it takes to learn the lesson you needed to learn; once this has been resolved you can move on. Of course if the lesson was whether or not you could spend a lifetime with that person then that is a different story.

Are some soulmates more significant than others?

Sometimes they are. I have already mentioned the fact that a soul's energy can split and enter two, or even multiple, different lifetimes on the earth plane, although this is pretty rare. These "split souls" may experience a craving for the missing part of themselves, without whom they struggle to feel whole.

Is there anything that can be done to remedy this?

If someone does have another part of their soul floating around somewhere else on the planet the feeling can only be fully remedied by reconnecting with their "twin" or "other" soul part. However this is also not always a romantic connection. Knowing what has happened can help a person to understand why they feel the way they do and can make things easier to manage.

I had one client who had really powerful awareness that she had a twin soul out there somewhere; she kept dreaming of a man, who was not her husband, and the dreams were very emotional and upsetting. She felt a longing for this man even though she was very happily married, and she was really worried that it would disrupt her life. She wanted to explore the connection and find out what it all meant. She found herself in a life as a young man who was deeply in love; he was prevented from marrying the love of his life as her family did not consider him wealthy enough. He went away determined to make his fortune and he succeeded, however by the time he returned she was already married to another and they never met again. He died with the feeling of longing still intact.

The object of his desire had, in fact, been a part of his own soul and when they met in the inter-life space it was very emotional. The challenge they had set for each other was all about separation and managing to deal with everyday life, regardless of whether they were together or not. Clearly in that life he had not succeeded. My client asked if they had both come to the earth plane in her current life and she was told that they had. She wanted to know if they would meet at some point, and this part of her soul smiled and said "Yes" they would meet. I knew that in order to deal with the longing something needed to happen, so I got her to go back and relive the life – only this time the young man would have already succeeded in gaining his wealth, this time he would be able to marry his love. She did this and was able to imagine a wonderful life, in complete harmony with her "other self."

Once the session was over the feeling of longing was gone. This was just as well as a few months later she attended a family wedding. A friend of the groom walked into the room and she knew instantly that this man was her twin soul. As he approached she could feel her heart beat a little faster, they smiled, and conversed for a time and she was hugely relieved to find that she felt no desire for him or need for anything more. They found they had much in common and when he laughed and said, "Its funny but I feel like I know you," she just laughed and said, "Yes, funny that." She decided not to share her secret with him, lest he think she was a bit strange.

What about people who don't have a twin soul but are looking for someone else to "complete them"?

If people who don't have a twin soul are looking for someone else to complete them, or make them feel whole, they are always going to be disappointed; because it really doesn't work like that. I understand that this is contrary to what Tom Cruise, or his alter ego Jerry Maguire, would have you believe.

I tell my clients that it is far healthier for them to work on themselves, to get into a place where they no longer feel they need someone else to make them feel good or complete. It is so much more important for them to love and accept who they are unconditionally, to reclaim their own inner power, to be in control over their feelings and emotions, and really appreciate themselves – accepting their faults as well as their talents and skills.

Once they feel good about themselves and their sense of self esteem improves, they send a message to the world that they deserve to be happy. Then they attract people who feel the same way. Instead of needing to fix the wounds that they recognize in each other, or fill in any "gaps" they may have, they can just come together and be happy– enjoying life and all that it has to offer. Of course, there may still be lessons to learn but at a very different level.

How would you know if you really had met a significant soulmate or even a twin soul?

It could be nothing more than a feeling, a sense that you have known each other for a very, very long time; perhaps you know exactly what the other is thinking and can finish their sentences, and perhaps it is just a strange sense of recognition from the moment you met, and perhaps it is a feeling of having finally come home. Or you could have a past life session and allow the information to emerge as many of my clients have done, often with incredible results.

If you are single, how do you find The One that is right for right now?

Once you have done the inner work that is required and have achieved a level of self-love and appreciation for who you really are then you will be ready to open your heart and share your life with someone else, if that is what you want.

I saw a post on someone's media site recently that said, "Don't change so that people like you. Be yourself and the real people will love the real you." When you are ready, your soulmate, or one of them, might just turn out to be the person next door, or they may appear in the most unusual of circumstances, like the airport or while you are waiting for a train. When you are really ready the person will come.

Waiting for fate and destiny to intervene is one way to do it, but sometimes you do need to give it a helping hand; so getting out and meeting people in different places, particularly doing things that you enjoy, is a good idea. Nothing like meeting someone that you have things in common with and in today's world of technology, even the Internet may be the designated meeting point for soulmates. I know several people who met online and who are now very happily living their lives together.

Once you meet your soulmate, or someone that you want to share your life with, what is the best way to make the relationship work?

The best way to make any relationship work is to make sure that you take care of, and honour yourself, while you are in it. By ensuring that you are happy and living life in a way that keeps you satisfied and fulfilled, you will be able to share those good feelings with a partner. In choosing the right partner, you might not necessarily want to go for the person that is the most gorgeous, sexy, and dangerous – but totally unavailable and unable to commit.

For the long haul you may want to pick someone that you like and that you can be friends with. The idea of romantic love that you see in the movies just doesn't really happen – well, not every day anyway; far better to find someone that you share interests with, someone who makes you laugh, who wants to share time with you, and someone who is willing to learn and grow as they go along.

Annie

Are all difficult romantic relationships that challenge you based on soulmate connections?

It would be more surprising if they were not. One of my clients, a woman called Annie, came because she had become aware of an unpleasant pattern in her relationships, and it seemed like way too much of a coincidence that the two major relationships in her life had ended not only very badly but there had been elements of them that had been almost identical. Her first serious, long-term relationship had been with a man who had been controlling in many ways but completely cold and shut off when it came to their love life. It was as if he had no interest in being intimate with her and eventually she had been left feeling unloved and shut out. After a turbulent five years they broke up and she decided to make some changes to her life.

Eventually she met another man, who at first seemed very different: for one, he was very passionate and affectionate. However, as time went on, the pattern of being controlled began to emerge again and this time it was even worse: he started telling her how to eat and how to dress. Their love life began to take an unhappy turn and she began to feel overwhelmed by his demands. Eventually, after another five years, the relationship broke down and after a holiday in South America, where things really came to a head, she was forced to instigate a break-up.

The break-up was very difficult and left her drained and exhausted. She was afraid of entering into any new relationships in case she found herself repeating the pattern all over again. After each break-up she had also put on a lot of weight, especially around her middle; it was as if she was trying to protect herself by building up a pro-tective layer. She wanted to put the past behind her so that she could meet someone and have a family; it just had to be with someone that was emotionally stable.

The journey began:

A: I am a woman and I am wearing North American Indian clothes, leather shoes, and a long leather dress. I am at a celebration; there is a big fire and there are lots of people dancing around it.

ME: What are you celebrating?

A: It is a wedding. I am the bride but I do not want to marry this man; he is not a Native American, he is a white man.

ME: What is your role here?

A: I am the chief's daughter, and he is the British captain of a ship; his name is Robert Marr. It was he who suggested the marriage; he persuaded my father

118

that it would be good for the tribe and good for trading relations.

ME: How do you feel about this?

A: I do not want to go, but I must do what my father says.

ME: What happens next?

A: I am taken away from my beautiful home, away from all of the people that I love and the traditional ways that I respect and I am to be taken to England.

ME: Tell me about your journey.

A: On the boat, my new husband, treats me like a servant; I do not want to be with him. He cheated us and tricked us; he is treating me like a puppy that you can train to behave. I am still just wearing my leather clothes, and I feel very cold.

ME: What happens next?

A: I slip on the floor and the other sailors just pretend that they do not see me; it is humiliating and I am angry and cold and I fight with him and in return he beats me until I submit to him. I want to go back home but it is so far away now and I am all alone.

ME: Tell me about the boat you are on.

A: This boat is pushed by the wind; it has huge sails and at high winds we travel at a very fast pace. We arrive in England and when we arrive at his home, he puts me in the cellar, locking me in there.

ME: Why has he put you in the cellar?

A: He wants to keep me as a servant, a whore. He did not tell anyone that he married me; he just said that he captured me. He is married to someone else as well.

ME: Tell me about his wife.

A: I meet her; she is nice, her name is Maria and she is Spanish. He is cheating on her too; he tells her that I am insane and that I am dangerous and that I need to be locked up in the cellar. She is very nice to me though; she comes to see me and gives me food.

ME: Are you able to speak to her?

A: We cannot communicate properly because I do not speak the language.

ME: What else are you aware of?

A: I know that he married her because he wants to pretend to the outside world that he is normal, but he is not normal; he has an insatiable sexual appetite – he likes to be with men and women, sometimes both at the same time.

ME: Is she aware of this?

A: She is not really aware and believes what he tells her; he is away most of the time, either on his boat or on horseback. He just likes to please himself.

ME: What happens next?

A: Robert spends most of the time in London now, entertaining, and I am still kept in the cellar. Maria still visits and brings me my food; she wants to help me but she cannot. If she were to let me go I would have no way to survive, so it is safer for me to stay here in the cellar.

ME: What is she afraid of?

A: She is afraid that bad things would happen to me; she is a good woman. I cannot understand why Robert has to be so cruel, why he is cheating on everyone the way he does.

She shakes her head in distaste and appears to be mumbling something.

ME: What are you experiencing now?

A: I am praying. Maria has taught me how to pray and how to speak in English; we pray together regularly.

ME: Tell me what happens next.

A: I am alone in the cellar; it is night-time and it is very dark and very cold. I can hear Robert coming; he wants me to please him. Maria is away visiting her family so he wants me to make love to him; actually, it is just sex – he does not know what love is.

ME: What happens next?

A: I do not want this with him; I wish I could tell him that he is just a horrible man.

ME: Is anyone else around?

A: I can hear some voices, but it is probably just the servants. He has taken me to a bedroom and he wants more and more sex; I try to resist him and so he is beating me and kicking me and once he stops he wants to have sex with me again.

ME: How does this make you feel?

A: I feel so dirty.

ME: What happens next?

A: He has fallen asleep now, and I am sitting in the corner of the room crying; I feel extremely cold.

ME: Then what happens?

A: He is waking and he wants more. He wants me to treat him like a god and please him. I think he is sick; I am just useless but what can I do, I am his wife even though no one else knows this but me.

ME: Then what happens?

A: Finally, he is done with me and he is taking me back to the cellar. I am only wearing a thin white nightgown and I am freezing; he is telling me that if I do not do what he wants that I will die here in this cellar.

I can see that she is feeling distressed and so I move things forward quite quickly.

ME: Please move on to the next important event.

A: Maria is back. She is coming to see me; she has bought me a dress and shoes and a coat, which keeps me warm. While he is away she has been, very patiently, teaching me English; I can now read and write and we have been making a plan.

ME: What is your plan?

A: She wants to run away from him; she knows that what is going on with him is wrong.

She sighs deeply.

ME: What happens next?

She catches her breath.

A: I am on a boat with Maria; we are trying to escape but he has discovered our plan and is following us. If he catches us he will kill us....

ME: Then what happens?

A: Oh god, he is just behind us; we are trying to hurry the oarsman on but he is alone and Robert has many men in his boat. They are gaining on us...Maria is screaming. Robert has caught us and toppled the boat and we have all been pushed into the icy water. He is hitting us on our heads so we will drown; his men turn their heads, they are loyal to him and ignore our pleas for help.

ME: And then what happens?

A: We are both pretending to be dead in the hope that he will leave, but he is pulling out a gun...oh god no, he has shot Maria...there is blood everywhere...I am beyond terrified.

ME: What happens next?

A: I hide under her in the hope that he will think that I am dead too; thank god, he is going away.

She is very distressed as she speaks.

ME: What happens next?

A: I manage to get out of the water and I am running in the forest; I am wet and freezing cold and I feel so alone, there is just no one that can help me...Oh no, I can hear them returning... he has come back for the bodies and as he can't find mine he knows that I have escaped. He is furious and starts yelling at his men; he shouts out that whoever finds me will get a high price for my head...

ME: What are you experiencing now?

A: Fear, Oh god, I need to run, I need to hide but I have no strength left and nowhere to run to; I try to hide in the bushes but it's no use as they have found me.

For a while it all goes quiet, when she speaks again her voice sounds tired and resigned.

A: I am back in the cellar. I am getting fat…oh no…I am not fat, I am pregnant.

ME: What happens next?

A: I am giving birth to a little girl. I am going to call her Maria.

ME: Move on to the next significant event and tell me what you are aware of.

A: He doesn't want me anymore; I have a big tummy and breasts. I am not slim like I was before.

ME: Please move further forward in time and tell me what is happening.

A: I am getting old; he keeps me in the garden in a small house with my daughter but he still doesn't allow me to leave him; for some reason I must always be near him.

ME: How does that make you feel?

A: Angry, I don't want that. I don't know why he doesn't just leave me alone.

ME: Do you have any idea of why he keeps you here?

A: I think he sometimes feels guilty that he cheated me and my family in America; but even then he is double-minded – the other side of him thinks it is normal to use his power and please himself.

ME: How much time does he spend with you now?

A: None, he spends most of his time now with another man. I do not think it is a sexual relationship; the other man is resentful about sex, he has some problems.

ME: What kind of problems?

A: They both believe in the stories of Ancient Greece and Rome where wisdom and power were only for men and that the purest love was between men; woman were to be used just for sex, for man's own purpose.

ME: What do these men do with their lives?

A: They are very rich and continue to live in the big house, the place where he used to live with his wife, Maria; he has told everyone that she was shot by robbers who came in from the forest.

She laughs bitterly.

A: I am one of the few to know that this is a lie; it just is not true, but no one will believe me even if I could tell them the truth.

ME: Does he ever visit you?

A: He hardly ever visits us; he sends us food and clothes from time to time. He is not interested in us and he does not like children – neither of them do. The other man comes sometimes and looks into the window when he thinks we cannot see him; he gives me the creeps.

ME: How do you feel about being kept here all this time?

A: I don't care about my life any more; I just worry about what will happen to my daughter; it is not good for her to be kept here with no chance of a life. She has done nothing to him! I kept trying to tell him this but he wouldn't listen.

ME: So tell me what happens next?

A: I am getting tired, I just want to go to sleep and never wake up; I hope and pray that my daughter will be safe, but I guess I may never know.

ME: I would like you to move on to the end of this lifetime and tell me what you experience.

She sighs and for a time it goes quiet.

A: I am dying; I have just given up all the hope.

ME: What are you experiencing now?

A: I am dying now…and then finally I will be free…be free.

She smiles, and it is over.

ME: What was the karmic lesson that you had chosen to experience in this life?

A: I wanted to experience sadness, and part of my lesson was learning to be careful with people; that unfortunately, in life there are some people that you just can't trust – some people just have different values and they are not always truthful.

ME: What did you learn from this?

A: I learnt that I cannot spend my life with people who do not know about love; it is not about money, it does not matter how rich a person is or isn't, it is what is in their heart that matters. I also learnt that there are some very good people around too and that angels are always by your side, especially in hard times. Maria taught me to have faith and to believe in something higher than myself; it is what kept me going through all of the hard times.

ME: Can you get a sense of why Robert treated you so badly?

A: Robert's family struggled with him. His mother was a very strong woman but even though she knew of his ways she pretended not to; she was too ashamed to address them. His father was an alcoholic and was much the same, except that he had not liked men. He preferred to keep many mistresses and had very little in the way of family values to pass on to his son. He had been raised to just have fun, please himself, and think little of the consequences of his actions, and his son had taken it all on board and then some.

In the therapeutic part of the session she released all the negative feelings that she had developed at having been so wronged and so cheated of her life.

ME: Is there anyone you recognize from your current lifetime?

She gasped in amazement.

A: Robert is my last boyfriend, the one who had treated me so badly; in fact, he was almost a carbon copy of him and more incredibly Robert's partner in later years, the man who had watched me silently through the window, was my other ex-partner. She felt astonished that these two men had once again appeared in her life, especially in such powerful roles. Both had cheated her of the life she was supposed to live in one way or another. She had learnt her lesson!

ME: What needs to happen for you to release this pattern from your life?

A: I need to thank them for all that they have taught me and let them go.

ME: Are either of these men part of your soul group?

A: Oh, they both are, both of them are soulmates. I had not expected that at all; they are telling me that it was hard for them to play those parts as they loved me very much, but it was part of the lesson we had agreed upon and so they had to be cruel; it was all prearranged by me. Wow, I guess I did want to learn the hard way.

ME: What is the theme of your soul group?

A: They are telling me that it was about learning faith and fortitude; I can see that is what I have been learning in this life too.

ME: If you have learnt all you need from them you can let them go now, knowing that you may see them again some time, perhaps in happier circumstances next time.

She smiled and with tears in her eyes she told them both thank you and said a final goodbye.

ME: Were there any unhelpful vows or promises made in that life?

A: I made a vow that I would always be fat, to protect me from men; I decided that I would not look after myself and then I would not have to worry about temptation or being trapped!

ME: I think it is time to release that vow now, do you?

A: Yes, please.

She smiled as she did this, and I could see a look of relief on her face.

ME: What would be a more beneficial promise to make yourself?

A: I will always be slim and healthy; I will always look after myself. I deserve to be loved and have a loving husband; I deserve to have children and, most of all, I deserve to be happy.

ME: Now store this message somewhere in your heart centre, where it will never be lost and you will always remember it; this is to be your new mantra.

ME: What have you learnt from all this?

She smiled.

A: I know now that there are always good people around, that God will protect me. I shouldn't be afraid. I came to learn and I can now leave all the bad things behind me; I see now that even in hard times you can have happiness.

The journey was over.

When Annie came to, she was amazed at how cold she had felt through most of the session; the room she was in was warm and toasty and yet she had been shivering. She was staggered at the comparisons with her current life. She could see the strange power the men had over her – it all made sense. It had just never occurred to her that they were both soulmates. She left with a great sense of excitement about her future, and she realized the extra weight she had been carrying was no longer necessary.

A year after the session she reported that she had lost more than four stone and was engaged to a wonderful man who made her very happy; this time she said she was looking forward to being tied down, and she knew there would be no more living in the cellar for her.

Samantha

Someone who had quite a different experience with regard to soulmates was a client called Samantha; she came because she had this very strange feeling that she would never get married. She wanted to be married and have children and so wanted to see if there was anything from her past lives that might be holding her back. As she explored her current life she saw that she had been drawn to men who were somehow emotionally unavailable, and she realised that she had been choosing men that allowed her to keep her own emotions closed off and therefore safe from any attachments. The final question that she asked before the session was, "Why can't I find someone to love?"

The journey began:

ME: Can you tell me what you are experiencing?

S: Oh, it is so sad. My mother has just died giving birth to me and my father is really not happy. It's because I am a girl and he is holding me responsible for the death of my mother, his beloved wife. He's holding his head and he is pacing the room, up and down, head down low, muttering to himself. He really is in despair and he doesn't know what to do; he wanted a boy, not some helpless girl who would demand his attention and especially now my mother is dead!

ME: What else can you tell me?

S: My father's name is Albert, and it is 1822.

ME: Is there anyone else there with you?

S: I can see the doctor now; he is an old, kind-looking man. He's just cleaning up. He is beside himself with grief. He doesn't know what to do for the best. My father is saying that he doesn't want me; he doesn't want to take me home. The doctor understands that he is distressed because of what's happened, but he is trying to talk him around. But it is no use, he is adamant!

ME: What is your father saying to the doctor?

S: He is saying, "I don't want her. It's no use, I cannot see any way around it; a girl can't ever help me, a girl is just going to get in the way, so as far as I am concerned. It is simple; I have to get out of here and she is not coming with me." He leans over me in the cot at end of the bed and as I lie there screaming he whispers, "I'm sorry, but I have no choice. I just can't take care of you, that's all there is to it. I have to go, God forgive me, but I really have to go!" and he leaves, without turning his head. He never comes back. The doctor covers the body of my mother with a sheet and then it all goes quiet.

A small tear trickled down Samantha's face.

ME: I want you to move on to the next significant event.

She takes a deep breath and begins to describe the next scene.

S: I am in an orphanage now.

ME: How old are you now?

S: I am still a baby, although I am now a couple of months old. Some people have arrived and are looking at me in my cot. I can see them looking at me. They look like nice enough people; they appear to have money as they are very well dressed. The lady is saying, "I'll take her, I want her." There is another woman with them, I guess she must be a nurse; they seem to have made their decision and they walk away to talk to the man from the orphanage. Even though I'm a baby I know they are not my real parents.

ME: How does this make you feel?

S: I am overwhelmed with the feeling that I just want my father, my real father. I don't want to go with them. What if one day he comes back to look for me and I'm not there? So even though they look okay, I want to be with my real father! I want him, not some unknown step-family. But I have no choice. They sign all the papers, pick me up and wrap me in blankets, and then they walk outside. It all seems so bright after the doom and gloom of the orphanage.

ME: What else are you aware of?

S: We are walking through narrow cobbled streets; I feel a sense of dread coming over me as I am carried off into a new life over which I have no control!

ME: Tell me what happens next.

She shifts in her chair uneasily.

S: I am 12 years old; they have called me Rebecca. I am outside a big house, where there are children playing in the street with hoops and things. I am sat alone watching them. As they run past me one boy shouts "no one wants you, orphan girl, we're not playing with you."

ME: How does it make you feel when you hear them say that?

S: It makes me feel very sad, and deep down it hurts so much more because I believe it to be the truth....I know that the people that have raised me are not my real parents...and it is true: I wasn't wanted, not by my real father at any rate; I wonder whatever happened to him and if he ever thinks of me.

ME: What is significant about this moment in time?

S: The children constantly tease me.

ME: What about?

S: Being an outsider; the family I live with has lots of money and I live in a very nice house, but it is not enough – all I want is a place where I feel I belong.

ME: What about the family, how do they treat you?

S: The family constantly reminds me how lucky I am that they took me in, but I get no love from any of them.

ME: Is there anyone that you can turn to?

S: None of the children will play with me, except for one boy – his name is Arthur.

ME: Tell me about Arthur.

S: I know that my "family" would highly disapprove as he has no home, but he wants to play with me.

ME: Tell me what happens.

S: At first I am hesitant because I know that the family would disapprove, but his kind eyes and his sweet smile win me around; he tells me that he will be my friend – and he tells me that he thinks I'm really pretty. I feel a sense of happiness and lightness for the first time in my life.

ME: I want you to move to the next important event.

S: I am a teenager now, and I am at some sort of wishing well, a place where Arthur and I regularly meet up in secret.

ME: What are you doing here?

S: We are throwing in stones instead of coins because we have no money, to make our wishes come true; we are always very careful that no one sees us together.

ME: What are you wishing for?

S: My secret wish is that my father would come back for me and Arthur and whisk us off to someplace where we can be happy.

ME: What about Arthur; what is he wishing for?

S: Arthur wishes that he can grow up and be a soldier so that he can make me proud and provide a good home for us both.

ME: What happens next?

S: I am older now. Arthur is still my friend; in fact, he is a lot more than my friend – we have fallen in love with each other. I steal food from the house and sneak it out to him as he still has nowhere to live; he stays around because he wants to be close to me. He has nothing to give me but his love and he gives this freely and openly; we dream of being together, having a home and one day a family.

ME: Please continue.

S: It is the summer and Arthur and I have spent a few hours together by the well, dreaming of our future together. It is time for me to leave and go back to the house. I don't want to leave him but I must; we are trying to think of a way that we can be together, and I am hoping that in time the family will agree to let me go and be with him, but I am waiting for the right time to ask them. I know that it won't be easy.

ME: What happens next?

S: I say goodbye to Arthur and we hold each other for a very long time. We arrange to meet at the same time the next day and he gives me a little flower, a daisy; I go home really happy.

ME: What happens next?

S: As I walk in the door my stepmother and stepfather are there, waiting for me; my stepfather orders my stepmother to leave the room; in a voice filled with venom he spits at me, "You have bought shame on this family, I know all about you and that little guttersnipe! I did not bring you from that place to bring shame on me and my family!" He shouts and rants at me like a madman. I try to explain and tell him, "I'm sorry, but I love him," but he just looks at me in horror and disgust. In my desperation I scream at him to let me go, to set me free. I yell out at him, "What do you care, you are not my real father anyway," and at this sees red, he lashes out and he hits me, and he keeps hitting me again and again. He screams into my face, "I forbid you to ever see that creature again."

ME: What happens next?

S: I am inconsolable and I cannot stop crying.

Through big wet tears she continues.

S: I am banned from ever leaving the house; I am forced to sit in my room, alone. The windows are boarded up so that I cannot see anything or anyone; I am sure that Arthur will think I don't love him anymore.

ME: What happens next?

S: I miss him like crazy. The days turn into weeks, then months, and every day I pine for him and each day that passes I miss him more; I have a horrible feeling that I will never see him again. Eventually my despair turns to numbness; I feel utterly desolate and heartbroken. I feel really sad because he has not tried to find a way to contact me or rescue me in some way. I can't help feeling that if he really loved me he would have at least tried.

She sighs forlornly.

ME: Then what happens?

S: Eventually the family decides to take matters into their own hands and be rid of me: They force me to marry someone else; in fact, what really happens is that he pays them a sum of money so that I will be his wife. They forced me into the marriage, but they could not make me love him; I couldn't love him even if I wanted to.

ME: What is he like?

S: He is much older than me, much too old; his name is Ralph. He has a funny moustache and greased-back hair; he is very strict and cruel.

ME: How does he make you feel?

S: I am so scared. Every day I worry that he might beat me to death; the only thing that I can do is to try to escape, to run away from him.

ME: What do you do next?

S: One day when he's out I manage to pry open a small window at the back of the house. I squeeze myself through it and escape – breathless and terrified, I run to the well. I see mine and Arthur's initials engraved on the wall and something inside me begins to scream. I don't know where he is, or what happened to him; perhaps he thought I hadn't loved him, but I never stopped. I remember how happy we had been the last time I saw him by the well and it breaks my heart!

ME: So what happens next?

S: I run away, I never go back. I just run and run, with no idea of where I am running to; I have nowhere to go and so I hide on the streets and eat any scraps that I find.

ME: Then what happens?

S: Time goes on and I am getting weaker and weaker; I am not feeling very well. I have no strength left inside me; I can hardly walk I am so weak.

ME: How long do you search for?

S: Months have passed and no one has found me; I have kept myself well hidden away. When I do venture out of the shadows looking for some sign of Arthur, with some hope of finding him, people look at me in disgust.

ME: How do you know that's what they are thinking?

S: I can see it in their faces; they look at me like I am scum. I can't breathe very well and I am just collapsing in the street, falling over; I have so little energy, I don't know where I am anymore.

ME: Then what happens?

S: I come to a little house and find the strength to knock on the door. I know that I need help; I am desperate. I hear someone coming to the door and then someone answers. She is a kind woman; she brings me in and I collapse into her arms. She calls for her husband and he lifts me up easily, there is very little left of me and he puts me into their bed. I can tell by the house that they are very poor and have very little, but what they do have they are happy to share.

ME: Then what happens?

S: As I lie in the bed the woman brings over a bowl of hot broth and tries to get me to drink some of it but I am too weak even for that and it just makes me cough; she tells me to rest, that I have a fever.

ME: How are you feeling?

S: I can hardly breathe. I try to talk, to ask them of Arthur, but I have not the strength to do so; all I can think of is Arthur, without him I have nothing to live for....

And then it all goes quiet, the silence is a little eerie and finally she speaks.

S: It's just blank now, not alive now…I am floating somewhere above it all.

ME: Can you get a sense of what your karmic lesson had been in that life?

S: It was the discovery that everybody is equal – it does not matter if they are rich or poor. Everyone deserves the same; class shouldn't separate people!

ME: Were you able to really learn that lesson?

S: I'm not sure that I did learn it completely as I always felt that I was never wanted because I wasn't good enough; the one person who did want me wasn't allowed to be with me and he thought I didn't want him. But…

Now she was sounding angry.

S: If he really had wanted me why didn't he come back? Why wasn't he there? He should have waited, he should have known I had never really left him or stopped loving him; why wasn't he there?

The anger subsided and she was sobbing again.

ME: Tell me what you are thinking.

S: It was all my fault, it must have been my fault; if only I had been a better person perhaps he would not have left me. I just wasn't good enough to make him stay.

The discovery of this powerful limiting belief meant that it was time to begin the healing part of the session.

ME: I want you to bring in Arthur and ask him what you were supposed to learn.

S: He was sent to show me that I am good enough, that I am worthy and special; he wanted me to really believe it. I just hadn't believed it when he said it all those years before and when he left me, even though it had not been his fault, I felt that I had been right all along. But now I can see that I need to heal the sadness between us and forgive him for not being there for me at the end.

She smiled.

ME: How does he respond when you forgive him?

S: Oh he's saying... "I never stopped thinking about you in that lifetime, I never stopped loving you – not for a moment – now you know this I can come back. I will find you again and this time you'll be ready; you need to know that you are very special, you deserve to be loved, and now that you have learnt this, I will come back again – I promise, we will be together again – this time you will be ready and you will know it's me. You will see it in my eyes; it will be the same eyes, you'll have to trust me. You will recognise me, you must believe in yourself, you must know that you are always good enough– truly believe it!"

She sat back in the chair not quite believing what she was hearing.

ME: I want you to ask him if he is part of your soul group.

S: He is saying yes, he is my soulmate; in fact he is telling me that he is my twin soul and we have had many, many lives together, always struggling with love and self-worth. We didn't manage to be together in that life, but he is saying that we will get another chance this time around.

Arthur had gone silent but his powerful words were echoing around her mind.

ME: Can you ask him what you need to do to really believe in yourself?

S: He says that all I have to do is appreciate all the wonderful things I already have, instead of looking at what I don't have.

It was time to move on so I asked her to look for any negative beliefs or vows she might have generated in that life that were no longer useful to her; immediately she spoke up.

S: I vowed that I would never love anyone again because it hurt too much.

She gasped as it dawned on her just how powerful this vow had become and with a great sense of relief she was able to let it go, replacing it with a promise to allow love to come into her life. And then the Universe, or whoever you want to think of as responsible, began its work. About a week later, she saw a photo of a man in a magazine who looked eerily familiar; a few days after that a woman she met insisted that she had to meet her son – he turned out to be the man in the photo. The minute they met they knew that they were meant to be together. They were married within a year. She has no doubt that he is the same soul; they both describe an uncanny sensation as if they had known each other forever. The strangest part of the story is that he had been a very good friend of her brother's and had attended both his wedding, at which she had been a bridesmaid, and his christenings, at which she had been godmother. They did not remember seeing each other. It was as if a veil had been between them, preventing them from meeting until she was ready.

So, you just can't help but wonder: If she had not experienced the healing in the session when she did, and had not allowed herself to let go of her negative beliefs and her blocks, would they have found each other? What if the healing that occurred that day really had opened up a portal that allowed their love to reunite? I believe that it did, and it is just wonderful to know that these twin souls are finally where they wanted to be: together, in love, and looking forward to a very long and happy life together.

EXERCISE 5: *Significant Relationships*

1. Make a list of all of the key relationships in your life.
2. How old were you when you met them?
3. How did you meet? Were there any strange synchronicities?
4. What were their key personality traits – good and bad?
5. What kind of a person were they?
6. How did they treat you at the beginning, in the middle, and at the end?
7. What impact did they have on your life?
8. How did they make you feel about yourself?
9. How long were you with them?
10. What caused you to break up?
11. How did they challenge you?
12. How did they support you?
13. Did you ever feel victimized, or abused, by them in any way?
14. Did you feel as though you were meant to be together?
15. Did you ever feel as though it was impossible to get away?
16. Did you feel safe and secure knowing that they were around?
17. Did you experience jealousy or obsessive attachment, or them towards you?
18. Were you free to be yourself?
19. Was there any sexual addiction?

20. Were you comfortable with the intimate part of the relationship?
21. Was the person not who you thought they were?
22. Did the person fulfill your expectations?
23. Which part of your shadow did you see in them?
24. What good things did you learn from them?
25. What did you learn about yourself as a result of being with them?
26. What happened to your self-esteem as a result of being with them?
27. Do they remind you of anyone in your family?
28. When you think about them, are the memories, and the feelings that you had about them still clear in your mind?
29. Have you been able to completely let them go?
30. Is this a pattern you have been repeating?
31. Are you ready to let any unhelpful patterns go?
32. Are you ready to love and accept yourself?
33. Are you ready to allow real, healthy love and joy into your life?

Exercise to Bring Love into Your Life

If you are ready to bring love (or if you are already in a relationship, even more love) into your life you may wish to take a little time each day to focus on this meditation. It is all about becoming the best you can be so that you can draw to you someone who is the best that they can be too. (Or allow your partner to be the very best that they can be.)

Sit down, make yourself comfortable, and clear your mind. Focus on your breathing and take a few deep breaths. As you breathe out, you can let your body relax and allow the sounds around you help you to relax – or you can choose to ignore them if you wish. As you relax a little more, you can imagine that you are drifting into a deeper and deeper state of relaxation and – as you relax even more deeply – I would like you to imagine that you are standing at the bottom of a mountain and there is a long, winding path that will take you to the top. Even though at times the climb may be a little strenuous, you find that you have all the energy you need to get to the top.

As you reach the top of this very high mountain, you step out onto a plateau; as you look out over the view you can see lots of people at the bottom running around – all frantically looking for something that will make them happy. But up here on top of your mountain there is nothing you need to make you happy; up here you already have everything you need. As you look up into the sky you allow yourself to feel a sense of gratitude for the beauty of the sky, clear and blue. You remember to say thank you for the sun and for the clouds. You say thank you for the air that you breathe, and the body you are in that allows you to breathe in that air. As you focus on gratitude for everything around you, you can be thankful for all the people that have come into your life to teach you so many different things. You can be thankful for the people in your family, for your friends, your teachers, and for all the people who have appeared in your life – your partner or previous partners, especially those who challenged you the most. You can be thankful for all the lessons you have learnt in your life and all the lessons you have yet to learn.

And as you stand here aware of all the gifts that life has brought you, you just take a moment to let that feeling of gratitude really settle into your body. And as you breathe in the energy of gratitude you can be aware of the energy in your body that feels a little stagnant – the energy that feels a little heavy – and you can allow yourself to breathe out. All the negative emotions you have been holding onto, all the perceived hurts, all the guilt, and the blame and the shame, all the disappointments, and the sadness, and the frustrations, all the feelings of powerlessness, and the feelings of unhappiness that have been stored deeply down in your body – as you release these emotions, as you set the intention to let them go, you can take some nice deep breaths and then release – just let that energy go. In your mind's eye see that energy float away as though carried away in a balloon by the breeze and as you let go, you say to yourself, "I'm sorry, please forgive me, I love you, thank you." You may be aware of all of those people that have appeared in your life, of the things that have happened to you, but you say these words to yourself: "I'm sorry, please forgive me, I love you, thank you," and you continue to say this until you feel the energy shift and you are ready to stop. And then, when you are ready to stop, you reconnect once again to the feelings of gratitude – gratitude for everything around you.

As you focus once again on those feelings of gratitude, just notice that there is so much more room in your body now to feel those good feelings. And as you bathe in those good feelings, I want you to imagine yourself in the future: happy and full of love, full of love and gratitude for the world, for the people in your life and – especially – for yourself. You can see yourself as you want to be: confident and happy and enjoying your life – no matter where you are, what you are doing, or who you are with. You are happy, and you can stay here and focus on the feeling of love and gratitude for as long as you like …returning back down the mountain whenever you are ready, bringing those positive feelings back with you.

The more you *let go* of what you *no longer need* the more room you have to bring good things into your life. The more you focus on the things you have to be thankful for, the more things – and people – will arrive in your life that you can be thankful for. It is the law of the universe and one that we should all acknowledge and respect. What you put out you get back; it really is very simple. The words in this meditation come from the ancient Hawaiian practice of Huna. The Ho'oponopono mantra "I'm sorry, please forgive me, I love you, thank you" is one of the most powerful mantras that you can ever say. It can be used whilst in meditation or just in your everyday thinking. The results that occur through using it can be remarkable.

In December 2012 I was in Upper Egypt on a spiritual retreat with Stewart Pearce. It was the most incredible journey; we visited two temples a day and in each temple there was an element of work that we needed to do. Unfortunately, in each temple the guards were aggressive and noisy, determined that we would not do any spiritual work while we were there. Apparently that required a huge amount more baksheesh (tipping) than we had paid. So, in the very first temple, a few of us in the group practiced this process, silently, as we walked around. We set the intention to heal whatever was disturbed within ourselves and as we repeated the mantra we sent waves of love to these men and then the strangest thing started to happen. Suddenly the men were smiling; we were brought into the inner chambers of the temple and asked to pray with them and when it was time to leave they hugged us, wanting to have their photos taken with us, and they thanked us for being there – even though they had no real idea of what we were doing. This continued in every single temple, and we managed to get access to some extraordinary places as a result and had some really unbelievable experiences; some of these men even cried as we left. If there is anything that you want to heal in your life, just practice this and see what happens.

So what is Ho'oponopono?

It is a Hawaiian practice based on the idea of forgiveness. It requires you to take full responsibility for your actions. The Hawaiian shamans believe that the problems you experience are nothing to do with what is going on outside of you but are a reflection of what is within you. The main objective of the Ho'oponopono is to heal and forgive everything within you and get you to a state of awareness where there is no separation from the whole of humanity, no separate identity, and no karma – nothing that needs to be forgiven. It is immensely powerful because as you recognize that you, and your consciousness, are part of the whole then any healing, or clearing, which you do for yourself heals, and clears, the global consciousness too. Heal self, heal the world. It's perfect.

6

How Do You Clear Away the Blocks to Your Success?

As Dorothy travelled along the yellow brick road with her dog, Toto, she came to a crossroads. There were no signposts to tell her which way to go. Out loud she wondered which way and she got a reply. She was very surprised to discover that the voice came from a scarecrow that had been tied to a stake in the middle of a cornfield. He had been stuck there for a long time and was very uncomfortable. He told her that he had no choice but to stay there as he believed that he didn't have a brain. Without a brain he was unable to think about, or understand, what he needed to do with his life and so he just stayed there, afraid to move. They decided he should join her on her quest to meet the Wizard to see if he could help him get the brain he so longed for, and the intelligence that went with it. Further along the way they met the Tin Man; he believed that he didn't have a heart and was afraid that he was unable to love anyone fully. He had become rusty and had been stuck on the same spot for many years. He joined them too, delighted at the thought that the wizard could grant his wish and bestow upon him the heart he had always yearned for. Their final companion was to be the cowardly lion, who was afraid of everyone and everything. He believed that he lacked the one thing that he needed to be the king of the forest: courage. All three believed that they lacked what they needed to succeed in their lives and as a result were too afraid to move on. They were all stuck, destined to repeat the same old experiences over and over again. They told themselves, repeatedly, that if only they had what they needed – a brain, a heart, the nerve – then all would have been fine. At least that is what they believed, and these beliefs led them to be stuck and full of fear. They had focused on what they thought was missing from inside them, and these thoughts led to them telling all kinds of stories about why they were stuck – all kinds of great excuses. These thoughts had conjured up all kinds of negative images inside their minds about what could go wrong if they did something else, and these images led to all kinds of negative thoughts, which in turn led to more fear; they went around and around until they really were paralyzed and completely blocked from going anywhere.

Ultimately, it was just the fear that they were not good enough, or that something was missing, that held them back. They were to learn differently as the journey went along, because as Dorothy and her companions travelled together to get to the Emerald City, the home of the Wizard, they were forced to confront these limiting beliefs and to face their greatest fears. It was only when they refused to be held back and really confronted these fears and the limiting ideas they had about themselves, that they learnt the truth: The truth that they already possessed the qualities they needed. They were within them all along. They never gave up on their dreams or each other, and their desire to reach their goals pushed them onwards, until eventually there was nothing left for them to fear; their limiting beliefs just fell to the wayside, having no power anymore. They learnt to see the world through different eyes and change their limited thinking to something far more productive.

What blocks people from achieving the success they desire, limiting their life experience?

The first thing is fear. And there are many, many different types of fears that get in the way. Often people are paralyzed with fear before anything bad has ever happened; just the fear of the fear stops them from moving forward and an inability to trust themselves to get things right. The saddest thing about it is that there are often simple solutions to overcoming those fears. Most people are just not taught what they are.

What is the second thing?

Limiting beliefs. Once you recognize what your limiting beliefs are, you can do what needs to be done to remove them once and for all.

How can people identify what these limiting beliefs are?

The patterns that tend to get played out in people's lives will often give away what the limiting beliefs are, whether they are connected to self-esteem, confidence, relationships, commitments, finances, or any other issue. When people replay over and over again the same story you can be sure that there is an unhealthy belief lying at the core of it – just like Samantha's belief that she was "not good enough" to deserve love in her life.

Where do these limiting beliefs come from?

They are picked up in childhood or may be carried over from past lives; either way, they can be very disabling and need to be cleared.

How can negative childhood experiences impact on the sense of self?

Often, when people have had upsetting, traumatic, or abusive experiences in childhood, a part of them becomes dissociated or fragmented and can hide away in a place that appeared to be safe at the time, which is deep within the subconscious. This part of them often remains at the age they were then and at the same stage of their development. You may see this with people around you who refer to feeling like a child, feeling helpless, or behaving in a childlike way – sulking, having tantrums, or not taking responsibility for things in their lives. Often the lost, or dissociated, part wants to be reconnected, and there is much that can be done to allow for a reintegration to occur. In psychotherapeutic terms this is known as the inner child: this inner child often just wants to be seen and taken care of. This can be done in the trance state and generally leads to feelings of much greater inner security and self-confidence.

I had one client who had suffered from sexual abuse as a child, and as a result a part of her had been locked away; it had been the only way to survive what was happening. In the trance state she was able to make huge changes to the way memories of her abuse experiences were stored. For years they had been haunting her, and each time they surfaced she would feel as though she was back there, reliving the event over and over again. It was bad enough that she had experienced the events in the first place but her mind kept on bringing these memories back. And the flags on these memories were huge. Her mind didn't know that this was not a good idea and that it was causing her great pain and distress; it just responded to the triggers in the outside world and every time she felt unsafe, there they were: The memories that proved that the world was not a safe place and that people could not be trusted. Needless to say this was having a devastating effect on her life and her ability to have any sort of relationship.

In the session she recalled these memories and was able to take control of the way they had been stored in her mind; in the way that I described earlier in the book, she diffused all the memories, took all the flags off, and relegated them to a safe place, right at the back of her mind where they would not be able to disturb her any more. When this was done she felt so much better. The process meant that she was unable to recall these memories in quite the same way ever again. The clearance process made it easier for her to remember the good moments in her early life, which she then did.

What happened once the memories had been dealt with in this way?

Once she was certain that she could control what she focused on, and felt much stronger and more in control, she called her inner child forward. Her inner child was around 5 years old and was very vulnerable; at first she did not want to sit too close. She began to make promises to her that from now on she would take care of her; she needed to let her know that she would protect her and that she would never let anything bad happen to her ever again. She allowed herself to come closer and eventually came and sat on her lap. This inner part of her had missed out on the joys of being a child and had forever been held in a space of fear and pain, and more than a few tears were shed as this energy was released.

Once her inner child felt a greater sense of trust and safety, and knew what it was like to be loved unconditionally, she was invited to imagine what life would have been like growing up with these very different inner feelings. She reported that she would have been more confident, that she would have been more outgoing, that it would have been easier to make friends and to do well at school. As she imagined getting older she saw how much easier it would have been to have loving and intimate relationships, a successful career, and even a family – something that had eluded her so far.

As she grew into womanhood and all the way up to the current age of my client, with the inner feelings of safety and inner trust getting stronger and stronger all the time, she was invited to reintegrate and merge fully with my client so that they could support each other as they went onwards, creating a powerful and positive inner resource that she could draw upon to feel totally different about herself.

My client reported that she had been through years of traditional therapy, talking and talking about what had happened to her, and that nothing had shifted; but after this session she felt free of the events of her childhood for the first time in over 50 years; she left feeling a sense of lightness, as though she had let go of a huge weight – a huge burden that she had been carrying, and said she now felt ready to enjoy the rest of her life. Moving and powerful stuff and incredible to see someone break free of inner pain and mental anguish for the first time in many, many years!

Can exploring past lives help with identifying and releasing these patterns?

Absolutely! The best thing about working at the subconscious level is that it enables you to get direct access to the memories where these issues originated, right to the source of the problem. All that is required is the right question, and your higher mind will take you to the first moment you experienced the problem. Once the knowledge of where it came from emerges, it holds no power over you, and of course the healing part of the session allows for a process of reframing – changing the story– which changes the way the memory is stored. This means that the memory can never be experienced in the same way and can never affect you in the same way ever again.

One of my clients, Sandra, believed that she was always going to have disastrous relationships; her first marriage had ended in tears when she found out that her husband had been unfaithful. Since that time all of the men that she had been involved with had cheated. She just could not imagine what a healthy relationship would be like and regularly pictured herself as old and alone, and feeling sorry for herself. Men seemed to see her as just a plaything and nothing more. She was becoming more and more insecure about herself, which was made all the more tragic because she was very beautiful and obviously had a very good heart. In the end she became convinced that it was something to do with her, that she must be the one that was doing something wrong, or "Why," she asked, "would this keep on happening?" When I asked her why she thought it was happening she said, "There must be something wrong with me. I keep making a mess of things; I am just an idiot and totally useless."

I wanted her to really pay attention to the language she used to put herself down, to identify the voice of her inner critic. She was really surprised when she realized that thought repetitively was "I am just useless and no one is ever going to love me now." She knew this wasn't helpful, and she wanted to know if there was something from her past that meant that she held on to this kind of thinking and, as a result, kept repeating this pattern.

In the past life session she found herself as a young girl, who had been rejected by pretty much everyone around her because she had displayed the gift of the second sight; her biggest mistake had been telling the leader of the community that she knew he was being unfaithful to his wife. She had seen it in a dream and had wanted to prevent him from hurting his wife, who was one of the only people who was kind to her. Because of his fear that she would reveal his secret, he had locked her away in a place far away from everyone and left her there to die, freezing and starving.

It had been a hard lesson for her, and she had died with a fear that all men were like this; that they all cheated and were cruel. In the session she was able to confront the man that had done this to her and discovered that he had only acted because he was afraid of her power, that he had been threatened, and in that moment she saw his fear and his weakness. He admitted that what he had done had been very wrong and asked her to forgive him, which she did. In that moment she was able to release her fears and the beliefs that she was unworthy of real love. In the session she was able to go back and see what would have happened if he had not ended her life the way he did, and she got to experience a very different life. This time she grew up and met someone very special to her; she got to have a family and feel what it was like to be accepted and loved for who she was. There were tears in her eyes as she experienced this. She left the session filled with optimism and real hope for the future as she saw that there were other options – much better ones.

What are the main unhelpful beliefs that people hold?

So many people believe that only if they had more confidence, more money, more education, more time, were younger, or had more luck then they would be able to succeed. They may tell themselves this over and over again, an inner voice that assures them that they are not good enough or do not have what they need. This inner voice, the negative inner critic, is often referred to as a chattering monkey; in many Buddhist or meditation circles, it is this part of the mind that they are trying to still.

It is probably no coincidence at all that the army that the witch uses to finally capture Dorothy and Toto is made up of noisy, winged, flying monkeys. This inner voice, which is made up of your own subconscious ramblings, can change the way you feel in an instant. It is almost like a recording that you listen to day in and day out; unfortunately, the words that are used by this inner critic part of you are not always very helpful, and the majority of people are completely unaware that it is there. It is only when you bring it into full conscious awareness that you can get a sense of how badly you treat yourself. I like to ask my clients if they have ever made a mistake, and the answer is usually "yes"; we have all at times gotten things wrong. It is the nature of being human.

However, what we do and how we treat ourselves in those moments can vary wildly; some may just shrug and say, "Oh well, I have learnt from that and won't do it again," and others berate themselves and call themselves all kinds of terrible names. This inner voice often has an energetic tone to it as well, a tone that sets off all kinds of inner feelings. I know that a particular favourite of mine used to be calling myself an idiot and a donkey, in a particularly sarcastic tone of voice. All this did was make me feel very bad and pretty useless and in no way helped me to learn from the event. But until I did the exercise, which I will share with you at the end of the chapter, I was not even aware that I was doing it.

How do you know what these unhelpful thoughts are?

You have to pay attention. The main thing that holds you back are the thoughts that you keep thinking over and over again, albeit that they are being played out in the back of your mind.

Whatever the thoughts are, be they thoughts of not being good enough, not being worthy, never having enough time or money or the courage to do what needs to be done, the worst thing about them is that they produce a kind of self-fulfilling prophecy; if people keep focusing on what doesn't work they will find it, and then the belief that lies behind the thought, gets reinforced over and over again until they think it *must* be true.

If a negative belief is something that we hold to be true, how can it be changed?

The wonderful thing about beliefs is that they really are only thoughts that you think over and over again. Just because you keep repeating a thought it doesn't mean that it *is* true. All it takes is a counter example, or an understanding of where it originally came from, and the whole belief comes crashing down and no longer has any power. You may need to make a very conscious effort to monitor any unhelpful thinking and stop giving yourself a hard time, and there is an exercise at the end of this chapter to help you do that. Being kind to yourself is one of the most important things you can ever do to help you improve your life because if you aren't kind to you, why should anyone else bother? Your outer world is just a mirror of your inner world. So if your external world needs to change in any way you can be sure that there is work to be done on the inside.

Donna

One of my clients, Donna, came to see me because she was feeling stuck. She was dissatisfied with her world and was having difficulties in getting motivated and getting her life in order. She had been working in the same job for many years. She had seen others in her team being promoted and moving up to bigger and greater things, and she knew that she was just as capable as they were, more so in many cases. But something was holding her back. She really wanted to make more of her life but every time she tried to speak to her boss about a promotion, or about stepping up into another role within the company, a little voice in her head said "Don't be ridiculous, he will laugh at you. Who do you think you are? Stay right where you are, where you know you are safe," and she would dissolve into a bag of nerves – reinforcing her belief that she was not ready or deserving of anything more in her life. She really wanted to unlock the key to her procrastination and let go of her inability to really move forward in her career.

The journey began:

D: I am a young woman, 17 years old.

ME: What are you wearing?

D: I am wearing long, green slippers made of felt and a long green dress; it is heavy and has lots of different layers. My hair is long and piled high with jewels in it, and I am wearing a beaded skull cap at the back of my head. I am also wearing a very heavy gold necklace with precious stones in it; the weight of it makes it very uncomfortable. In fact, everything I am wearing feels heavy and cumbersome.

ME: Where are you?

D: I am in a large, cold, stone room; it has a large open fireplace where wood is burning. There are some women in the room with me; these women are not my friends but my servants. I do not want to be here. I am being kept a prisoner. I am being kept against my will.

ME: Who is keeping you here?

D: My husband.

She spoke with despair in her voice.

ME: Where are you, and what year is it?

D: It is 1622, and I am in France. I am being kept captive in a castle by my husband who I despise.

ME: How did you come to be here?

D: I was born into a wealthy British family who were of noble descent. Some time ago I was chosen by this French baron because he had admired my energy and my tenacity. As a young girl I had been involved in the day-to-day running of my father's house and I had loved the challenges; the Baron, who had been visiting, had seen this and had decided to take me for a wife. My father had seen this as a great honour and had given his blessing. However, what he had not counted on was the fact that I had other ideas. Not only was I *not* in love with the Baron, but I was in love with a young man from the court.

ME: Tell me about these men.

D: The man I loved was the same age as me, and we had many things in common. This strange older French man seemed like a barbarian in comparison; he was loud and rude and used to having his own way. He barked orders at everyone and consumed huge amounts of wine and the local beer. He found my polite refusals amusing at first, as though I was playing some kind of game with him. But then he became tired of the chase and insisted that I marry him and leave for France forthwith.

ME: What happened next?

D: At first I refused to marry him, but my family gave me no choice; without this alliance there would be no future trade with the baron and his king, and the family would be destroyed. I had no choice; and so, I was married.

She sighs deeply.

ME: Then what happened?

D: We left for France within a few weeks. I never even got the chance to say goodbye to my loved one. I arrived in France bitter, angry, and in despair. I refused all of my husband's advances; I refused to co-operate in any way and eventually when he could take it no more the baron had locked me up in the tower. He could not understand what was wrong with me; he called me the "stupid English girl"; he had given me the best of everything – beautiful clothes, silks, jewellery…everything that money could buy – but nothing would change my mind. I would have traded every cent of the wealth that he lavished on me for a moment of real happiness with the man who genuinely loved me.

ME: What is happening now?

D: Here I stay; I tried to plot a way to escape, but it was impossible. I was never allowed out of my room alone.

ME: What happens next?

D: Due to the lack of fresh air, my refusal to eat, and my general feelings of deep despair, I am very sick. I just keep telling myself over and over again that I was stupid and that if I had not been such a show-off this would never have happened to me. The women of the court have tried everything they can to revive me, but I have no desire to live. I have lost all hope.

Once again a silence filled the room.

ME: What are you experiencing now?

She spoke in a very soft and serene voice

D: My death was very quiet. I had so little energy left, and I was so weak that I had simply faded away. No one had even noticed for quite some time after I had gone.

ME: What happened after your death?

D: My husband had already moved on to another woman, so my death just meant that he was free to marry again – so I was no loss to him. He had been angry that I had not obeyed him as he felt that I should have done.

ME: What was your last conscious thought as you left that body?

D: If only I had been less noticeable, if only I had stayed hidden away and had not been shown off to this terrible man then perhaps I would have remained at home and would have had the life I desired.

ME: What were the emotions you experienced as you left that life?

D: In the end I died feeling desperately sad at the waste of it all and remained angry that my outgoing and ambitious nature had led to my ultimate destruction.

ME: What needs to happen in order for you to release these emotions?

D: I need to understand why this man insisted on taking me away from everyone I loved; I don't understand why he needed to make me suffer like that.

ME: Let's invite him in; what do you want to say to him?

D: I want to tell him how unhappy I was, how difficult it was to leave the people I loved behind.

ME: How does he respond?

D: He was not aware that he did anything wrong; he thought that he was offering me a chance of a good life and thought that should have been enough. He sees now that he had not stopped to consider my feelings, and he is sorry for what he did.

ME: How do you feel knowing that he is sorry?

D: It is a relief; I can see now that he was not a bad man, he just did what he thought was normal and was right for the times. It is sad that he was not aware of his or anyone else's feelings, and I feel sad that he missed out.

ME: Is there anything that you wish to say to him now?

D: Yes, I want him to know that I have forgiven him; it was not really his fault, and I could have been a little kinder to him.

ME: Was there any previous agreement between you with regard to this life or any lives that you may have shared before?

D: Oh, we have had lives together before, although in our last life together he was my father. I never did what I was told in that life either.

At this she laughs.

ME: Has there been a theme to the lives you have had together?

D: The theme has always been one of battling with authority. I have always struggled with being told what to do.

ME: Is it time to let go of this battle now?

D: Yes. He says that it is good that I can see this now as he is tired of playing the bad guy in my lives and would like another role next time.

ME: Will you agree to this?

D: Yes, happily.

ME: I want you to see the contract that the two of you had between you and then in whatever way makes sense to you – you can tear it up or set fire to it, whatever you like – but I want you to set yourself and this other soul free.

D: It is like an old scroll; I am tearing it up and then burning it. I want to make sure it is properly gone.

ME: Now, what would be a better commitment for you to make to yourself now, a new contract that would be more beneficial?

D: I promise that from now on I will make the most of every opportunity that comes my way. I will be kinder to myself and support myself in whatever I am doing. I will be stronger and clearer in what I say, and I will never call myself bad names ever again. From now on I will accept that I am worthy of success and will allow it to come into my life.

ME: Excellent! You can thank this soul for assisting you in these lives and check if he has a message for you before he leaves.

D: He is just smiling and saying "thank you"; he says he is free to move on now and so am I. He is also telling me to get on with things and enjoy my life this time around.

She was amazed at how relevant this story was to her current situation; she realized that this reflected her fears of standing out and being noticed in this life. These fears had produced a very active, and very protective part of her that was terrified she would suffer if she stepped into the limelight and it forced her, by putting her down all the time, to stay in the background and never obviously stand out. She understood that this was no longer relevant, not in this lifetime anyway, and she recognized that she was now free of the need to hide away. Some time after the session, through the recommendation of one of her friends and co-workers, she was headhunted and found herself working within a large organization in a role of real responsibility. She is now thriving and no longer needs to hide. Through her new-found belief in herself, and her new, more supportive and positive thinking, she has changed her world beyond recognition.

Veronica

Another client, Veronica, came for a session because she was struggling with achieving her desired weight loss; she had been trying to lose weight for as long as she could remember and it was the same every time: She would go on some crash diet, starve herself for a few months, lose some weight, and as soon as she came off the diet all the weight would go back on, plus a little more.

By the time she came for her session she was at the end of her tether and was really beating herself up mentally. She was convinced that she had no willpower and that she was, in her words, "just a bit rubbish at getting things right." She worked through some hypnosis sessions, helping to change her lifestyle and getting her to recognize some unhelpful patterns that she had in relation to food. But these patterns seemed intent on staying, no matter how hard she tried she kept referring back to her old habits – habits of comfort eating whenever she felt bad and continuous feelings of really intense hunger, even when she knew she couldn't possibly be hungry. Every time she sat down to eat she would shovel her food in really quickly, and as soon as she was finished she would feel terribly guilty and really abuse herself verbally, calling herself a "lazy, fat cow." She was really fed up of having such a hard time with food and of beating herself up all the time, and she was terrified that she would never be able to move on. She wanted to know if there might be a past life connection and decided that it would be worth exploring.

The journey began:

ME: What are you aware of?

V: I am barefoot, and I am wearing nothing but animal skins.

ME: What are you doing here?

V: I am a lookout, a sort of scout for my village; it is my job to sit high up on a hill and watch out for attackers from other nearby villages or for wild animals. I am in Africa, and even though the sun is shining I am very sad; my job is very lonely, and I miss my family.

ME: Why were you chosen for this role?

V: I am not sure; my father is the leader of the tribe, but maybe they do not think that I can do anything else.

ME: What is significant about this time for you?

V: I have to rely on people from the tribe to bring me food and water, and often they make me wait and wait until I am almost faint with hunger; their belief is that hunger will keep me vigilant and awake, so my father encourages them to not overfeed me.

ME: What happens when you do get food?

V: When food does arrive, I wolf it down as fast as I can, trying to quell my vicious hunger pangs.

ME: I want you to move to the next significant event.

V: One of the men from the tribe has come. He has stolen some extra food for me. I have taken great delight at this, and I have wolfed down every mouthful until I am stuffed full, unable to move.

ME: What is important about this moment in time?

V: I use the memory of this moment to appease me whenever the hunger becomes unbearable. But there is no peace as my thoughts torture me, and I think that I must be bad or worthless to have been sent out to this terrible place and made to suffer like this.

ME: I would like you to move to the end of this lifetime and tell me what happens to you.

V: I got killed by a large bear that crept up on me while I was sleeping; by the time I woke, it was too late and the bear was upon me.

ME: What was going through your mind as you died?

V: All I could think about was my relentless hunger, of how unfair it had been and how angry I am that they made me suffer like that! I am also aware that if I hadn't been asleep the bear wouldn't have killed me, and so I was angry at myself, as well, for letting my guard down.

ME: What needs to happen for you to let go of some of that anger?

V: I need to forgive myself and see that it was not my fault; I need to let go of the guilt too, the guilt that I failed everyone and that I am rubbish.

ME: I want you to bring in the people who were part of your village and ask them what they thought about you and what happened.

V: Oh, they are saying that they were very proud of me and that they thought that I was incredibly brave to be out there on my own like that; many of them could not have done what I did. But I never thought of it that way; I was just too upset about being left out there to be worried about anything. I can see now that it was quite a dangerous position to be in and that I was brave; in fact, I was much stronger than I realized. And I was a good lookout for most of the time; I saved the villagers from more than one situation of danger.

ME: How does that make you feel now?

V: I feel much lighter, as if a weight has lifted. The people are saying "thank you," and they are all lovely. I feel very grateful to them for coming.

ME: I would like you to call in your father from that life. What would you like to say to him that you were not able to say back then?

V: I am really angry that you left me out there in that place all alone.

ME: What does he say?

V: He tells me that he had been thinking of the good of the whole tribe, and not just about me, and the position that he gave me was one of great honour and trust, and only those who were deemed worthy were ever given the position. He had been immensely proud that his child had been the chosen one. It never occurred to him that I would feel any differently.

ME: Now that he understands what you went through, how does he respond?

V: On reflection he is deeply sorry and asks me for forgiveness.

ME: Are you able to forgive him?

V: As a result of these new insights, yes, I can forgive him completely.

ME: Now that you have let this go I want you to let go of these thoughts that you kept repeating – the ones that said that you were not worthy or good enough, or that you were just a bit rubbish. I would like you to create a new mantra.

V: Oh, it's wonderful. I tell myself that I am good enough, that I am brave and strong, and that I can do anything that I set my mind to.

As a result of this session, she was able to release the feelings of anger, unfairness, guilt, and the terrible feeling of hunger that she had always felt, which were the same feelings that drove her to eat more than she needed in her current life. She vowed to be kinder to herself and found that she didn't need to comfort eat any more.

In less than a year after the session Veronica reported that she was feeling happier and healthier than ever before. She had lost around four dress sizes, and this time there was no suffering – no diets and no depriving herself. She just started eating sensibly, exercising more regularly, and going to Zumba classes so that she could dance her way to being fit, which of course is one of the most enjoyable ways to exercise you can find.

Most importantly, she remembered to be kind to herself and any time she found herself being mean in her head she simply refused to listen. Instead she focused on her positive mantra, and this kept her moving in the right direction. She is now free from her old compulsions, has much more energy, and is really enjoying her life.

EXERCISE 6: *Inner Critic*

PART A

1. Become aware of a memory, of a moment in time when you got something wrong, where you made a mistake; take yourself back to the moment when you realized it had happened. If you close your eyes and imagine that you are back there, then you can really get a sense of what was going on.
2. What were you saying to yourself at the time?
3. Become aware of the tone of the voice; is it angry, disappointed, sarcastic, matter of fact (which is usually the worst of all, because it feels so normal)?
4. Where do you hear the voice? (This may feel strange as you will not have thought of this before.) Do you hear the critic part of you at the front of your head? To the side? Behind you?
5. Is it your voice? So many people learnt how to give themselves a hard time by mimicking people who were there at the early stages of their lives: parents, teachers, caretakers. Many people think, as this was what they experienced, that this is normal and acceptable, and the harsh reality is that so often it is not. This is not to cast blame on the caregivers or the people we learnt this from,

they would just have been doing what they thought was normal and what was shown to them as they were growing up. But even still it does not make it right or acceptable.

6. Once you recognize the words, the tone, and the quality of the voice, I want you to close your eyes once again.

7. Imagine that you have been assigned an apprentice for a week. This person is going to have to be you for a week. They are going to have to carry out all the daily tasks that you carry out, take care of all of the things that you take care of, and it is your job to motivate them to be the best you that they can be. There is only one catch: You are only able to talk to them in the way that you were talking to yourself when you made a mistake. You are only able to use the same tone of voice, use the same words that you used to berate yourself. And you are to imagine saying these things over and over again.

8. Think about the impact this would have on the person in front of you.

9. How would this make them feel?

10. How successfully would they be able to carry out the tasks assigned to them, and how motivated would they be to even carry them out in the first place?

Most people that I work with are horrified when I ask them to do this. They shake their heads and tell me that this would destroy the person; that they would not dream of speaking to someone like that as it would be very destructive, undermine their confidence, and prevent them from being the best that they could be. They insist that they would never do this – until I remind them that this is how they have been talking to themselves inside their head. It can come as a bit of a shock to know that they can be so abusive to themselves and then wonder why they don't always do as well as they would like.

I believe that it is hugely important for everyone to be aware of what they are listening to internally. For the majority of people if they turned on a radio and the station was negative and critical, fearful, whining, or complaining they would turn it off. Most people would take control of the situation and choose something that would be more enjoyable and more productive. Of course, there are some who just enjoy a good moan, like Victor Meldrew, but that is another story; and, as they say, "to each their own."

But if you are someone whose sense of self could do with a boost, you may wish to take some time to tune in and really become aware of the background station that you are tuned into. Once you become consciously aware, it is very difficult to ignore.

So how do you change it if this is a habit that you have had for life?

Well, awareness is the biggest key; once you recognize that you are doing this, and are aware of the inner voice, you can choose to take control.

PART B

1. Really focus on the inner critical voice, remembering a time when it was active and really giving you some stick. Identify how it sounds – what it is saying and where around you, you hear it. It might be in front of you, or behind you, or above your head.

2. Imagine pushing that part of you away; usually about a foot in front of you will do.

3. Then, imagine that you have a volume switch, and experiment with the volume.

4. Turn it up really loud so that the voice is shouting at you; for some people the unpleasant feeling that goes with this inner critic gets worse, for some it is not as bad as it is so obvious and harder to accept.

5. Then turn it down so that it is really quiet, almost to a whisper; for some this is much better and for others it is much worse as the sounds becomes insidious and difficult to escape from.

6. Then push the voice way off into the distance so that it can hardly be heard; this distance can be very helpful.

7. The next stage is very important. Saying bad things to yourself that make you feel bad is a bit of a silly thing to do – again there is no blame here, people just do what appears to be normal from what they see around them; however, with this now in the open there is only one way that makes sense and that is to choose the most ridiculous voice that you can think of – it could be a cartoon character like Mickey Mouse or Donald Duck. Homer Simpson seems to be a popular choice, or anyone that seems ridiculous – do not pick someone that you do not like or it will make it worse – just choose someone or something that you cannot take seriously and change the inner critic's voice to the ridiculous voice.

8. Then bring that part of you back and listen to it give you a hard time in the silly style of your choice.

9. You will find that it is very hard to take it seriously after this, and in the future any time that you become aware that you have slipped back into the old way, all you have to do is stop it, interrupt your flow, and take control, changing the voice in any of these ways that help you most. It is a bit like having a bully bother you; once you acknowledge that you are no longer afraid of them or willing to take their nonsense, they leave you alone.

The best bit of this exercise is that once you have turned off the inner critic there is usually a supportive, loving, and encouraging part of you hidden in the background trying to be heard. This is the part that pushes you forward even when you are terrified and keeps you from missing out on life and the things that are important to you. Once you have shut off the critic, you can hear what really needs to be said.

PART C

1. Once the inner critic is silenced, pay attention to what you can hear instead.
2. Write out the new positive statements and use them as personal mantras that you repeat to yourself each day.
3. Allow this to become the new inner program that you listen to.
4. For example: I AM WORTHY OF HAVING GREAT LOVE AND JOY IN MY LIFE; I DESERVE ALL GOOD THINGS; I AM LOVING, LOVEABLE, AND I AM LOVED.
5. These mantras can be written on cards and put in places where they will be seen – like a purse or a wallet, or on a bathroom mirror – as regular repetition of them will help them to sink deep down into the subconscious where they will become the new "belief" program behind the scenes.
6. Be aware that for these mantras to be fully effective you must take yourself into a good-feeling place first. If you are feeling low and depressed and feel that the world is a terrible place, no amount of repeating "I am amazing" is going to work; to change your state, just remember a time when you did feel great first.

COWARDLY LION:
*"I do believe in spooks, I do believe in spooks.
I do, I do, I do, I do believe in spooks!"*

7

What Are Spirit Attachments?

With a little help from Glinda and some well-appointed snow, Dorothy and her friends, were able to remain awake, conscious, and on the right path. Eventually they arrived at the Emerald City and had a very pleasant time recuperating and preparing themselves for their audience with the Wizard. All of them were hugely excited to know that the realization of their dreams was only a short time away and so, understandably, they were all devastated when they were refused entry by the doorman at the very last moment. He told them that no one got to see the Wizard: Not nobody, not no how.

All of them were distraught, because at that point he had been their only hope. It was only when the doorman, who was actually the Wizard in disguise, saw Dorothy's tears that he changed his mind. He was reminded of moments of sadness and loss from his own life, and so he relented and allowed the group inside. Apparently he too had once lost an Auntie Em; coincidence, or perhaps not? Once they were inside the inner sanctum the Wizard appeared to them on a screen. He looked big and powerful, and he terrified them all. He insisted, in a very big voice that reverberated throughout the room, that Dorothy and her companions complete a task before he would help them. And of course no heroes' quest would be complete without one.

Their task was to bring back the broom of the Wicked Witch; no small task, as there was only one way they could do this and it meant killing the witch. As a testament to their commitment, the four friends agreed, although the lion was more than a little reluctant and threw himself out of the nearest window before anything else could be said. The four friends set off into the unknown, ready to face whatever trials lay before them – and there were many challenges for them to face along the way. Even though they were deeply afraid, each member of the group held true and they never gave up on each other or themselves.

One of their biggest challenges came when they arrived at the haunted forest; a big sign greeted them saying "I'd go back if I were you." The Cowardly Lion tried to turn around but the others stopped him just in time. The Scarecrow and the Cowardly Lion looked around nervously, convinced that there were spooks in the forest, but the Tin Man just scoffed at them. Moments later he was hurled into the air by unseen hands and came crashing down with a very loud bang. This resulted in the whole group dropping into a state of deep fear – the very state that the wicked witch wanted them to experience, because as soon as they were in a mental state of fear they could no longer think clearly. Their vibration had shifted, and their energy became weak.

As a result of this inner shift they were open to attack and soon Dorothy and Toto were captured by the Wicked Witch's winged monkeys and carried up into the air and away to the Witch's castle, leaving the other three devastated at their loss. Unsure what to do next, they vowed to keep going until they found them both and could set them free. Toto – as the animal figure representing Dorothy's instincts – managed once again to escape from the dangerous clutches of the Wicked Witch – the personification of fear and negativity – who was determined to destroy him. Once free, he ran all the way back to the forest and was able to lead her friends right back to the castle where she was being held. As they waited outside, the Scarecrow devised a cunning plan, the Tin Man gladly offered his life to save Dorothy, and it was the Cowardly Lion who bravely leapt into action as they battled with the Wicked Witch's army. Dorothy was locked in the castle with time running out, and all she could do was pray for help to come. The prayers were heard. Her loyal and trusted friends, who disguised themselves as guards – now afraid of nothing and no one – were able to sneak their way into the witch's castle. They were determined to set her free, and all they needed to do was work out how. Once again it was Toto – her instincts – who led them right to her door, right to where they needed to be.

Do ghosts really exist?

Yes, they do. Ghosts are merely different forms of energy: spirits, souls, or fragments of souls that are not in a body – disembodied souls who are lost, in some way, and unable to get to the light.

How do these spirits or souls get lost?

If at the point of death someone experiences trauma, shock, or confusion, it is possible for the soul, or spirit, of that person to get lost or stuck on the earth plane.

If for some reason they miss the portal of light that opens to take them back, then they must wait for another one to be opened before they can return home to their loved ones on the other side.

If you have ever seen the movie *Ghost*, with Patrick Swayze and Demi Moore, you will have seen this portrayed almost perfectly. Swayze's character is murdered and he fails to go into the tunnel of light where all of his loved ones are waiting because he is worried that something bad will happen to his girlfriend. He is then stuck on the earth plane and cannot escape, not until he has solved the mystery of who killed him and ensured that his girlfriend is safe; only then can he return safely to the light.

So why do souls not go straight back to the light when they die?

Sometimes souls do not depart fully because they don't want to leave their loved ones, they have unfinished business to attend to, they just don't know where to go, or they are just unaware that they are dead. It is these lost souls that people refer to as ghosts, and they can be attached to people or to places.

How do they become attached?

If it is to a place, it may be because they are familiar with it; they may have died there or perhaps they have powerful memories connected to the place. These can be fond memories or traumatic ones, it really doesn't matter. If it is to a person, they may become attracted to their energy; there is something familiar in it. If they died feeling very fearful and they happen to pass a person who is feeling fear in that moment in time, then they are able to connect – the similar vibration of the energy creating a link for them to connect to. They then stick to the person's energy field as though it were Velcro. It is usually negative emotions that attract the attachments, and the more intense the emotion a person feels the easier it is for them to climb aboard. They are also attracted to people who have been drinking, taking drugs, or are vulnerable after an accident or operation because their energy fields, or auras, tend to be wide open.

This makes hospitals a prime place for energies to be collected; these are places where people die and then a whole host of possible candidates arrive, whether from an accident, an operation, or whether they are under the influence of some harmful substance. Watching violent and scary horror movies, listening to music that is angry and aggressive, or playing computer games that are filled with death and destruction are also good ways to let them in. I worked with one young girl who had been watching horror movies and because she was so sensitive it opened her up to all kinds of energies. We managed to remove them fairly easily as they were not particularly bad spirits; they were just a bit lost, but they had been affecting her sleep and also her health. At the end of the session her higher self came in with a very stern warning for her to not watch these films any more.

How do they attach to a person's energy field?

In order for a spirit attachment to get on board there is usually some kind of "emotional wound" that the person has; this may have been created in childhood or may come from a past life. This may be in the form of a negative emotion or some trapped feelings that have been unresolved. The negative emotion causes a weak spot in the energy field and an attachment that resonates with the same emotional energy is able to use this as a sticking point – or a hook, as we like to call it. Once the attachments are released, the emotional hook needs to be dealt with to ensure there are no return visitors.

How do you get rid of them?

Once upon a time, freeing earthbound spirits from people was called an exorcism. This is a process that is quite brutal and shows very little or no compassion for the lost soul that has been caught up in someone's energy field. Nowadays there is a much better approach and that uses what is called spirit release therapy. This process ensures that there is unconditional love and compassion for the spirit, or soul, that has been caught up in the wrong place. The spirits are not just cast out but are helped back into the light and returned to their loved ones in the spirit realms

When I was doing my training, my energy field was clear and so I invited a spirit to come in so that my colleague and I could practice. It was a really emotional experience; the attachment turned out to be a young girl who had been playing with her friends. They had been rolling down a hill together and at the bottom of the hill she hit her head on a rock and broke her neck. She floated out of her body but was really worried that her friends would get in trouble so she stayed with them. Of course this meant that she was stuck on the earth plane and had no way of getting back to the light. We were able to open a portal for her and bring in the spirits of her friends and her family. It was a very tearful reunion, and as she left I could feel how grateful she was to be finally going home.

How many kinds of attachments are there?

There can be many different types, from lost loved ones, thought forms, elementals, humans living or deceased, guides, young children, people from past lives, groups of souls –particularly if they came from a scene of a battle or a natural disaster, curses, hexes, and, what is referred to as "dark" energy.

Does this include demons?

From time to time there are entities, or spirits, that claim to be "dark," negative, evil, or connected to the devil himself. Hollywood has had a field day portraying them and wouldn't survive without them, and there are many stories that range from the bible to Harry Potter that promote the idea of evil forces at work. But in reality it is all just energy, and these beings – who have strayed off the path of light and love – just need to get a little reminder of *who they really are,* which is ultimately a being of light who got a bit lost or waylaid.

These souls are treated with the exact same love and compassion, which can be really annoying for them if they are trying to insist that they are big and bad and ugly, or they can be persuaded to leave by means of a little trickery – getting them to see the spark of light that exists within their being is usually a good way to get them. Most of them have just forgotten that they originally came from the light, and once they see this they can no longer insist that they are part of the darkness; failing that, they are lovingly put into the custody of angels who know exactly what to do with them and where they need to go.

How do you know if there are attachments present?

People will usually report that they feel drained and exhausted all the time; they may feel itchiness or strange sensations in their body. They may find that they have acquired new and unsavoury habits, like wanting to smoke, drink, or take drugs. They may have sharp mood swings and get angry or anxious really easily. They may find that they have strange twitches happening, especially in their fingers. They might have intrusive thoughts that don't seem as though they belong to them and feel a general sense of unease. They may find that things start to go wrong in their lives, in a way that cannot be rationally explained. In his book *Transforming the Eternal Soul,* Andy Tomlinson says, "The physical effects of dark energy on a client can include a depleted energy field, sudden exhaustion, the inability to think clearly, irritability and lack of motivation."

How can you find out for sure?

Once a person is in a hypnotic trance it is fairly easy to establish whether there are any attachments or not. The "ideomotor signals" that I spoke of previously are a perfect way of finding out, or you or someone else can use a pendulum to find out.

What needs to be done once they have been discovered?

First, the host needs to be reassured that there is nothing to worry about. These spirits or energies cannot do them any serious harm; they are just an irritant to their systems. Then the spirits, or energies, need to be released and safely sent back to the light.

How does the release take place?

The release can be done in person or it can be done remotely. Once attachments have been identified, and the number of them that are present has been confirmed, they are asked, one by one, to use the vocal chords of the host body. If there is more than one, it is usually best to work with the strongest one first, as they can sometimes act as a guide to take the rest with them to the light; or, once they have gone safely, the others are more willing to leave. Sometimes a spirit may try to hide if they are afraid, and so it is really important to be gentle and reassuring all the way through the process.

Once you have established contact with a spirit, a dialogue then occurs that helps to understand what caused the spirit, or entity, to be there in the first place and find out what impact it has been having on the host. It is important to find out what happened to end the life of the spirit and what they need to be able to go free. This might be a reunion with a loved one, a reconnection to something they loved, or they may just want to find a place where they can continue to do whatever they want free of the restriction of a body. This one is quite helpful when working with souls that are a bit tricky, and once they agree to leave they are directed to a place in the light where they can no longer do any harm.

What do people experience when they have a spirit released?

People often feel a shift in their energy while the release is taking place, as if a weight has been lifted off them, or they may find they feel different over the space of a few days. They may experience mood changes, a release of bad habits, or even experience a complete detox where they let go of the physical and mental effects of the energies. Afterwards, once their energy has settled, they get to experience greater feelings of well-being.

Can these attachments prevent people from achieving what they want in life?

Yes. If spirit attachments, or energies that do not belong to people, have attached to their energy field, they can really trip people up. They can be responsible for creating blockages and enhancing challenging emotions, particularly those of fear, anxiety, and anger.

How do you deal with curses or hexes?

Curses and hexes work in a similar manner to attachments; they are negative forms of energy. It is just that they are usually sent deliberately. However, they can also happen unintentionally, for instance, when someone is having very strong negative feelings about someone else and keeps focusing on them. On many occasions there may be no intention to do any real damage, but in some cases the negative thoughts act like spells and "energies" are conjured up and sent to do their bidding.

Do spells really exist?

Most people are familiar with the idea of voodoo or being able to cause harm to another, with just the power of thought and intention; it is the flip side of prayer, and you would be surprised at just how prevalent this way of thinking still is, in many places all over the world. For some people this can lead to sickness, chaos, and problems in their life. However, it is important to note that if they have no belief in the curse or the spell and are strong and grounded within themselves, with no unresolved emotional issues to deal with, then the spell will have no effect.

How do these spells work?

When a spell is cast, lost souls or spirits get called up and become responsible for carrying out the sender's wishes. These souls usually died with little or no self-belief, thinking themselves to be unworthy or bad in some way, and some may have believed that they did not deserve to go to the light. Some get lied to once they die and are told that they are being taken to the light – but in reality they are just being taken to a holding place. It is clear that these souls are not malevolent or bad; they were just misinformed, and with the right communication it is possible to free them and return them home to the light where they belong. Even the darkest and scariest of the attachments respond to love, forgiveness, and the acknowledgment of who they really are, which is a being of light, a fact that so many forget once they come to earth and live in a dense and heavy vibrational body dealing with the negative emotions that can arise in a lifetime. Thankfully there are many things that can be done to negate these energies and to deconstruct the hexes, and transformation always occurs once they are back in the light. Working for the highest good, and working with love, always wins in the end.

How can these energies be removed or cleared?

First you need to find out where they came from and who sent them; once the source has been identified, and the reason for it understood, it is then possible to get a resolution. This usually means talking to the person that sent it in the first place, usually via their higher self, and a negotiation then takes place. But even if the person who sent the curse is hesitant about letting it go, with the right encouragement and the right motivation, the energies who are responsible for carrying the curse or the hex, will, once they have been freed from their task, be willing to leave and go back to where they belong.

What needs to happen to these attachments?

They need to be set free from any unsavoury tasks they have been set, like creating chaos in a person's life; any contracts they have been given need to be destroyed, their higher selves called in to remind them who they really are, and then they need to be guided safely back to the light; this is always done in a very loving and gentle manner, even when the energies claim to be dark or unpleasant – especially when they claim to be dark and unpleasant. The angrier and scarier they claim to be the more fear there usually is, and once they are reassured that there is nothing to be afraid of the mask of darkness usually drops away to reveal a terrified soul trapped underneath.

Do people always know when a hex or a curse has been sent?

Not usually, but if they are constantly feeling under the weather or life just keeps feeling like a terrible struggle and no matter what they do things just seem to keep going wrong, there may well be something in place that needs to be cleared.

Can this be the cause of what some people think of as psychotic behaviour?

Thankfully, more and more people in the medical profession are starting to understand that there is more to life on earth than just what the eye, or the microscope, can see, and there are now many medical doctors who fully accept that there may be souls, or fragments of souls, that get lost in transit from time to time. Many in the field of psychiatry are accepting that some of the more unusual things that happen to people may be connected to attachments. In many countries, such as India and even the United States, there is a much wider acceptance of this idea and the negative effect it can have, and many doctors there are working with spirit release therapy. Dr. Shakuntala Modi, in her book *Remarkable Healings: A Psychiatrist Discovers Unsuspected Roots of Mental and Physical Illness,* says that many acute psychological and psychosomatic symptoms that patients present with are due to these spirits. As a result, medication or traditional talking therapies cannot cure them; as long as the spirits remain, they will continue to suffer with their symptoms. She describes hundreds of cases she has worked with and reveals how she was able to set them free. Louise Ireland Frey, MD, in her book *Freeing the Captives,* also deals with the impact these attachments can have on people, and in one chapter she talks about releasing entities who claim to be dark energies that haven't been in a body before. She confirms that these lower-level "dark" entities attach because they are confused and deluded, having been told by their leaders in the nonphysical world that the "darkness" is all there is and that the "light" would destroy them. However she points out that the dark forces are never as strong as the bright powers and once they are made aware of this she is always able to get them back to the light.

How can you be certain that they have gone?

Ideomotor checks, while the person is still in trance, is the clearest way to test if they have gone, but a person will know, depending on how they are feeling, if the attachments really are gone.

How can you prevent spirit attachments from getting into your energy field?

The best way to ensure that you do not pick up any attachments is to use a form of energy protection. You can do this by using certain crystals, such as black tourmaline or rose quartz; you can use protection sprays or oils; or you can set an intention for protection and visualize a protective shield around you. This can be made of white light or any colour that feels right to you. You can visualize protective symbols such as the Eye of Horus around you or perhaps Reiki symbols. Some people like to imagine that the shield is concave, meaning that any energy that is sent to you, or tries to get into your energy field, bounces back to where it came from. I always set the intention that any energy that bounces off me is transformed into love before it goes anywhere else, because as we know what goes around comes around. It is also very important to deal with any unfinished business or unresolved emotions, as this is what allows the attachments to stick in the first place. If you are clear on the inside, or holding a powerful vibration of love and gratitude, then there is nothing for them to attach to and they simply float away.

Alice

One of my clients, Alice, came to see me as she had been struggling to move away from an unhappy working situation; she was working for her family business in a role that she didn't like and even though she knew that she *should* leave and find a new job, where she could step up to her highest potential, something stopped her. She could not explain what it was; she just knew that every time she tried to speak to her parents a huge wave of anxiety came over her and she would be unable to speak, frustrated and angry with herself. She would often go home and row with her partner over her inability to move on. He believed she was capable of a lot more than she was doing, and she was struggling with a sense of loyalty and duty versus her own fulfillment and satisfaction. What she really wanted was to focus on her Reiki and become a healer, but she could not see how it would ever happen. She told me that she really needed some help because it felt like there was a part of her that was sabotaging all of her attempts to be happy, and she couldn't understand it. Once she was in trance and in a safe place I asked to speak with her higher mind, using the finger signals that I mentioned earlier; when I asked if there were any "energies" in her energy field that did not belong to her, the signal said "yes." I asked if there was more than one and the finger signal said "no," just the one. In order for me to communicate with this energy I asked it to come up to her vocal chords so that I could speak with it. She was quite safe and comfortable whilst in the trance state so this happened quite easily, although it does feel a little strange. When I asked the energy if it had a name it said, "Yes, Anthony," in a deep male voice and the session began.

ME: So, Anthony, how long have you been here in this body?

A: About four years.

ME: What brought you here?

A: There was a feeling of frustration going on.

ME: Was the feeling of frustration familiar to you?

A: Yes, very.

ME: What were you frustrated about?

A: That my life came to an end so suddenly before I got to do all the things that I wanted to do.

ME: What happened to you?

A: I was murdered.

ME: Who did this to you?

A: My family.

ME: What happened, and why did your family want to kill you?

A: I was shot, because they were a bunch of cowards and they didn't have the nerve to stand up to me.

ME: What had you done to them to make them want to kill you in this way?

A: I set up a deal with a rival gang, which would have brought in a lot of money, but they didn't like it; they were afraid that they might try to stitch us up. I told them I would take care of it, but they were too stupid to see that I could.

ME: Wow, so I imagine that you have been affecting this body while you have been here.

A: Yes, I get angry when things don't move on; it drives me a bit crazy.

ME: Yes, I can imagine that it must be a bit frustrating for you being stuck here. So when you died, what happened?

A: I was angry with my family; I couldn't believe what they had done to me so I wanted to stay and get them back.

ME: What happened?

A: It was a waste of time; I couldn't get at them, and it was hard just floating around.

ME: Is that why you picked this body?

A: Yes, it seemed like the best option.

ME: So when you had your own body, I imagine that it was big and strong.

A: Yes, I was very fit.

ME: So how does it feel to be in the body of a young girl?

A: What?

This was said with some surprise.

ME: Yes, Alice here is a young woman and you are in her body.

With this there is some patting of the body.

A: Oh great, that is all I need. Now I feel really angry.

ME: Would you like to come out of this body now?

A: No, I don't have anywhere else to go; I have to stay here. You can't make me leave.

At this point Anthony was getting a bit agitated.

ME: I would never force you to do anything, but I wonder, would you prefer to have your own body back, the fit and strong one that you had when you were alive?

A: Yes, I would.

The anger had subsided, and Anthony was decidedly more willing to listen to me.

ME: And would you prefer to be somewhere where you can make sense of everything that happened to you, instead of unsettling a young girl and her life?

A: Yes, I want out of here before anyone sees me.

ME: Good. Well I am going to call in your spirit guide and ask him to locate your body and bring it here so that you can reunite with it. Then we are going to open a portal of white light and you can use it to get back to the spirit realms where you can meet with your soul group and find out what your life on earth was really about. Would you like that?

A: Anything is going to be better than being stuck here. So, yes, I will go.

ME: Thank you. And when you go will you take all of that frustration and anger with you?

A: Yes, it wasn't her fault.

ME: Good, I want you to look up now. Can you see your guide and your body and the white light?

A: Yes, I am going now; and thank you.

ME: You are welcome.

Alice's body was shuddering as Anthony left.

In order to ensure that we cleared away the hook that Anthony had attached himself to, we found the past life where her frustration had initially started. In that life she had been the daughter of a wealthy land owner. She had lived in a castle with her family and her younger brother, and they had been very happy. Her family was preparing a huge feast for her eighteenth birthday and she had decided to go out for a ride on her horse. Her mother had asked her not to as the weather was not looking so good, but she had insisted that this was the thing that she would enjoy the most on her special day. She loved riding with a passion and was very close to her horse; they set off at a gallop.

While they were out a storm began and rain started lashing down; some lightening startled her horse and she was thrown to the ground and was knocked unconscious for some time. Eventually the horse nuzzled her awake, and she managed to climb onto his back. They returned to the castle but by now the ground was wet and waterlogged. As they approached a search party came to meet them and in the rush to get her and the horse back into the castle her horse slipped and fell into the moat. One of the men dived in to save her and pull her to safety; her horse was not so lucky. He got caught up in some reeds, and the more he tried to break free the more entangled he got. Several of the men dived in to try to cut him free, but in the struggle the horse was drowned and it was only his body that was pulled from the water.

The birthday girl was taken to her room where she was dried and put into warm clothes. She managed to join her family for the feast that they had prepared but was unable to eat a thing. A chill set in; the loss of her beloved horse had stolen her will to live and within a few short weeks she was dead of a fever. She died angry and frustrated that she had let her family down, especially her little brother who she had promised to care for.

In the session she met with her family and asked them to forgive her for leaving the way she did; they told her that there was nothing to forgive, they had just been sad that a beautiful life had been wasted. They insisted she take the opportunity to really live her life fully in the present and no longer feel as though she were obligated to stay with them. They wanted her to really live and make up for the life she had missed; they joked that she should stay away from horses, whatever else she did. She was amazed to discover that her parents then were her parents now and that they had chosen to come back with her again to test her resolve and her desire to live life in her own way. She recognized her partner as her brother and saw that he had chosen to come back and help her to live her life fully this time. She was even more surprised to find that the soul that had been her horse was now her cat – a cat that was always over protective and trying to prevent her from going out.

Soon after the session Alice enrolled in another Reiki course; she made a promise that she would spend less time at work in the family business and use the rest of the time to do the things that she loved. She got to practice her healing skills on everyone, so in the end they were all happy.

John

John came to see me because he had been experiencing major problems with his relationships. No matter what he did or how much he tried to convince the women in his life that he was not a womanizer they would always end up jealous and accusing him of cheating on them. This pattern had been going on for his whole adult life, and he was really upset by the whole thing. He had married young and the relationship had not worked out; his wife had been very angry with him when he left her 12 years ago and had never really forgiven him. He knew that she had friends who dabbled in magic and witchcraft, and he was a little concerned that they might have put some sort of spell on him.

Five years previously another woman, who he had considered to be a good friend, had fallen for him and had been very angry when he spurned her advances. This had led to some very unpleasant situations, and he had been forced to cut the communications with her completely too. He was in a new relationship with a woman that he adored, and intended to marry, and he wanted to make sure that nothing got in the way this time and that the same arguments didn't happen again. This time he was determined to get to the bottom of it and nip it in the bud, and so he came for some help.

The session began and I quickly established that there were three energies in his energy field. Two of them had been sent to him from external sources.

ME: Can I please speak to the first of the energies? Hello, what is your name?
J: Sacha.
The voice was timid and quiet, and he sounded very young.
ME: How old are you Sacha?
J: I'm seven.

ME: How long have you been here?

J: A long time, since John was seven.

ME: What happened to you when you were in a body?

J: I got sick and I died.

ME: What attracted you to this body?

J: It was very light; I was stuck in the dark, and I was afraid.

ME: What was going on in John's life when you joined him?

J: He was frightened about something, and he was speaking to his grandfather who had passed.

ME: Were you close to your grandfather?

J: Yes, and I miss him.

Sacha was quite emotional and seemed a little scared.

ME: Would you like to be reunited with your grandfather?

J: Yes, and my mummy and daddy.

ME: Okay, I want you to look up and see a portal of white light; we are going to go and get your guide who will find mummy and daddy and your grandfather and bring them to the light so that you can go home and be back with them. Can you see them up there now?

J: Yes, I can.

Sacha was very happy, and there were tears running down John's face.

ME: Off you go now, sweetie; you can go back home and be with your loved ones. Will you make sure that you take all of the fear that you were carrying with you?

J: Yes, I will do that; I am going now, thank you for your help.

ME: You are welcome. Now can I speak to the second of the energies please?

John's face began to change and this time it was a very deep male voice that greeted me.

J: My name is Roger.

ME: How long have you been here Roger?

J: Twelve years.

ME: What brought you here?

J: I was sent here by an evil man; I was sent to create chaos and make bad things happen, to attract difficult people and situations.

ME: This man that sent you; was it his idea or did someone ask him to do this?

J: He was paid £50 to send a spell.

ME: How does that work?

J: I died in the 1800s. I was murdered and was unable to get back to the light because I got a bit lost and confused and had nowhere to go so I was just wandering around. This man appeared and told me that he would take me back to the light. I believed him. He told me that I had to do something for him first and I agreed. I was just happy to be getting out of limbo; but he lied to me. Once I was in the body I had no way to escape, and I have been here ever since. I feel bad that I have created all this chaos; I just didn't know any way out.

ME: That is okay, Roger, no one is blaming you, and I am really sorry for what happened to you and for the lies that were told that have kept you trapped here, doing something that you don't really want to do, and I think you have done more than your £50's worth by now. So tell me, when you were alive was there someone that you loved?

J: Yes, my wife.

ME: What was her name?

J: Rebecca.

ME: I am going to ask your guide to go and find the soul of Rebecca and bring her here, into the portal of white light. If you look up can you see her?

Johns face breaks into a huge smile.

ME: How does she look?

J: Beautiful.

He starts to cry.

ME: Would you like to go back to her now?

J: Yes, please.

ME: Will you ensure that you take all the energy of the chaos with you?

J: Yes, and I am very sorry for what I have done.

ME: Don't you worry, you were just following orders and you did a really good job, so you have nothing to worry about; you are completely forgiven for all of it. You can go home now and be with your loved ones.

J: Thank you. Goodbye.

ME: Bless you. You are so welcome. Can I speak to the third of the energies please?

J: I have no name.

ME: Okay, and what brought you here?

J: I was sent by a witch.

ME: And what was your job?

J: To keep relationships away, to keep chaos in them and to keep money away.

ME: Why did the witch send you?

J: She was rejected and angry and her thoughts called to me; I had no choice but to follow the instructions.

ME: Why did you have no choice?

J: I was a slave and was bound to do what I was told. It is all I have ever known.

ME: What happened to you at the end of your life?

J: I was whipped and beaten to death.

ME: I am so sorry that you had to suffer in this way and now you have been trapped here. I am sure that this is not a satisfying place for you to be.

J: No, it is not.

ME: Would you be happy to go home to the light if we could find some people that you love?

J: Yes. I had a wife and two daughters before I was stolen and sold as a slave.

ME: How old were your daughters?

J: Four and seven.

ME: Okay, well I am going to ask your guide to go and find them for you and bring them into the light. Can you see them there?

Once again John's face broke into a huge smile and the tears began to flow.

J: Yes, I can see them; they are so beautiful, and they are so happy to see me. I thought that I had lost them forever. Thank you so much, I thank you – really, I thank you….

ME: Bless you, you are welcome; my job is just to help you get home and to get back to those that love you. Are you ready to go now, and will you take all the chaos with you?

J: Yes, I am ready and sorry for the chaos.

ME: Don't you worry, it is all forgiven. You are a free man now. Go enjoy your freedom and your family.

With that John sighed and the last of the energies left his body.

ME: I would like John's higher mind to create a protective shield around him to protect him from such energies returning. This shield will allow all good energy to come in and send all bad energy back to where it came from – transforming it into love as it returns.

His higher mind confirmed that this was happening via the finger signals and the session came to an end. He determined to return at another time to establish what the past life hook might have been, but he was amazed at how much lighter he felt and how emotional the experience had been for him. He was delighted to find that the problems he had previously encountered in his relationships ceased, and his wedding is planned and he is looking forward to a long and very happy marriage this time.

EXERCISE 7: *Identifying Spirit Attachments*

Do you ever:

1. Wake up in the early hours after going to sleep and find it hard to get back to sleep?
2. Sense or see presences?
3. Have the feeling of nits or fleas in the hair?
4. Receive a sharp, pin-prick feeling over your legs, hands, and arms?
5. Have phantom illnesses where the doctor insists that you are OK?
6. Have phantom lovers?
7. Have a feeling of something crawling under your skin?
8. Have horrible nasty thoughts in your mind and sometimes hear voices that aren't yours?
9. Have the feeling that something is crawling in your hair?
10. Have really sudden bad thoughts (you think them) but you know they are not yours?
11. Have a feeling of despair and want to end your life?
12. Have bad dreams with unusual creatures in them or night terrors?
13. Had one of your eyes mist over at any time (a bit like they can in the morning)?
14. Have uncharacteristic changes in personality or behaviour; bursts of anger or sadness, unexplained fatigue or depression?
15. Have panic attacks for no known reason?
16. Have unexplained fears or phobias?

If you have answered "yes" to several of these questions you may wish to find someone who can check whether you do have any unwanted energies and, if so, help you clear them. There will be details of reputable practitioners at the end of the book. To keep your energy field clear, you may wish to practice some energy protection.

Protection

To keep spirit attachments and any unwanted energies at bay, it is best to keep your energy vibration high; if you can stay in an energy of pure unconditional love then they cannot come near you. This high vibrational energy helps to keep the chakras clear and energy flowing freely through your system. However, it is not always easy to remain in this state at all times, and so it is a good idea to have another form of protection in place until such time as you are able to manage this.

Close your eyes and imagine sending roots down from the soles of your feet into the ground; imagine sending theses roots down like the roots of a tree. Allow the roots to go all the way to the centre of the earth and find a large rock or a crystal to tie these roots around – allowing you to be grounded and safe and connected to the earth.

Allow a cleansing, brown earth energy to come up from the centre of the earth and flow right into your body, clearing away any unwanted energies. Send the brown energy back into the earth where it can be transformed.

Reach up to the highest point of light and visualize a beam of pure white light coming down into your body, right down through the central column within your body, all the way from the top of your head to the tips of your toes.

As you fill your body with this pure white light, see it expand, allowing the white light to form an oval shape around you – a protective bubble of light. You can ask for this bubble of light to protect you and keep you safe. The edges of this bubble can be made concave so that any energy that comes to you that you do not want can be sent right back to where it came from; you can ask that any energy that is not for your highest benefit be transformed into love – and returned.

You can visualize protective symbols around this bubble, perhaps the Eye of Horus, the Star of David, the Hand of Fatima, or the Symbol of the Cross. This bubble and the symbols around it will keep you protected and safe at all times. While you are within this bubble you can ask to connect with the angels – your guides and your higher self – to guide you, guard you, protect you, and direct you onto the right path.

And you can give thanks for all the gifts in your world, focusing your attention on the feeling of unconditional love within your heart, and you can take this feeling of love with you into your day or your night, knowing that you are now safe.

8

Is It Possible to Release Your Karma?

The Wicked Witch of the West is killed when Dorothy's house lands on her head; now some may say that this was just karmic retribution for all the bad things that she did in her lifetime, or even in other lifetimes too. And in what could be seen as a karmic exchange, Dorothy is granted her magic shoes in return. Was this a karmic payoff for saving the Munchkins from her tyranny? These ruby slippers had all the power she needed to get back home – she just had no idea of this at the time. The shoes carried Dorothy all the way to the wizard and the Emerald City, and it was these shoes that convinced the guard at the door to let her in because their ownership cast her in position of importance. But it wasn't all good because it was these very same shoes that had driven the witch to want to kill Dorothy, as killing her was the only way she was going to get her hands on the shoes and have the power they possessed for herself. At this point in the movie, it seemed that the witch had Dorothy right where she wanted her, locked in her tower with no way out; the shoes would soon be hers, and then she would be in control; she would be unstoppable. Whilst in the tower Dorothy was kept in a place of fear – her thinking was no longer clear and she felt completely helpless.

She longed to reach out to her Auntie Em – a feeling made all the worse when she saw her image in the witch's giant crystal ball: She saw her aunt searching for her and calling out her name, but she had no way of reaching her and as she watched the time she had left slip away in the giant hour glass she felt nothing but despair; all she could do was hope and pray that someone would save her.

And help was at hand, and her brave friends were about to stage a heroic rescue. The Tin Man used an axe to break down the door and soon Dorothy was released but, just as they were about to escape, the guards spotted them, and the four friends and Toto were driven into a tower even higher up in the castle.

As the witch and her Twinkie army approached, it seemed that their time had come. The Wicked Witch thought she could destroy them one at a time while the others watched helplessly. She decided to attack the scarecrow first and used the flame from a burning torch to set him on fire. Dorothy leapt into action and threw a bucket of water over him to put out the flames, and she ended up with a huge surprise because the water was all that was needed to melt the Wicked Witch and her "beautiful wickedness" away. This wicked witch, who had provided Dorothy and the others with the greatest challenges throughout the story, got her comeuppance from a simple bucket of water – water that was intended to save the scarecrow's life. It is interesting to note that in many spiritual circles water is used as a symbol of rebirth, of baptism, of the washing away of sins, the doorway to new beginnings.

By confronting her head on, Dorothy had found the way to deal with the fearful shadow side of herself and by this act transitioned into a new, more empowered phase in her life. The witch's army was delighted to be free and gladly gave Dorothy the witch's broom to thank her for saving them – another karmic gift it seemed. The jubilant friends, who had now passed the test assigned to them by the Wizard, were very excited that their wishes could now be granted. They were ready to receive their proper and full karmic rewards for setting the residents of Oz free from the clutches of the Wicked Witch. However, things were not as simple as they seemed.

Upon return to the Emerald City, the friends, who had risked life and limb for one another and for the accomplishment of the Wizard's request, discovered with the help of Toto and the removal of a very large curtain, that he was not really a wizard at all. He was merely a humble Kansas balloon man who had floated into Oz in his hot air balloon one day and hadn't been able to leave. He had created the scary and powerful persona of the wizard to fit in with the expectations of the people, and up to now he had been able to provide people with what they wanted: a wise word or a symbol to represent that which they thought they needed. At first they were very angry, upset that he had lied to them but when he was confronted he assured them that although he was in the wrong, he was not a bad man; he was an old man with a good heart – he was just a very bad wizard.

So shouldn't karma mean that bad things only happen to bad people?

That is very much related to your interpretation of what is good and what is bad. If it is true that we have chosen our lives, and the lessons, and the circumstances that we will live, then is anything that we experience ever bad? In real life bad things do happen; how you interpret them is up to you. There is a great story about a man who lived on a farm. One day his horse ran away and the people in the village said, "this is terrible, what bad luck," and he said, "maybe it is, maybe not." The next day the horse came back with 20 beautiful wild horses and they ran straight into his corral. The people in the village came and said, "this is wonderful, what great luck," and the man said, "maybe it is, and maybe not." The next day his son went out to train one of the new horses, it threw him to the ground, and he broke his leg, putting him out of action for several weeks. The people in the village came and said, "this is most unfortunate, what bad luck," and the man said, "maybe it is, maybe not." The next day the king's men came and took all of the young men from the village to fight in a war; the young man with the broken leg was the only one who couldn't go. The rest of the young men were killed in action. The people from the village came and said, "it was a great fortune that he broke his leg, what great luck," and the man said… well, you know now what the man said. How we see things determines how we respond, and how we respond affects everything we do. We can see the idea of karma as a negative thing – or maybe not. So, bearing that thought in mind, how do you judge what is a good or bad life? Perhaps those people living a "good life" this time around have had previous incarnations where they were the bad guy. Their good deeds in this life might be their way of making recompense for something terrible they did in the past. What if they did all kinds of good things in their previous life and their lesson this time is to learn all about being harsh and mean? It is a question that raises much debate. What is important about the principle of karma is that the way you lived in your past lives will affect your experience of life in the present, and how you live in this life will most certainly affect how you live later in this life and in your future lives.

So what does karma really mean?

The principle of karma implies that you get nothing more than you deserve and that what goes around comes around; so karma can be seen as a blessing or as a curse, depending on how you look at it. Russian theosophist Helena P. Blavatsky said that karma is a basic cosmic law, in which the physical, mental, and soul world connects cause with its effect. She described karma as an invisible law that wisely, righteously, and providentially connects every effect with a corresponding cause and its originator.

Where does the idea of karma originate?

The concept of karma has been around for aeons; it is mentioned in the bible within the statement "as ye reap, so shall ye sow" and relates to the fact that every thought, word, and deed has an action and a consequence. In spiritual terms this means that everything that you send out, be it thought, word, or deed will come back to you – eventually – in the same way.

How many types of karma are there?

There are several kinds of karma, the kind that you bring back with you from previous lifetimes and the karma that is created within your present lifetime – be it good or bad.

How long does it take for the effects of karma to come back to you?

It varies depending on the strength and magnitude of the action that was taken. Some say that because the energy vibrations of the planet are quickening, karmic effects reach you much more speedily. I know mine does these days. I have to be very careful with my thoughts and actions, because there are times when I can almost see them coming right back at me.

What creates bad karma?

If you are experiencing misfortune in your life, there are three things to be aware of: 1. you may have an attachment causing the disturbance in your life, 2. you may have chosen to have this experience so it is nothing to do with karma at all, or 3. it may be a response to something you did in a previous life or from things that happened earlier on in your current life. You may be experiencing the karmic pay-back for things that only you were responsible for.

Why are more people not aware of this idea?

Unfortunately, many are aware of this idea but choose to ignore it. Just imagine how great it would be if more people took the time to think about the consequences of their actions, towards each other and towards the planet. It would go a long way towards making this a better world.

What if you were a bad person in your previous life?

At a soul level, there is no judgment about whether one life is better than another, one more worthy of praise or punishment than another; they are all just parts of the soul's journey to wholeness. When you consider that, ultimately, everyone is connected and that at a soul level are all one, it becomes clear that when you judge another you are simply judging a part of yourself. This concept can be a little difficult to grasp sometimes, which is understandable when you look at the actions of some of the people who have left their mark on the planet. How can you possibly be connected to, or "one and the same" as, the "bad" guys. This concept really tests the ability to experience unconditional love, for all, to the limits. I like to point out that it is far easier to love everyone unconditionally, than it is to like them, or the way they behave; and it is easy to forget that people are not their behaviours. It is essential to remember that people's behaviours usually reflect their deeply buried shadows – shadows that all possess, but not all are prepared to face.

One of my clients really feared that she was being punished for her actions in a previous life and was worried that she had been a very bad person. "I must have been really bad in a previous life to deserve this," was a phrase that she used all the time. It was not a helpful belief for her to have, even if it *was* true. In her session she returned to a life as a Mongol soldier who had brutally killed hundreds of people. The valuable learning from the experience came when she realized that, at the time, the soldier had fully believed that what he was doing was right. He was following orders and had no choice but to rid the area of people who were not conforming to the law. He had not had any thought for the victims or the impact of his actions throughout most of his life; however, as he got older, and some might say wiser, he began to question what he was doing. At one particular village, where there were only women and children present, he felt his first pangs of guilt and remorse at the brutal way in which they were slaughtered. Not willing to shame his family or go against his orders, he chose to enter the next battle with his weapons lowered and was killed instantly. His final thoughts at the end of the life were of regret and sorrow for all of the lives he had taken. In the session my client was able to receive forgiveness from all of the victims who knew that the soldier had just been doing his job, and she was able to forgive herself as a result.

Once she had released all of the negative emotions I asked her to explore some other lives, to help her to get a greater understanding of her soul's journey so far. She found herself in a life in France as a healer; she had been persecuted for her abilities and drowned, accused of being a witch. Her last thoughts in that life were of real frustration that she had been prevented from doing her healing work. In another life she found herself as a nurse in France at the time of the First World War, tending to the sick and the dying. She had died young of a fever, in terrible circumstances, and left regretting that she had not been able to be of more help to those that were suffering. She recognized that there was a balance in her experiences, and a duality of good and bad, and she let go of her fears that she was a bad person. She no longer needed to beat herself up mentally, and she was finally able to believe that she did deserve happiness in this life.

What about fate, or free will; how does that fit in?

Karma is not to be confused with fate, because as this book shows, life on earth provides the chance for people to experience free will and create their own destiny. Even when a life path has been deliberately chosen, or a desired outcome preset before a person arrives, once on earth all plans can change – and they can be changed in an instant. One different choice can change the whole meaning of a life. Think *Sliding Doors,* the movie, in which we see two versions of Gwyneth Paltrow's character, who live very different lives, based on whether she turned left or right as she left the train one day. Ultimately she ends up in the same place but she has a very different experience along the way – all down to the choices that she made in that one moment and the ones succeeding it.

So karma or no karma, right now everyone has free will. In this lifetime only you hold the secret to your success or failure with nothing more than your thoughts, your actions, and your deeds. Every person living on earth is free, to some degree, to choose the path they wish to walk and, for certain, free to choose *how* they wish to walk it. However, being able to uncover previous karmic lessons, and understand whether they were completed or not, offers the chance to see what is yet to be cleared, or completed, in this life and ensure that old patterns are not repeated over and over again until they are resolved.

How can you ensure more karma is not accrued?

Your karma can be kept clear by focusing on positive, loving thoughts and actions.

Is it possible to release the bad karma you have already produced?

Yes, a lot can be done to release karma.

How does this happen?

In a past life session, the karma is revealed and the lesson is immediately dealt with.

Why is it important to understand what karma you may have been carrying?

The reason for understanding your karma is so that you can deal with anything that is pending. Once you are free of your karma, you have much greater freedom to enjoy your life and will be set free from the cycle of birth and rebirth when your life comes to an end. The release of your karma, and the negative vibrations that go with it, will go a long way to helping the planet heal too.

What about negative thoughts about others – can that produce bad karma?

People really have to take responsibility for their actions and especially their thinking, particularly negative thoughts aimed at another; otherwise, the negative vibration of that thought will not only have a negative effect on the other, but it will come right back to them.

Is this what they mean when they talk about the law of attraction?

Yes, everything in the universe has a specific vibration, and this will eventually attract to it events of a similar vibration. So if someone has been guilty of bad actions and bad thoughts, in their present life or somewhere in a past life, the chances are that it will come back to bite them – often in ways that are unexpected.

If all people are connected, can the karma of one person affect the whole planet?

Yes, despite the good intentions of many it is clear that there is still much karma that needs to be cleared. All over the world people are suffering and struggling to survive; there is much unhappiness brought about by greed and selfishness, wars and battles being fought over land and resources, all the things that should, by rights, be shared by all. But as we have discussed previously, when you seek to heal yourself and free up your own karma it affects the whole – in a very positive way; all positive change in the world starts with you.

What about good karma?

The principle that says what you reap you sow also applies to good karma; good deeds, compassion, and loving kindness will reap more of the same. And this is so often true. And yet, you still hear stories of the good dying young, of accidents and terrible tragedies befalling good people. What needs to be understood is that they may not necessarily be experiencing karmic retribution but may have chosen those experiences before they arrived so that they could learn from them; it may be that they had chosen to experience suffering so that they could understand how it felt, and allow others to benefit from their experience.

One of my clients had a son who died very suddenly at the age of 17; all through his life he had been gentle, kind, loving, and hugely popular with his friends at school and had been a role model for all the younger children around him. His sudden death, from a heart defect that had been undetected, caused a huge upset for many people and at the same time created bonds that brought many people together.

In her past life session she saw that they had been together in many lives, and that his role was always to help her experience unconditional love. He had been her child many times but also her brother, her teacher, even her father in one life; in this lifetime they had agreed that unconditional love and loss would be the experience, and so he had chosen to leave early. Knowing this helped her to let go of the pain of her loss and she was able to move on; she was also reassured by the fact that she would see him again, that death was not the end.

Are there themes to each life, karmic lessons that are being played out?

Yes, each life has a theme, a karmic mission to be fulfilled. In some lives people make all the right choices; the mission is found, the lessons learnt, and they can move on to the next theme. But in many lifetimes this is not the case and sometimes people fail. This means that they will have no choice but to return and do it all again until they get it right. They may choose to come back for joyous reasons, to be a guide or a help to others, or because they desired to experience life with another member of their soul group; even so there will always be some reason why people are here, and this is very rarely obvious. Many people spend their entire lives wondering why they are here, and the fortunate ones – the ones who explore beyond the remit of their everyday lives – get to find out.

One of my clients, the man who found himself in the dark wearing a toga and a sword, discovered that he had committed a murder in his past life; he had been set upon by a gang of young men and in an instinctual response to protect himself and his girlfriend he had pulled out his sword and before he had a sense of what was happening a young man was dead. His girlfriend had rejected him, thinking him to be violent and weak; he was unable to forgive himself and spent the rest of his life alone. He avoided all contact with people and died alone, sad and full of regrets. At the end of the life there was a sense that the life had been wasted, that nothing had been achieved, and that there was a huge burden to be carried – the burden of the guilt at taking a life. And yet when he was reunited with the young man that he killed he was amazed to find out that this was exactly what he had been sent to do; this had been a karmic contract, and he had fulfilled his mission perfectly. The young man was thankful to him, and as a result he was able to let go of the guilt that he had been carrying with him; it had been a heavy load, and he was glad to see it go.

Caroline

Another client, called Caroline, was concerned that she may have been a bad person in her past and that her karma was affecting her in this life. She came for a session because she had been suffering from recurring nightmares of being attacked; the nightmare was always the same: She was being dragged out of her house and beaten by a group of men. This anxiety and fear affected both her sleep and her daytime anxiety levels, and although she had tried other ways to deal with the underlying anxiety, the feelings remained. Some time previously, a woman who claimed that she was a "witch" told her that she had probably been a murderer in a previous life and this was why she was being haunted in her sleep. This suggestion had not only been unhelpful but had added to the bad feelings, adding a sense of guilt into the mix. She decided that the best way to remedy this would be to explore her past lives and see if there was something that would be relevant to her problem.

The journey began:

ME: What are you aware of?

C: I am a young man of around 18 years old; I am wearing a white shirt, a white tunic, and breeches, and my name is Haden. I am wearing strange suede shoes and my clothes are made of old cloth.

ME: Where are you?

C: I am in an inn; there is lots of wood, lots of beams, and a low stone ceiling, surrounded by countryside. The year is 1490.

ME: What else are you aware of?

C: I can feel a sense of anxiety or excitement; I am not alone, there are others around.

ME: What are you doing here?

C: We are here to take over the inn; the others are checking to see if anyone else is around, to see if anyone is coming.

ME: Why are you here?

C: We are here to either arrest or kill the owner of the inn; it is a sort of military coup. There is more activity, more people arriving, soldiers all moving around me swiftly. I am not feeling at all happy about being here.

ME: Tell me what happens next.

C: I begin, slowly, to move up the stairs, knowing that the aim once there is to kill the man.

ME: Who is this man?

C: He is an old but very powerful person; the people are afraid of him.

ME: What is he doing at this moment?

C: Right now he is asleep in bed. His wife is with him, and there are maids somewhere else in the house.

Suddenly, recognition dawned and her voice went very quiet.

C: I am supposed to kill his wife, but I do not want to; it does not feel right. She is innocent of whatever crimes her husband may have committed.

She shook her head and, as she was getting a little upset, I moved her on.

ME: I want you to move to the next significant event.

C: I am in a house now; I am older, about 24 years old.

ME: Is anyone else with you?

C: I live here with my wife and my child, who are asleep in bed.

ME: What can you tell me about this place?

C: There is a great feeling of love in this house, a feeling of warmth that cannot all be attributed to the open fire that burns in the hearth.

She jumps in the chair.

ME: What are you aware of?

C: There is a banging on the door. This is most unusual, as it is very late at night. I feel great apprehension and when I look outside I see the men from the inn.

ME: Why have they come here?

C: They have come for me; they say that I am a traitor and that I failed to fulfill my part in their plan.

ME: What happened on that night?

C: I chose not to murder that man's wife and fled from the group; they have been searching for me ever since, and now they have found me.

ME: What happens next?

C: I very quickly wake my wife and insist that she take our child and hide. They are only here for me, and I want to ensure that no harm comes to my family.

ME: Then what happens?

C: Eventually the men get into the house; they find me and begin to beat me, they tie me up, and they take me away.

ME: What about your wife and child?

C: They are safely hidden away at the top of the house.

ME: Where do they take you?

C: They take me away out into the countryside where they beat me to death.

ME: I want you to float up and out of that body now and tell me what you are aware of.

C: I have my hands tied behind my back; I am wearing a grey powdered wig, breeches, and a dark blue coat. The night sky is incredibly vivid; it is winter and there is a frost, but it is a really clear night and the sky is full of stars.

ME: How does it feel to witness this scene?

C: I feel a great feeling of sadness but also a sense of resignation, as I had brought the whole thing onto myself.

ME: What was the last thought that you had as you left that body?

C: My last thought as I died was that "I didn't get it right."

Later Caroline noted that this was something she was aware of saying to herself in this life on a regular basis.

ME: Can you get a sense of why you experienced this?

C: I have a very powerful sense that I should not have been in the army, that as the young man I should have not had any part in this group's plans and schemes because I did not believe in their cause.

ME: Is this something that feels familiar to you now?

C: Yes, I have always felt that it would be impossible to work for something that I did not believe in.

ME: What happened to your family?

C: They were safe, and they did survive.

ME: How do you feel knowing that now?

C: I am happy that they survived, but I feel a great sense of sadness and feel so bad for putting them in that position and then leaving them behind.

ME: How did you get involved in the military drama in the first place?

C: I was just a pawn in someone else's game and did not take full responsibility for my actions; I paid the ultimate price though: my life.

ME: What needs to happen now?

C: I need to heal the wounds that were inflicted onto the physical body, and the emotions – the sadness at the loss of my wife and baby.

Healing energy was sent to the body and the wounds were repaired, then he was reunited with his wife and child, who insisted that they were proud of him and had forgiven him for leaving them; they were just sad that they had been separated and had not had the chance to live their lives together. There was a powerful release of the guilt that had been carried.

ME: What do you need to bring in to allow this healing to fully take place?

C: I need to bring in a feeling of acceptance for all that had occurred; I am aware that what had been missing was a sense of recognition and accomplishment. The life felt wasted.

ME: Bring in the men that attacked you and ask them if there were any contracts set between you.

C: Yes, they tell me that we agreed to this, as I wished to be tested, to see if I would hold true to my own values and beliefs.

ME: Was this accomplished?

C: Yes, but I went around it the wrong way; I should have spoken up sooner instead of running away. I think they would have respected me more if I had said "no" in the beginning.

ME: Were there any unhelpful beliefs that were carried over from that life?

C: In that lifetime I felt as though I was weak, and I died berating myself for it; I died feeling like a failure.

ME: As you review this lifetime now, how do you feel?

C: I can see now that I had been much braver than I had ever realized. It was a lot braver for me to not do what these people wanted and stand by my convictions, because I was fully aware that they would hunt me down.

ME: What else are you aware of when you really tune in to those choices that were made?

C: In my last moments I had no fear, just resignation that this was how it would be.

ME: And what does that tell you?

C: I can see now an inner strength and an ability to make the right choices when it is most important, that I was someone who would do the right thing. I can now acknowledge that there was a deeper sense of bravery within me than I ever thought of.

ME: Now that you have this understanding you can release the contract that requires you to be tested, and you can create a new contract that will be of more benefit to you.

C: I commit to trusting and believing in myself.

ME: Good. With all of this new knowledge and awareness, I want you to go back to the moment when you were asked to join this group and tell me what happens.

C: I am called to the leader and I tell him that I am unable to join his group as I have important commitments elsewhere.

ME: How does he respond?

C: He laughs at me, pats me on the back and says, "So be it, young man, go well and live a long and healthy life," then he winks at me.

ME: Good. Is there any recognition of this soul in your current life?

C: He is my father now, who challenged me all the time when I was younger. I can see now that it was all part of the same test, and I am really relieved to be able to let this go. At the end of the session she was given a gift, which was a medal, an old-fashioned medal made of brass. When I asked her what the medal represented she immediately said "courage." Not that surprisingly, the experience fitted perfectly with Caroline's nightmares. Since the session Caroline's nightmares have completely ceased, she has lost the sense of anxiety that she felt at night-time, and she feels much safer in general. She is sleeping better and has a much better relationship with her father too.

Pam

Earlier in the book I mentioned a client who had found herself in a life in the year 525; her discovery of a life where there was a residue of a karmic issue led to a profound shift for her too. Pam came for a session because she was feeling as though she never quite got where she wanted to be; everyone around her seemed to be moving on and she just felt stuck. Whether it was in her career, her friends, or her love life, it seemed that she always gave a lot but got little back. She was left questioning why it was that she was able to take such great care of others and not so much care of herself. She wondered if it was something karmic.

The journey began:

ME: What are you experiencing?

P: I am a man, and I am 35 years old.

ME: Can you describe what you are wearing?

P: I am wearing sandals on my feet and a white robe with a cord around the middle. I am holding a spear; I am very big and strong.

ME: Tell me about your character.

P: I am a good person; I look after other people, like a guardian.

ME: Where are you?

P: I am in a Roman bath. It is steamy; there are lots of people in the water.

ME: What are you doing here?

P: I am watching them, just keeping guard; they do not speak to me, but they are laughing and having fun.

ME: What year is it?

P: The date is 525; I can see it carved into a stone block in the wall in front of me.

ME: How do you feel about being in this job?

P: I am proud of my job, and I am happy to serve.

ME: How are you treated?

P: Everyone likes me, but they are not allowed to speak to me because of my position.

ME: How do you feel about that?

P: I don't mind, it is my job.

ME: Is there anyone significant there with you?

P: There is a man to my right; he is important.

ME: Who is this man?

P: He is the king; his name is Darius.

ME: I want you to move on to the next significant event.

P: There is a chariot race, lots of horses and dust everywhere. It is a big competition, not a battle; it's a race and everyone is happy and smiling. Lots of people are watching the races and laughing, having fun.

ME: What are you doing here?

P: I am in one of the chariots. I am wearing red and brown leather armour and my helmet has a gold emblem on it. I can see the wheels going around and around, I am going at a great speed around the track.

ME: What is happening now?

P: I am racing against the other guards, and I am winning. That's why they all like me, I am the first one to cross the finish, emerging from the dust victorious. The men were betting, and I have made them large sums of money. That is why they like me so much; I am a great racer, also I have a good heart and a very strong will.

ME: It sounds as though you are well regarded by the people here; are you a soldier?

P: I will never be just an ordinary soldier; I am a guard and a good one at that. I keep people safe and they trust me.

ME: Why is that?

P: Being a guard, and an elite one at that, is better than being a soldier; I feel very proud of myself, but I know that I will never be like Darius. He has money – lots of money – and status, and he is very clever.

ME: What else can you tell me about this King Darius?

P: Actually, he kills people to make money and he robs people; I don't really like him as a person, but he is very powerful.

ME: How does he feel about you?

P: He likes me, but I don't like him; I can sense that he is someone very special, very important, and it is my duty to protect him. He is my king, and the leader of a great army.

ME: Tell me what happens next.

P: Darius is looking at a map, and moving things around; the map is showing a desert.

ME: Where are you now?

P: We are in a large tent, and the landscape is very dusty and barren; the map is showing mountains and a river. There is something about the river that is important.

ME: What is significant about the river?

P: I have to do something to protect it.

ME: Who do you need to protect it from?

P: There is no battle to be had; we just have to do something here. I thought perhaps that we were building something, perhaps a bridge of some sort, but we are not; I know that it has something to do with the water.

ME: What is important about the water?

P: We need the water for something, almost as though we are trying to stop it flowing. Oh, he is trying to stop other people getting to the water in order to beat them.

ME: How will you do that?

P: We are building something over the river to stop the water, some sort of a dam, so there is to be no battle but we are going to kill these people without a fight.

ME: How will you do that?

P: It seems that this is their only source of water and so they will die without it.

ME: How do you feel about that?

P: It is a horrible idea, and I do not like it; but I can't say anything – it is not my place.

She sighs.

P: It is very, very hot where we are; these people are going to die, just because he sees them as the enemy. I don't think that they have even done anything wrong.

ME: Why does he want to kill them?

P: The only difference between us and them is that they worship a different God and he wants their land and their riches.

ME: How does this make you feel?

P: I feel so sad, but there is nothing that I can do; I am torn between being happy that I have a good job, where I do not have to work hard, and my outrage at the unfairness of what is going on around me.

ME: What else are you aware of?

P: I know that I am lucky; I do not have to work hard like the slaves do, I get plenty to eat, but I am frustrated at not being able to speak up. If I do, not only will I lose my position but I will most likely be put to death.

ME: Let's move on to the next significant event.

P: I am racing, in my chariot; once again King Darius and the men have wagered lots of money on me to win. I cannot help feeling angry at them and their callous behaviour, and I no longer have the desire to serve him. I can never escape this place, not alive anyway.

ME: What happens next?

P: As I round the corner, I lash out at the horses with my reins; all around me other chariots are vying for position, they all want to beat me; one comes very close, he has large knives jutting out from his wheels. Usually I would find the strength and the speed from the horses to move out of his way, but this time I hold my space. His knives cut away at my carriage, sparks are flying, and I feel myself flying through space. The last thing I see is King Darius screaming as he realizes his wager will be lost.

ME: What is the last thought that you have as you leave this lifetime?

P: I am glad that it is over.

ME: Can you get a sense of what the karmic lesson was you had chosen to learn?

P: My karmic lesson was about patience, and about learning to be humble, about not being too proud to be humble.

ME: Did you learn that lesson?

P: I definitely learnt that; unfortunately, I died with a huge feeling of guilt at what we had done to those people, the ones down river.

ME: I want you to call them in. What would you like to say to them?

P: I want to tell them how sorry I am that I was a part of that. I didn't agree with it, but there was nothing that I could do at the time.

ME: What do they say?

P: They are telling me that I must not worry, that they know it was not my fault; they are saying that they had all agreed to it beforehand anyway, their contract was with Darius. I was just doing my job, and they say I did a good job. They also know how much I suffered at the end of my life as a result of this, and they are saying that I must let this go now. They forgive me, and they are saying it is time for me to forgive myself.

ME: Is there anyone there that you recognize?

P: Yes, one of the women there, she says that she is part of my soul group, and that our group is working on forgiveness. She says that I must let this go now in order to help our entire group; as I let go I release the energy of guilt for them all.

ME: Are you able to let this go now?

P: Yes, I can see that it no longer serves me to hold onto this.

ME: Is there anyone else there that you recognize?

P: Incredibly, I recognize my horse; in this life he is my dog.

ME: I want you to check and see whether you had picked up any negative beliefs in that life that no longer serve you.

P: Yes, I did feel as though I was not as good as everyone else, that I was not worthy. But I can see now that I was strong, that I was respected and loved by many; I chose to take control of my destiny and not be pushed around by Darius anymore.

ME: It is time for you to let any residue of that thought of being unworthy go now. We allowed a symbolic release of these feelings to occur.

ME: I would like you to check in with your spirit guide and see if they have any words of wisdom for you. What are you aware of now?

P: I have the strangest feeling; it is hard to put it into words. It is as though I am being told that I don't have to sit around and wait for success. I spent my life feeling as though I was not good enough. I can now see that I don't just have to put up with whatever is thrown at me. Darius wasn't better than me, just different; he didn't have my heart. Ultimately he used his power to serve his own ends; he will have to deal with his own karma when the time comes.

As she spoke a huge tear ran down her face.

ME: What is the most important thing that you have learnt from this?

P: I have learnt that I do not need to be afraid and that I must believe in myself. I need to show others how to break free, to not be scared of what is inside them

After the session Pam was very emotional; she was amazed at the clarity of the messages. She decided to explore the Internet to see if there really had been anyone in those times called Darius; it seemed like a name that neither fit with the time or the place, so she was stunned when she tapped in the name Darius and the year 525 to find that there had been a king of that name in Persia and that he was famous for overthrowing many of his enemies, for having his own elite guard who were called the Companions or the Immortals (depending on which translation you used) for designing and constructing several large dams – one of which was over a mile long and for constructing canals. The modern-day Suez Canal follows the path he opened up.

In 1866 when they were rebuilding it they found a pink granite stele with an inscription on it, in four different languages. It stated that he, King Darius, had ordered the canal to be dug from the river Nile to the sea that began in Persia. Since the session, Pam has managed to get rid of people in her life that were wasting her time; having recognized her inner strength and her desire to help others in a fair and caring way, she has had a complete change of career and has set up her own company. The business is going from strength to strength, and she has finally found her niche and her road to success.

EXERCISE 8: *Negative Events*

List the key negative events that have happened in your life. Grade the experiences from 1 to 10, with 10 having the most impact and 1 the least.

1. What were your greatest fears?
2. When did you doubt yourself the most?
3. What were your lowest moments?

4. What are you most ashamed of?
5. What are you most angry about?
6. What or who has brought you the most unhappiness?
7. What or who has brought you the greatest fear?
8. What were the key challenging events?
9. Who were the most challenging people?
10. What effect did this have on your life?
11. Were you defeated by these events or were you forced to move forward as a result?
12. What were the key physical and emotional impacts this had on you?
13. What effects, if any, are they still having on you now?

GLINDA TO DOROTHY:
"The ruby slippers had the power to take you home all along."
SCARECROW:
"Well, why didn't you say so?"
GLINDA:
"She had to find that out for herself!"

9

How Do You Discover
Your Life Purpose?

Dorothy and her friends had learnt that the Wizard was not really a wizard, and felt sure that none of their wishes were going to be granted. But as is so often the way in life, they got just what they needed, although not necessarily what they thought they wanted. For many years the Wizard had been ruling in the land of Oz because he had a good mind and he understood people's thinking. He knew that it was just the limitations of people's beliefs that held them back. He knew exactly what the four friends needed to be happy, and from a small black sack the Wizard produced just what they needed to change their beliefs. For the Scarecrow he found a diploma, and awarded him with the title of Th.D, Doctor of "Thinkology"; he had, said the Wizard, proved himself by way of his deep thinking and his plan to save Dorothy from the Wicked Witch. At last he had the recognition that he needed that he had always had a brain. He told the Tin Man that a heart was not judged by how much you love, but by how much you were loved by others. As he looked around at his new-found friends who all loved him dearly, he knew then that he must already have a heart. The Wizard presented him with a testimonial for his devotion to Dorothy and his friends in such a difficult time. It came in the form of a heart-shaped clock that was ticking; for him it was proof that not only did he now have a heart but that he had known how to love all along. He told the Cowardly Lion that he had his thinking all wrong. He said that avoiding danger was not cowardly and that he lacked not courage but a medal for bravery against wicked witches. He was then awarded the Triple Cross for "meritorious conduct, extraordinary valour, and conspicuous bravery against the Wicked Witch of the West." This medal stated very clearly that the wearer had demonstrated the highest order of courage. The friends were overjoyed. But when it came to Dorothy's turn they felt sure that there was nothing in the sack that could get her back to Kansas. And they were right.... But the Wizard assured them they shouldn't worry as he had a plan. He would take Dorothy back to Kansas they way he had come in – in his balloon.

It was simple: The next day the balloon was ready, Dorothy and Toto were on board, and the four friends were getting ready to say their goodbyes. The Wizard instructed the people of Oz to welcome their newly appointed leaders, namely the Scarecrow, the Tin Man and the now courageous Lion, who would reign in his place on account of their superior minds and hearts and bravery.

And then disaster struck.

Toto spotted a cat in the crowd and once again his instincts kicked in; he leapt from the balloon, forcing Dorothy to leap out after him. The balloon broke free and the helpful, but hapless, wizard had no way to bring it back; he had no idea how it worked. Once again Dorothy was lost – or so it seemed – and then, just when she needed her the most, Glinda the Good Witch (her intuitive higher self) appeared. She asked Dorothy what she had learnt along the way, and Dorothy told her that she recognized that what she needed was within her all the time, in her own back yard, as it were; that she didn't need to go running off to other places but that she could choose to be happy and to have gratitude for all that she already had. She had found all the love she needed in her own heart, and she would carry it with her wherever she went. Glinda was delighted; this was the lesson that Dorothy had needed to learn. And, once learnt, it meant that she could return home to Auntie Em and to the farm in Kansas. Dorothy and her friends were amazed to discover that the ruby slippers had always had the power to take her home at any time. Her power had been right under her nose the whole time, and she had simply failed to recognize it. Just as the Scarecrow had been intelligent all along, the Tin Man loving and the Lion brave – but they all had to find this out for themselves, no one else could have made them see the truth. Once they acknowledged their power they were free to move forward and live their lives in the best way possible. After some very emotional goodbyes Dorothy was on her way home, in no more than the time it took her to click her heels together three times and repeat to herself: "There's no place like home. There's no place like home. There's no place like home."

And then she was back, at home in Kansas, in her own room with Toto, her Auntie Em and Uncle Henry, the farm workers, and even the traveling Mr. Marvel. She regaled them with her adventures of Oz, but she was very glad to be home. And they were very happy to see her too.

How enlightening would it be if you could discover the theme of your previous lives?

The discovery of themes in your past lives allows for a real sense of clarity and an understanding of why you are here. If you and the members of your soul group are working towards a particular cause, then you may replay the theme again and again. I saw this so clearly in my own past lives, when I came back time and time again as a healer or a teacher of some sort. These themes explain why you are drawn to the same type of person or situation over and over again, either to redeem some lesson that needs to be learnt, balance some event or experience, or just fulfill your life purpose.

Does the life purpose remain the same in every life?

These same themes may be repeated again and again, although there may be many very different ways of being challenged on that theme and many different tests to overcome before you get it right. As each soul advances up the ladder of experience, the lessons become more intense and challenging, and the lessons in the lifetime itself are usually more prominent, more obvious, and happen at a much quicker rate.

How many different types of experiences does a soul have to go through to get it right?

That all depends on the soul. Some may have very few lives but manage to do what needs to be done quickly and efficiently; they may not want to keep coming back. They may decide that they would rather work in the spirit realms or in other dimensions, which is entirely up to them, but some souls really want to go for the full-on experience – trying out everything that is on offer. I think I was one of them.

In order to make some sense of it, you may wish to think of the soul as the owner of its very own DVD store. Now some souls, especially those that are fairly advanced, will only need to watch a select few movies to get the learning and the experience required before they can move on to the next level; they may choose to only look at love stories or action adventures. But some souls might need to go through every movie in the store to get the message and learn what they need to learn. Now each store is unique in itself, and yet it is made up of many different, contrasting movies, each one telling a different story, each one whole and complete in itself, and yet each one a part of the whole. One does not exist without the other. In order for the "store" and the lesson, the message or theme it is carrying to be fully realized every movie would have to be experienced, whether it is an action, drama, comedy, farce, violent, black comedy, sexual, love story, adventure, tragedy, or even just a short snippet of a film, like a trailer. What can be a little daunting to realize is that all of these films co-exist together – all at the same time; however, here on the earth plane we are only able to focus on one at a time – until you enter the realm of the unconscious, that is.

And so, each lifetime within the store needs to be experienced, and some will be more significant than others. In fact some of the stories may have very little significance at all, such as the ones where you led a very simple life and where not much happened; these ones can be discounted in past life work, which explains why people usually go to lives where dramatic things happened. These more dramatic lives are where the big lessons were learnt and can be incredibly valuable. And so, the earth can be perceived as a place of opportunity, where souls come to play out these great dramas, to learn the lessons that they need to allow them to move to a higher plane.

How does this work?

The fact that each soul carries with it the vibrations and the imprints of all its other lives explains how you access those past and future life memories; and once you tap into the collective unconscious, all you have to do is go to the library, the storehouse that is contained there, and choose whichever DVD that is relevant to you to put into the player. Then you can learn all you need to. And of course, there are movies and stories there that are set in the future – things that in your earthly time frame haven't even happened yet. You need to be aware that what you choose to do in your current life will have an impact on the outcome of those future lives, as well as the ones in the past.

Are you only able to see your own soul's stories in this place?

No, this system means that if you really want to you can explore the lives of any other souls, including the souls of those who were famous, for one reason or another; this explains why so many people over the years have claimed to have been Napoleon or Cleopatra. They may have experienced their lives, but it doesn't necessarily mean that they were them.

Can you do healing work on these souls while you are there?

It is sometimes possible for people to act as a proxy for other souls, in order to do any healing, or spirit release work, that is needed, whilst in this place, but only when permission has been granted by the soul or higher self of the soul, who is being healed.

If there is a predestined purpose to your life, are you at the mercy of fate, or do you really have free choice in your life?

You do have complete free will to choose the life you want to lead or whether or not to fulfill your life purpose. No one will stop you from doing whatever you want to do. However, many people choose their life paths not based on what they want to do but based on what is expected of them. Often parents and peers will have a huge impact on career choices. Upon leaving school the pressure is on to get an education, get a job that will provide a level of security, perhaps to get married and have a family. All this leaves little room for "following your bliss" as Joseph Campbell advised people to do. But if there is a life path that you were "destined to follow," and there really is a path that will allow you to be fulfilled at every level, wouldn't you want to know what it was?

Can you discover what your destiny, or life purpose, is by looking at the past?

Yes, you can get a really clear idea of what you are meant to be doing once you see what your mission was throughout your previous lives. In these lives you get to see what your strengths were, the unique talents that are carried with you from lifetime to lifetime, and once you see what they are you can put them to full use.

How can people recognize their own inner strengths?

I hear so many stories of people who have spent a lifetime totally unaware of their inner capabilities, and these same people usually take for granted the things that they are good at, focusing instead on what they can't do or what they have failed to achieve. It is always easier for people to talk about what hasn't worked in their lives than what has worked. Of course it is a good idea to take stock and become aware of the challenges and adversities that you have faced to learn the lessons that you need from them; however, time and consideration needs to be made to remember all of the good things that have happened, and the positive talents and skills that a person has or has had.

How can they be remembered?

The easiest way to remember positive inner resources is by remembering the times when you succeeded at things in the past or when you overcame adversity – remembering times when you refused to allow anyone or anything to get in your way. Remembering times when you pushed through and survived against all the odds reminds you of just how powerful you really are. It reminds you that you can be who you want to be in your life.

What kinds of different life purposes are there?

In the past many people had much less choice in the career paths that were available to them. Often their life, regardless of what their life purpose was, was already mapped out for them. They would follow what their families had done for generations before them, hence the commonality of names such as Smith or Baker. People were named after their occupations, and it was expected – certainly more so of the eldest children – that they would follow in the footsteps of their forefathers.

Some families saw the opportunity to achieve a certain status by entering their children into the priesthood or into a convent. The vocational search or spiritual journey was seen in many countries as something that would bestow blessings on the families involved. The navy and the armed forces were once thought of as the greatest opportunities. Today these are much less popular options, particularly the religious orders. People are no longer satisfied with the way some of these institutions are run and are staying away.

What about those who chose not to follow what the family decreed?

Some people were happier to just go with the flow, and some were determined, from an early age, to stand out from the crowd and do something different – whether it be something that is just radically different from their family before them or whether it is to really make a difference to themselves and the world. Today there is a lot more freedom, which on the one hand is great but on the other hand can lead to a lot of confusion and can lead many people to travel along pathways that are way off what their true life purpose really is.

What about those who choose slightly unrealistic life goals?

We see this more and more today, with the celebrity culture that has sprung up, and with the advent of TV shows like the *X Factor* and *Britain's Got Talent,* where thousands upon thousands of people appear with dreams of fame and fortune driving them on. Some are realistic, but sadly, many of them are completely unrealistic – their talents being something else entirely that they have yet to discover.

Does everyone have a particular life purpose?

Each person does have their own unique and special purpose, and whether you came here to sing songs, climb mountains, build bombs, heal people, have a family, or simply experience the beauty of living here on earth, it is ultimately your choice. Doing what you love has to be the key. Joseph Campbell said that if you did let go of fear and follow your bliss then you would be put onto the right track, a track that was waiting for you all along. And when you were on the right track you would meet the other people in your field of bliss, and the right doors would open for you – doors that would only open for you and not anyone else.

How can you be certain what your life purpose really is?

You can look for themes in your past lives or you might want to explore some of your more positive past lives to discover hidden talents you didn't even know that you possessed. When you relive these positive lives, it can help you to reclaim those skills and abilities.

What if you fail to recognize what your life purpose is?

Some of my clients discover that there was a mission in their past lives that did not get realized; they may have had a skill or a talent and they did not utilize it fully and as a result it got wasted. This can often create a burning desire to use that skill in the present life. Sometimes the person does utilize it and they get to step into the joy of their purpose and really embrace it.

What kind of impact can it have when people know what their life purpose is but it doesn't fit in with the world around them?

Sometimes the missions or lives with great abilities carry a heavy price, and great talents end up being unappreciated or even ridiculed and despised. Oftentimes there is jealousy and envy, and this can leave behind a residue that needs to be cleared. When you look at the lives of some of the most talented people that the world has known, such as Mozart, Beethoven, Galileo, and Van Gogh, you can see that the path was not always an easy one to travel.

Andy

What if someone discovers what their life purpose is but doesn't have time to complete it?

Sometimes the journey just gets cut short before people are ready to leave. This was the case with my minister, Andy, whom I mentioned earlier in the book. He came to see me because he was curious as to why he was so passionate about communicating and teaching people about the link between mind and body. He felt that he had some sort of mission to teach and could not understand where it came from as there was no one in his family that even remotely thought the same way.

He really wanted to know where these strong feelings had come from.

The journey began:

ME: What are you aware of?

A: I am a man, around 28 years old.

ME: Where are you?

A: I am in a tropical jungle; my feet are bare.

ME: What are you aware of?

A: I can see ahead of me a large mountain; actually it is not just a mountain, it is a volcano.

ME: Can you describe the scenery?

A: It is very lush and green here.

ME: Where is this volcano, what part of the world?

A: I am on a Fijian island.

ME: Is anyone else with you?

A: No, I am alone, and I am hunting for food for my family.

ME: Tell me about your family.

A: I have two boys; right now they are with their mother.

ME: What else can you tell me?

A: I am not local to this place.

ME: Where are you originally from?

A: My family and I arrived here on a large boat – a tall ship, with high sails.

ME: Where did the ship come from?

A: We set off from Southampton.

ME: Where were you going?

A: We were on our way to Australia, but when I saw the beauty of these islands I felt compelled to stay; it just felt so good here. I fell in love with the place, and I have never looked back.

ME: What was it about the place that you loved so much?

A: There is a wonderful sense of freedom here that I never experienced in my life before. The people are incredibly friendly, the sun shines most of the time, and even when it rains the rain is warm and the tropical storms are incredible to watch – really exhilarating.

ME: What do you do here?

A: I am very lucky that I have been accepted here. The local people are very open to new ideas. My role here is as a Methodist preacher; albeit that many of our ways in the West are different, the principles of loving kindness and respect for man and nature are the same.

ME: How do you get on with the local chiefs?

A: The chief supports me and is happy that I bring some order and, what he perceives as, civilisation to his land.

ME: What kinds of things do they support you with?

A: Happily they support me as I choose to build a small church, where we can gather to worship the Lord; it is one of my proudest endeavours and the locals do a wonderful job. Life here is wonderful, and I am so passionate about teaching these lovely people about God and his word.

He smiles and sighs contentedly.

ME: I want you to move on to the next significant event in this life.

A: I am about 50 years old now.

His voice has an edge of concern to it.

ME: What are you experiencing now?

A: I am having a confrontation with a Belgian settler.

ME: What is the confrontation about?

A: He is a very bitter man and is jealous of the success that I have made of my life here on the islands.

ME: What is he jealous of?

A: He feels that I have it all too easy, and he appears to have been drinking.

ME: How do you feel about this confrontation?

A: I am very sad that I cannot appease him.

ME: What happens next?

A: Before I can react he pulls a musket out from his shirt and he shoots me in the chest.

ME: What happens next?

A: It is over!

ME: What are you aware of now?

A: I am floating out now, and I am feeling a huge sense of frustration that it ended too soon; I was living such a great life and felt that my role was really important.

ME: How were you feeling at the end?

A: I felt very sad that it had to end like that.

ME: From this higher perspective can you get a sense of why this happened?

A: This man was so caught up in his own misery that he couldn't bear to see my joy; he despised me because I was loved by the people, and he was too proud to listen to my sermons. He had decided that he would rather kill me than actually listen and take on board what I was saying about love and the possibilities of the great joys that were to be had on earth.

ME: What can you learn from this?

A: That for some people life can be very sad. I see now that he was a man that had a lot of fear; he just didn't know how to show it, and his anger was his front.

ME: Let's invite him in; what would you like to say to him?

A: I would want to tell him that there was nothing to fear, that he had so much potential but he failed to recognize it and that if only he had stopped to listen, I could have been a friend; I could have helped him.

ME: Are you able to forgive him for ending your life in the way that he did?

A: Yes, I can let that go now.

ME: How does he respond when you forgive him?

A: He is crying and is really sorry for what he did. He can see now that it was wrong and that I could have been a good friend to him if he had let me.

ME: Are there any negative emotions that you are holding onto?

A: I feel very sad for the family that I have left behind. I wanted more time there; it really was paradise.

Andy was able to reconnect with the people who had been his family and apologize for leaving them. They told him that it had not been his fault and that he had nothing to apologize for; he was able to forgive himself and release the residue of sadness that had been held for so long.

ME: Can you tell me what the main lesson was for you in this life?

A: My mission was to learn to understand fear in others, to really recognize the power that fear can have.

ME: Did you learn this?

A: Not completely. I don't think I was able to see how others felt as I was so in love with everything and everyone at the time.

ME: What else were you supposed to learn?

A: It was about courage, the courage to stand up and speak my truth, and it was about living life fully and passionately.

ME: And did you succeed in this?

A: Yes, I found my voice in that life, and I did stay true to what I believed in, right until the bitter end.

When Andy woke up he recognized the feelings of wanting to speak out and share what he had learnt with others – the real passion that he still felt for his work. He had always had a desire to travel, and he now travels around the world running workshops and yoga retreats; he recognized that if he had done it once he could do it again. Only this time he is free to return back to London whenever he wishes, air travel having made the world so much easier to navigate these days. After the session he decided to investigate the Fijian islands on the Internet and was staggered to find that there was an island in the region that had a volcano on it.

Even more astoundingly he found that a Methodist church had been built there in the year 1860, the very year that he found himself there. It was the earliest church in Fiji, and it is still there to this day. He found photographs and was able to verify that it was exactly the same as he had seen it in his session.

Brian

Brian, who we met at the beginning of this book, had come for a session because he was having trouble determining what he was meant to do with his life; he just wasn't quite sure that he was on the right path and wasn't convinced that he trusted his instincts when he thought about what he wanted to do versus what he thought he should do.

He had grown up in an Irish family where men were men and had to be tough. He had battled with his father many times over the years, but one of the biggest things that they had fought about was his boxing abilities. As a young man he had demonstrated great skill in the ring, but no matter how hard they pushed him to go for it, something somewhere within him always prevented him for going for the kill and he would often walk away from a fight rather than finish his opponent off with the killer blow they all knew he was capable of.

He was deeply unhappy with his career; he worked as a sales rep for a courier company and spent his days trawling around to different companies trying to persuade them to give his company their business. It was no easy task. What made things worse was that his passion lay somewhere else entirely.

Some years beforehand he had been viciously attacked and stabbed several times; the knife had punctured his heart each time. He was rushed to hospital where the surgeons told his family that there was little hope of him surviving the night. He did survive and was told that he would have to have surgery to repair the damage to his heart. The doctors told him that the recovery period could be as long as a year and that he would have to take it easy and rest. Not being a patient man, he soon got bored of the hospital and vowed to be home in a few months in time for Christmas. The doctors laughed and said it would be impossible; however, he had improved so much so that they decided to do a scan and assess how much damage was left to repair.

When they checked the results they were astounding. Within just a few short weeks Brian's heart had completely healed itself. The holes had all closed up, and they were looking at a perfectly normal healthy heart. Brian packed his bag and went home. From that point onwards they referred to him as "the miracle man." He grew very curious as to how this "miracle" may have occurred; he was not the most deeply religious man, so he was not convinced of a heavenly intervention.

He did, however, on his travels meet a man who opened up a whole new world for him. He was an ex-military man who had by chance met a healer who had changed his life. He in turn was to change the whole way of life for Brian; he introduced him to Reiki, a hands-on healing process, and Brian felt that he had finally found something that made sense to him. His ability to heal went from strength to strength and soon he was being called upon to heal both animals and humans alike.

The results were astounding: remissions of cancer, chronic pains simply disappearing. He became very sought after, but the one thing that got in the way was that no one in Brian's world, his friends or his family, really believed in what he was doing. They thought it was psychic mumbo-jumbo, and they refused to take it seriously. As a result, Brian himself had doubts and so he would only offer his services for free during the evening and weekends.

This meant that by day he was still travelling the lengths of the country trying to generate business for something he had no interest in. He was tired and he was confused; he could not see that his healing work could be any more than a hobby, even though he felt so passionately about it. Doing the work for money seemed wrong, and he had a very strong feeling that he was letting his family down. He really wanted to know what his destiny was; why was he here, was there something that he really was supposed to be doing with his life?

The journey began:

ME: What are you aware of?

B: I am a man, 33 years old; I am wearing sandals of dark leather and a long robe.

ME: Where are you?

B: I am in the woods searching for herbs to use for medicine.

ME: What year is this, and what country are you in?

B: It is 1872 and the place is called Viola, in Italy. I live in a village with many people.

ME: What is your role here?

B: I heal their wounds, especially the soldiers, when they have been attacked.

ME: Who is attacking you?

B: We are at war with France. Oh, the children! They kill the children.

He is upset as he speaks.

B: It is wrong, it is so wrong. I have to bring the medicine back.

ME: I want you to move to the next significant event.

The scene shifts.

B: I am in a castle courtyard in the mountains, watching…watching the burning.

ME: What is burning?

B: They are burning the Protestants; it is horrible, cruel.

ME: Who is burning them?

B: It is the authorities from the Church.

ME: Why have they brought you here?

B: The soldiers brought me here to train me to fight. I say, "NO! I don't want to fight!"

ME: How do they respond when you say "no" to them?

B: When I tell them they laugh; I end up having to fight with them just to leave me alone.

He sighs.

ME: What happens next?

B: They lock me up for almost three years, and when they release me I am so angry; I run away, to the forest, I hide in the trees. I am hunted. It is horrible, but I realise I can do some good; I can protect those that are being persecuted.

ME: And what happens in this time?

B: The soldiers come through the forest with their prisoners, and I ambush and kill them – freeing the Protestants. I get to set them free.

ME: What happens to them after this?

B: There are lots of children; some of them stay with me. I am almost 30 now, and it is good here, yes good. I stay and help them until they grow, and then the children can fight; then they can leave.

ME: What happens next?

B: It is time for me to leave and so I go home.

He grimaces slightly at the thought.

ME: What are you aware of now?

B: I am inside the castle. I can see my father, his name is Leonard; he is the ruler here.

ME: What are you doing here?

B: I am tending to him; I have come home but it is too late. He is dying, and even though I know that he was wrong, what with all that killing, I am still sad.

ME: What are you sad about?

B: I am sad that even at this point, at the end of his life, he is still trying to insist that once he is dead I fight the Protestants.

ME: How do you respond?

B: I say "no," but he just doesn't understand.

ME: What is it that you want?

B: What I want is peace; I am filled with such a great sadness. In their blind hatred they killed so many children; they paid no heed to the future, to the new generations who could live together in harmony. All they care about is riches and gold and silk and horses and armies – not people or God!

ME: What is it that you care about?

B: I care about people, about our connection, about God; I care about peace and love, and acceptance and friendship. We are all the same people, all God's children, all equals.

ME: I want you to move to the next significant event in that life.

B: There are many people. I am in church; I am being crowned. There is an air of excitement.

ME: What else are you aware of?

B: All around me there is a sense of peace – people peaceful, quiet, no more begging, no more people starving.

ME: What has happened to change things?

B: It has all stopped because of the new farms. I gave land to the people, and they are happy. But the priests are walking away; they are angry, and many of them are leaving.

ME: Why are they leaving?

B: They are angry with me because without the land and the wealth that went with it they have no power, not any more – their way won't work.

ME: Tell me what happens next.

B: Time moves on; I can hear horses coming.

ME: Who is coming to you?

B: It is a contingent from Rome, from the pope; he has sent the army.

ME: Why has the pope sent his army to you?

B: The church wants our gold.

ME: What do you decide to do?

B: My men want to fight but I say "no"; I want to deal with this the peaceful way. I offer forgiveness to these men who come and loot and steal and take what is not theirs to take. I can only pray to my God, to my loving God, that he will spare us.

ME: What happens next?

B: There is chaos and mayhem as these men destroy our homes and steal everything of value. Men are slaughtered, and the women and children are running for cover.

ME: How does this make you feel?

B: I am unmoved and still I will not fight.

ME: What happens next?

B: My family turns on me with contempt, especially my son; he implored me to let him train, to let him prepare an army to save us from such a fate, and I had said "no" to him too. I wanted him to understand the principles of loving kindness and to see that all this fighting was unnecessary.

ME: How does he respond to the attack?

B: I stay his hand and we can only watch as they take it all. My heart is heavy for their loss, but I am certain in my heart that this is the only way; I will not take a life in exchange for the riches of a court.

ME: What about your people? How do they respond?

B: People are leaving because of the army; they are afraid that they might return. Those that are left are very sad.

ME: How does this make you feel?

B: I am heartbroken; what had promised to become a wonderful place to live has become a nightmare. My son and the people believe I am weak and can't fight; but I will not fight.

ME: What happens?

B: We struggle on, but there is little left for us to survive on; the soldiers took our livestock and raided our cellars. All around me I hear the cries of death. My children are crying in the castle. They are struck with a terrible fever, my son, Roman, and three daughters, Isabelle, Amy, and Cherie.

ME: What about your wife?

B: My wife, Grace, is already dead; she died of the fever already. I tried to save them but I just could not do enough. I feel ill now too; I am tired and so sorry that I have failed them all.

My last thought as I die is how much I loved them all.

Brian was able to speak to his son and tell him he was sorry that he had not been able to do things his way. His son apologised too. He saw that war and fighting was not the answer and realised that far too much pain was caused by it. He discovered that they were from the same soul group and that they had been working through a series of lives where they were tested to see if they would stay true to their spiritual values and continue to use their healing gifts. Brian saw that even though he had suffered considerable loss in his own family, he had saved many lives, and all of these souls came to thank him. His spirit guide also appeared and told him that it was now time for him to reclaim his healing gifts, that there were people who would need his services. He was told that doing a normal day job was no longer going to be appropriate and that he should trust that all would work out fine. He was going to be protected and watched over, and he had many beings that were going to be helping him from now on. He was told to let go of his guilt and all of the fears he had around being a healer and to get on with it. That it was time.

Once the session was over Brian decided to explore whether any of the details that he had talked about in the session made sense; he had never heard of the place he mentioned and was not at all sure that it really existed. The dates for burning Protestants seemed wrong too. He was worried that perhaps he had just been making it all up. He was amazed to discover that Viola is a town in the centre of Italy and was even more astounded when he found a document that stated that the last of the Protestants had headed into central Spain and Italy to escape the end of the inquisition around the year 1872.

Since the session Brian has made huge changes to his life. His healing work has gone from strength to strength. In fact, as the time went on and his abilities grew he found that he had the ability to do psychic surgery. His acclaim began to spread far and wide, and soon he was inundated with patients who had been recommended to him. He had been forced to recognize that there was a need for his particular skills and that in order to proceed he would have to allow it to become his main focus. He quit his job at the courier company, sold his flat, and began to travel around the world providing healing for those that needed it. He now has a very successful business as a healer and continues to travel all over the world with his healing work. His life's purpose was discovered and is now, thankfully, fully embraced.

EXERCISE 9: *Purpose in Life*

PART 1: Make a list of all your successes and achievements from your life, all the things that you have done that you are proud of, no matter how small or seemingly trivial. It may be things like:

1. passing your exams,
2. your driving test,
3. buying your first home,
4. buying your perfect car,
5. the birth of your children,
6. getting a job that you love,
7. learning how to cook your favourite meal,

8. when you won at sports,
9. having and raising a child,
10. maintaining a relationship, or
11. going to that holiday destination that you always wanted to visit.

Everyone has at least some small thing that they can feel proud of, and if they don't then it is high time that they began to think of the kinds of things that would make them feel proud and make sure that they happen before it is too late and time here runs out. It really doesn't matter what the thing is – it is the feeling of success that goes with it that counts.

PART 2: Why Are You Here? Ask yourself some questions:
1. Who am I really, have I been here before, and why am I here now?
2. What kind of mission did I choose before I got here?
3. What did I dream about doing when I was a child?
4. What, who, and where do I love?
5. What am I passionate about and why?
6. What, potentially, is my life purpose?
7. Is there something that I agreed to do before I arrived here?
8. Who are my soul group, and are any of them with me now?
9. Have I met my soulmate or even soulmates?
10. Who are these people in my life, and why are they here?
11. What can I do to really be the best version of myself?
12. What, if anything, can I do to help the planet and ensure that our life here can be sustained?

10

How Can You Reach
Your Full Potential?

At the very start of the film, when Dorothy chose to walk past the challeng-ing and difficult Miss Gulch and Toto took it upon himself to run into her garden in order to bite her, a whole train of events were put into motion: Dorothy running away, her failure to reach the tornado shelter in time, and the subsequent adventure that she experienced in Oz.

In this transformational journey she was challenged and learnt more than she could ever have imagined about what was really important to her, which was that everything she ever needed was already inside her – all she had to do was take the time to go inside and look. But was Dorothy, the vibrant and curious girl that she was, really destined to live her whole life in grey, dusty Kansas, without ever really being challenged or learning about life and love and her real hearts desires, without ever finding out what she needed to be happy? As the hero of the story, the answer has to be…probably not!

So what is the true route to finding happiness?

When you make the decision to find your life purpose, you set off on a quest along your own metaphorical "yellow brick road"; this is a road of learning and discovery, a road filled with adventures, where you will get to live more fully, more vibrantly, and have a greater chance of reaching your highest potential. On this journey of life you have a choice about whether or not to learn all you can about who you are, why you are here, what can be learnt from all that has gone before, and what you are going to do with the time that you have left in your current life.

You have the chance to find a sense of contentment and fulfillment and real inner freedom and in doing so can show the world that this state of being really is possible. Being the best that you can be and living your life to your highest potential does not mean that you need to climb the highest mountains or run the longest marathons or become a world leader; creating a happy family, doing rewarding work that you love, and creating a beautiful garden is as valuable as is keeping the streets clean. Whatever your chosen path may be, it is your state of mind that counts. Often all you have to do is to open up your imagination, find ways to reframe your unhelpful thoughts and feelings in a more positive manner, and learn how to reconnect to all the wonderful resources that are already within you. Once you learn how to view the world with more positive eyes, so much more becomes possible. When you begin to focus on your goals and plan for them in a logical and sensible way, then – and only then – can your dreams really begin to come true.

What is the most important thing to be aware of once you decide to go for your dreams?

You need to learn that *all of your thoughts matter*. Your thoughts are the most important tools you have to change your life. Your power to change and live your dream is held within your imagination.

How can you use your imagination to help?

Your life is like a book; your experiences are what fill the pages. You can choose to write the script as you want your life to be. All you have to do is to change your thoughts and you start to change your reality. Your thoughts and beliefs determine how you are going to feel and how you are going to respond to all of the people and the situations in your life. Only you are responsible for all of your feelings. You choose how to respond, how to act, or how to react to people and the circumstances of your life, which means that no one can ever do anything to you against your will. You can choose whether to clear the past, plan the future, or just go with the winds of chance – hoping that they blow you in a direction that you will enjoy. You can choose. You can decide. You are responsible for your life and everything that happens to you. No one else! *And all of your thoughts matter!* It is up to you to make them work for you.

How can you make sure that you master your thoughts?

As I explained to you at the start of this book, you are a product of your past experiences; everything that you have ever known is stored away at the back of your mind and is having an impact on every thought you have about yourself and your future. The patterns and the clues you need to help you discover your life purpose are right there, contained within the story of your life. Being able to identify these beliefs and patterns can help you to become free of the limitations that may have been imposed, so it is a good idea to do a regular check-up on the story of your life so far – just like an MOT for the soul.

Suzy

How can visiting a past life help you to achieve your full potential?
Your past lives can reveal hidden strengths and show you what you are really capable of, once you set your mind to it. Suzy came because, as a very successful business woman who had created a very comfortable life for herself, she was curious as to why she felt so driven to compete in a very male business world – a place where she often had to work doubly hard to prove herself. Her drive and determination was leading her to achieve more and more victories over the men in her world, but there were moments when she was unsure whether she was doing the right thing and she felt that sometimes – just at crucial moments – she would back down and not live up to what she knew to be her highest potential. She really wanted to see what her highest potential really was.

The journey began:
S: I'm in a cave; my name is John, I think.
She paused and shook her head as if uncertain.
S: It is something like that.
She seemed a little confused.
ME: What are you doing here?
S: I am fighting; it is a war between Greece and Turkey.
ME: How do you feel about the fighting?
S: I am feeling proud that I am here.
ME: What are you doing in the cave?
S: My men are hiding in this cave so that they can have a rest; some of them are injured.
ME: Are you in charge of many men?
S: I have many men below me, around two hundred; but I am not in charge completely. There is someone in authority above me.
ME: Can you tell me about the men?
S: Some of the men are very young and they are scared; they need me to be their strength. One of them is dying; he is very frightened.

ME: What can you do for him?

S: I can only comfort him and encourage him; I try to give him some sort of peace.

ME: How do you do this?

S: By kneeling by his side and letting him know that I am there for him; he wanted to die for his country, but now he is scared. I tell him that he should be proud, that he has fulfilled his ambition.

ME: What happens next?

S: Other soldiers are coming in now; the enemy is advancing. We have to go back and fight; we grab the torches as it is dark in the cave, and head for the horses.

ME: What will happen to the young man?

S: He is at peace now; we have to leave him where he is. I cover his face with his cloak and we head off; there is no time to look back. We charge into battle.

ME: Tell me what happens in the battle.

S: Some of the men are knocked off their horses, and the battle is violent and bloody.

ME: What is the outcome of the battle?

S: We win the battle; I knew we would.

ME: How were you so sure?

S: It was no real heroism, we just did what had to be done; I am sorry for those lives that we lost, but I am glad for the ones that are okay.

ME: Can you tell me about your relationship with the men?

S: The men all look up to me, but I am just doing what I have to do; this is just another day. But they are grateful for our survival; they are patting me on the back.

ME: How does that make you feel?

S: I feel proud; it is a good feeling to be looked up to in this way. Although for me, it is just another battle and another day.

ME: If you feel that way, why are you fighting?

S: I thought that I had done the right thing joining the army.

ME: What made you decide to join in the first place?

S: I am all alone; I have no family, no one close. That's why I joined.

ME: How do you feel about that?

S: I don't really think about it.

ME: what happens next?

S: We are sitting around a fire, eating, laughing, and drinking; I check around the camp to make sure they are okay. I feel a bit removed from it all though, a bit empty; it feels just like any other day and it shouldn't. We have had a great victory.

ME: What is it that you need?

S: I need to find some sort of fulfillment.

ME: I want you to move on to the next significant event.

S: I am at a banquet; there is lots of laughing and drinking and noise.

ME: What is the banquet in aid of?

S: It is a celebration.

ME: Who are you celebrating with?

S: I can see the emperor, the Roman emperor; he is wearing a white robe and a red cloak. He has a wreath around his head and is drinking out of a big goblet, drinking red wine; on his finger he is wearing a big ring. There is much laughter.

ME: What is the celebration for?

S: The Roman emperor has just crowned me; he has just made me pope. It is such an honour and yet, it is strange, there is no one here of any significance for me.

ME: How old are you now?

S: I'm still quite young, in my early twenties.

ME: How are you feeling about the celebrations and your success?

S: I feel as though I have done well, but it's almost as if it is not real or maybe it just doesn't feel the way I thought it would; something is missing.

ME: Can you tell me what is missing for you?

S: I have success in society's terms, but I think it's about belonging; there is no one special to feel proud of me. People are pleased for me but there is just no one significant. It's a bit weird, all this power; I should have someone significant to share it with.

She begins to look a little confused.

ME: What is it that you are finding strange?

S: It's weird. I'm not sure that I am a man. Something is weird; it's like I'm playing a man but I am not a man. It's confusing me.

ME: Take a closer look at yourself and tell me what you are aware of.

S: Oh, I am a woman; it's just that I couldn't do this as a woman.

ME: Do what as a woman?

S: Travel, fight, be in the army, and now come to power as a pope; I had to pretend, that is why there is no one significant, no lover in my life; I am a woman but I am better, in many ways, than all of the men here.

ME: What makes you better than the men?

S: People rely on me to make their decisions; I have a great mind for strategy and structure. I can do all of that.

ME: So what are you sad about?

S: I am lonely; I am somewhere that I shouldn't be and really I am a bit of a misfit; it's a bit like playing a part.

ME: What made you decide to play this part?

S: I played it knowing that I was worth so much more. I wasn't ever going to be satisfied with an average life, I needed some sort of recognition. I also needed to prove my ability and my worth; I did that – I achieved huge success but now it doesn't really feel like it.

ME: Why does it not feel good now, what have you realized?

S: I was doing it for all the wrong reasons, and I am bound to get found out at some point.

ME: Is anyone aware of your secret?

S: No, no one knows just yet, although I think that my right hand man is suspicious.

ME: I want you to move to the next significant scene.

S: I am on a horse.

ME: Where are you?

S: Outside, in the town. It is a procession of some sort; there is lots of blood.

ME: What has happened?

S: I have given birth to a child whilst on my horse as I parade through the streets.

ME: Is anyone there with you?

S: My right hand man is there; he says that he will protect me, he tells me that he loves me and that he will keep the secret.

ME: What is the secret?

ME: What is happening now?

S: The blood is flowing out of me; I am getting weaker and weaker.

She sighs deeply.

ME: What is happening now?

S: That's it….it's over.

ME: How do you feel as you leave the body?

S: Death brings a sense of peace but not release. My last conscious thought as I leave that lifetime is that nobody knew the real me and that I never got to own my own power. The people would never know the real truth because my lover kept his secret; he never shared my vision of greatness with the others. And my name wasn't John, it was Jeanne.

ME: How do you feel now as you view this?

S: I am aware of that real lack of fulfillment – a real juxtaposition between success in society and the failure that was felt as a human being. I was hailed as a hero on the outside but on the inside I was in pain and afraid of being judged.

ME: What was the karmic lesson in that lifetime?

S: It was about being great, about giving everything, doing your best, despite your birthright; in other words, being whatever you wanted to be.

ME: Did you accomplish that?

S: Not quite. I nearly got there but I slipped at the end. That drive is still there within me.

ME: What beliefs did you hold about yourself in that life?

S: I had a strong belief that I had to be someone; I wasn't going to get what I wanted being a woman, so I had to play a part. It was as though I was born into the wrong body, although I can see now that this was part of the test.

ME: What did you need to learn from this?

S: I needed to know that if I really believed in myself then it was possible to have it all.

ME: And what do you need to believe now?

S: I need to believe that I can be accepted as I am and still have it all. Man or woman, it really doesn't matter.

ME: Is there anyone that you recognize from that lifetime that you know in your current life?

S: Oh Lord, I see that my brother, in this life, was my right hand man, my secret lover.

ME: Does this have any bearing on your relationship with him now?

S: He was the only one, then and now, who really knows the real me; he believes in me more than I do in myself.

ME: Was there any agreement between you before you came into these lives together?

S: He came to support me and remind me what I am capable of.

ME: What is the most significant thing about this for you now?

S: I can still remember the determination I had in that lifetime, the feeling that I would not let anything stop me – not even being born as a woman. I still have that tenacity and strength, and I can draw on that whenever I need it.

She smiled.

S: It feels really good knowing that is there; it makes me feel that I can get what I want.

After the session Suzy was amazed at the story that had emerged; to her it seemed to be incredibly far fetched, and she was struggling to see how something like this could have happened in the realms of history without there being some kind of reference to it. She went onto the Internet and typed in the word "pope" and the name "Jeanne." She discovered that in the year 850 AD there had indeed been a pope Joan or Jeanne, who had been masquerading as a man and who had died in childbirth whilst on her horse.

In fact for centuries, as a result of this, there had been a very important addition to the pope's coronation: A marble chair had been specifically designed with a large hole cut out in it and the newly crowned pope was forced to sit in the chair and allow members of the clergy to view him from below to ensure that he was indeed a man. Engraved onto this chair, in Latin, were the words "He has testicles and they hang well." The practice continued on for many centuries. Thankfully, it is no longer still in use. Since the session Suzy has reported that she feels even stronger, and her consultancy business has reached greater heights than ever before. She has recognized that her talents and skills are just as powerful as any man's, and she is now going for whatever she wants.

Sara

Sara came to see me as she was really in need of a spiritual MOT. She was torn between her successful career in the corporate world that provided her with a much appreciated healthy wage and her real love, which was her role as a homeopath. As a result of the challenges she was being faced with every day from the pharmaceutical world and the governments trying to do away with alternative practitioners, homeopaths in particular, she was at a point in her life where she was not sure which way to go. At one level she knew that the healing was the right way, but the fear of survival and the ability to generate the money she needed to survive was another matter altogether. As we dug a little deeper into the feelings that came up for her she became aware of a belief that she was afraid that she would fail, that she was not good enough, and that speaking the truth was dangerous. It was time for her to let this go so she could get onto her true path, step up to her highest potential, and do the work she was sent here to do.

The journey began:

ME: What are you aware of now?

S: I am outside, alone in a field. I am wearing moccasins and a velvet dress. I am 21 years of age, and I am in Norway. I have very long red hair.

ME: What year is it?

S: It is 1843.

ME: What are you doing here in this field by yourself?

S: I have come to be alone. There is a celebration going on in the town, and I do not want to be a part of it. There are tents and coloured flags.

ME: Why are you not celebrating with the others?

S: Because I am sad. I want to be out here in nature.

ME: Why are you sad?

S: My father is gone; he was killed. He was a good man, an inventor. He was a genius and they killed him because he was doing good work. He knew stuff; he was into magic.

ME: Who killed him?

S: Soldiers were sent by the king; they stabbed him with their swords just because he was able to invent things that would help to heal people. He created lights and knew about herbs and food that could keep people well. He was ahead of his time.

ME: Why was this a problem?

S: The king didn't want people to have this knowledge; knowledge means power, and he needed to keep the power for himself. I feel so angry. Not at the soldiers – I know it was not their fault; they were just carrying out orders, but I do not want to be a part of this society. I don't fit in anyway.

ME: Why not?

S: I see things that they can't and it upsets them sometimes. They treat me as though I am odd. Some of them try to be kind, but they just don't know how to deal with me.

ME: Who do you live with in the village?

S: I live with my grandmother. We have a simple house but it serves us well.

ME: What are the people celebrating?

S: There is a marriage; one of the princes. I am not going; I don't want to be one of their slaves.

ME: What happens next?

S: My friend comes to find me; he cares about me. Oh my god, I can see that he is my brother now.

ME: Tell me about your friend.

S: He has come to tell me not to be so sad. He wants me to come and play and have some fun. He tells me off for always being so serious. I feel dearly connected to this boy. Thank goodness he is around, and it is a joy to know that he has come back to be with me again in this life. I am very lucky.

ME: And then what happens?

S: We are going back to the village; he gets me a toffee apple, and we play some games. He is so strong and kind; when others take the "mickey" out of me he always defends me.

ME: What do you do with your time here in the village?

S: I help people, secretly. I help to heal them and I see things for people. They don't tell each other that they come to me – it is all hush-hush. There is one girl in particular; she is young and blonde and very lovely. She had a strange sickness and couldn't walk, and I have managed to help her to get well. She doesn't say much; she just giggles a lot. I like her a lot.

ME: Good; tell me what you are aware of now.

S: It is night-time; we are sat around the fire, people are still celebrating and laughing. I feel better now. I don't dance but my friend Jay is with me. He tells me it will all be okay. When it gets very late he walks me back to my grandma's and I go to sleep. She is very old and she is a very practical woman. She works hard and she is very grounded – just as well as I am not very grounded at all.

ME: What happened to your mother?

S: My mother died when I was really young, and I never knew her. I think she died shortly after giving birth to me. The whole family helped to raise me – we were one big family.

ME: I want you tell me about the next significant thing that happens.

S: I am up in the mountains and I love it here; I feel so free. I love the feeling of freedom. I am collecting flowers and herbs that I will need and am connecting with nature and the animals. When I tune into nature she tells me what I need to get. I have a cave up here, a secret one where people come to see me. There are very ancient drawings on the walls. It is a powerful place.

Her face clouds over.

ME: What is wrong?

S: Something terrible has happened to the village. The soldiers have come and smashed everything up. A few of them manage to get away and find me in the cave. Jay is there; there were a few people with me in the cave and altogether there are about 15 of us. Some of them have been wounded and so I start to prepare some tinctures. Jay doesn't get it, but he helps me anyway. He helps to grind the herbs. Some of the men had been out hunting when the attack happened, and some of the children had been playing away from the village. My grandma is not with them; she died at the village. I think she suffered from a heart attack as a result of the shock because it was so terrible what she saw. They killed most of the men, but many of the women were taken away in carts to be used as workers in the noblemen's houses. They claimed they were dealing with civil unrest, but there had been no challenges for them from our village.

ME: What will you do now?

S: We have to cross the mountains. We are hoping to find another village that will take us in; we have some simple provisions that we carry on our backs. Some of the men have brought drums and small instruments. We have cups and plates and as much food as we can carry. We survive by making fires, eating small animals and the plants that we find along the way. The music helps to uplift us as we go, and we try to raise our spirits by singing.

ME: And what are you aware of now?

S: It is snowy and cold. There is a place that is inhabited by Eskimos, a village in the snow. They have welcomed us in and have prepared fish for us to eat. They do not speak the same language so it is a little difficult, but we stay as we have nowhere else to go.

She starts to sob.

ME: What is wrong?

S: Jay didn't make it; he couldn't handle the travelling and the cold; he got sick and died. He left me.

ME: And then what happens?

She settles down.

S: I get married to one of the men and I have a baby. But it is the life of an outcast again. I feel cut off. I miss my home, and I don't get to do the things that I used to love. No more mountains and herbs and freedom. I lost everyone that was important to me, and I just have to live the life of an outcast. I am not connected to my husband and I feel so alone – even with my baby.

ME: Let's move to the next significant event.

S: My baby is 8 now. She is amazing; she fits in here in this society perfectly. I still don't fit in, with my red hair and my pale skin. But she is dark like them, and she is going to be alright. They are good people; it is a simple life.

ME: And what happens next?

S: She gets married and is happy. No one disturbs us here; it is safe. I am old now; they call me a wise woman. I feel safe, but I still miss the world and feel so cut off from it. I was too frightened to leave in case the soldiers came again, but I do miss my homeland. I missed out on so many opportunities, but I never felt as though I had a choice. In the end I just got old. I lived until I was 89 and I died surrounded by my family and lots of grandchildren. I felt a lot of love and kindness and was able to go to sleep and just not wake up.

ME: What was the last thought that you had as you left that life?

S: That I didn't live my life fully.

ME: What were the emotions that you took with you?

S: There was a lot of grief and sadness at the loss of my family and my dear friend. I lost all the people that I was truly connected to. I know that I should have left there but I was too afraid. I chose to marry someone that I didn't love for the security, and I know that if I had been brave and carried on with my travels things could have been very different.

ME: I want you to find out what the karmic lesson was that you had chosen to experience in this life.

She takes a big breath at this point.

S: Oh, I had chosen to experience loss. It was all part of the plan.

This recognition was powerful for her as she had been wondering why all the bad things had happened in this life, and now it all made sense. This meant that she was able to heal her heart – the heart that had been shut off as a result of all the pain she had experienced. Once she saw that she had been responsible for choosing this path she saw that the others involved, who she had blamed for her suffering, had just been playing their parts perfectly and she was able to let go and forgive them, and then she was able to heal her liver, which had been hardened from all the anger.

ME: I would like you to invite in your grandma now. What would you like to say to her that you were unable to say back then?

S: I love you.

ME: And how does she respond?

S: She tells me that she wishes she had been more kind; she did care about me, she just didn't always know how to say it or to show it. She thinks that what I did with the healing was good, not strange. She says I was just like my mum. She says that the challenge we set for each other was to not be afraid to speak our truths. She needed to learn acceptance, and I had to learn to stand up for myself. She is laughing now and saying that finally she does accept me, and I am speaking my truth so we no longer need that contract.

ME: Bring the contract in. What would you like to do with it?

S: I want to set fire to it.

ME: Good, go ahead and do this now. Once that is done, what would be a better contract for you to put in its place? What would be a better commitment to make to yourself?

S: It is safe to speak my truth; I am loved, and I am safe no matter what.

ME: Wonderful, let's write that onto a scroll that you can store in your heart centre so you always know where it is and can refer to it whenever you need it.

She is smiling now.

ME: What are you aware of now?

S: Grandma wants to hug me; she is free now too. She tells me that she loves me.

ME: Good, we can let her go now, and I would like you to bring in your father from that life. What would you like to say to him?

S: I am so proud of you; you were so courageous. I want to be more like you. You know that I loved you, but I want to tell you again.

ME: How does he respond?

S: He wishes that he had spent more time with me; he was so caught up in his work but he always loved me and I knew that. He is telling me that he is a member of my soul group and that we have had seven lives together. It was always the same theme: he was the strong one and I always wanted to emulate him instead of standing in my own power. I was always a little afraid to stand on my own two feet and own my own power.

ME: Is there any recognition of this soul in your current life?

S: Oh, my goodness, it is my homeopath; she is so amazing.

ME: And what was the contract between you?

S: He was supposed to learn to take time to love and care for people, and I was supposed to learn to not be dependent, to learn to step into my own power.

ME: Now that you understand this do you need to keep the contract running?

S: No, definitely not. I want to clear it now.

ME: Good, then bring it in and set fire to it. Now, what commitment do you want to make in its place?

S: I courageously step into my own power; I am worthwhile in my own right; I am free to be me.

ME: Excellent, and what is happening now?

S: He is holding both my hands and smiling, telling me that I have my own gift and he is thanking me.

ME: I would like you to ask him about your soul group.

S: He is telling me that there is a group of healers, 12 of them in total, and that four of us have chosen to return at this time. My homeopath is one of them, and I am not sure who the other two are at the moment; perhaps I haven't met them yet. He is blessing me now and telling me to remember to bring in the light. He says I am not alone and that his spirit will be with me every step of the way.

ME: I would like you to let him go now and bring in Jay. What would you like to say to him that you were unable to say before?

S: I love him and care about him; I want to say thank you for all he did for me. I am so grateful for all his support – in that life and in this. He is joking with me and says that I am daft, that of course he was going to support me – we are best friends. He is also a part of my soul group and we have had seven lives together; the theme is always of supporting each other.

ME: I want you to ask him if he had agreed to participate in helping you achieve the life lesson of experiencing loss in that life.

S: Oh, he says "yes," he wanted to stay and help me but it had been pre-agreed that he would go.

ME: What exactly did the agreement say?

S: It said that I was going to lose him and everything that was important to me. He was the last thing that went, and I was supposed to remember that I still had God's love. The test was to see if I could still fulfill my life purpose and step up to my highest potential, with nothing but my connection to God to get me through. I think I failed.

ME: Ah, but in the spirit realms there is no such thing as failure; there is only learning. Now that you understand this lesson, I suspect that this is also an agreement that you would like to let go of.

S: Oh, definitely, yes.

ME: So let's bring it in and set fire to it so that you are free from its power and it can no longer have any hold over you; you also release any impact this agreement may have had on any of your other lives, and this healing will reverberate through all of those lifetimes, clearing the way for greater success in the future. Now what would you like to commit to instead?

S: I can ask for help and receive it when I need it. It is okay to look after others and to look after myself. I can work with my guides and him to fulfill my purpose, and I can work with others to achieve my goals.

ME: What are you aware of now?

S: Jay is smiling. He is saying that now I am going to be unstoppable. He is very excited and thanks me.

ME: Good, we can thank him now and let him go because now I need you to bring in the soldiers that were responsible for killing your father and the people in the village. What would you like to say to them?

S: I forgive you. I know that you were just doing your job. They are bowing their heads now; they are all very sorry for what happened.

ME: How do they respond when you tell them that you forgive them?

S: They are very relieved and happy; they have carried this guilt for a long time. It is good that they can let it go. They are free now to move on.

ME: Wonderful. Now I would like you to bring in some assistance to help you; it might be your spirit guide or perhaps someone from the animal kingdom that will have strength and the qualities that you will need to deal with the leader who had sent out these orders to kill those you loved. Who do you want to call on?

S: I will call on my spirit guide and an eagle because the eagle had strength and power and has great insight.

ME: Good, then bring in the leader and tell me what you would like to say to him.

S: Oh, my god; it is my father in this life.

ME: What would you like to say to him?

S: I am angry. I know he is weak and can see that he was doing the best that he could, but he was deluded; being angry with him is not going to help.

ME: Ask him why he behaved this way; what did he want?

S: He wanted power and he wanted to please his superiors. He had his own agenda; he felt as though he had to take revenge on the whole world.

ME: I want you to float all the way back to his childhood and see what happened to him. What are you aware of?

S: He was very badly mistreated all his life, since he was very small. He was abused a lot and has a very low energy vibration as a result; there is so much pain in him.

ME: I want you to send a beam of love to this child; send it right into his heart centre where it can illuminate the little spark or light that is there within him; the light that he has forgotten that connects him to who he really is. And what happens now?

S: He is starting to glow a little and his dark heart is softening.

ME: And then what happens?

S: It is hard for him as he can feel the pain now; he was numb before and now he has great remorse for what he has done. He feels confused and lost.

ME: Now that he is sorry and you can understand why all of this occurred, are you able to let it go and forgive him?

S: Yes, I can.

ME: What was the agreement between you?

S: Mine was to learn forgiveness and his was to learn mercy. I am not sure whether he has completely gotten it but he is on the way.

ME: Okay, well let's bring in the contract and destroy it so that you are free of it forever.

S: Yes, please.

ME: Just watch as the words written on that contract go up in flames and notice how wonderful it feels to be free. What would you like to commit to as your new contract?

S: I see all beings compassionately; I have love for everyone and I see the divine in everyone.

ME: Perfect, and you can allow that contract to sink deeply into your heart centre too and allow all the healing that is needed, throughout this lifetime and any others that you are connected to, to begin. How does this soul respond to you now?

S: He says that he is sorry; he didn't know what he was doing really. He says that I should go and use my power to do good things, and he wishes that he had the sort of abilities that I have.

ME: Good, you can continue to send light into his heart centre so that his healing can continue at the appropriate rate for him. Let him go now, with thanks, and I would like you to bring in your daughter from that life. What would you like to say to her?

S: I want to tell her that I am sorry that I was so distracted; that I did care about her and love her. It was just hard to stay present. I do regret that.

ME: How does she respond?

S: She is very forgiving and always thought that I was just a little bit strange, although she is laughing as she says this. She loved me anyway. Oh lord, she is one of my sisters in this life.

ME: Are there any contracts or agreements that need to be changed?

S: No, not with her.

ME: Okay, good. I would like you to bring in your husband from that life. What would you like to say to him?

S: I want to say that I am sorry that I wasn't in love with him and that I did try to do my best; I just hope that I didn't stop him from marrying someone that he could really love.

ME: What does he say?

S: He says that it is all okay and that I mustn't worry. We were happy in our own way, and I gave him the freedom to be who he was. Others did not have that, and I gave him a beautiful daughter and many grandchildren so he is grateful.

ME: Good. Is there anyone else that you would like to connect with?

S: Yes, the blonde girl that I healed in the village.

ME: What do you want to tell her?

S: I want to tell her that I am sorry that she died in the village after we took all that time to get her well, just for her to be killed senselessly.

ME: What does she say?

S: She says that she is grateful for what we managed together and that I must let that go. Oh goodness, she is my little sister and we have come in with a huge contract.

ME: What was it?

S: I was not supposed to rescue her but love her as she was; to be kind to her but let her find her own strength. She was supposed to learn not to lean on me. Well, we have messed that up so far.

ME: Let's bring in the contract, shall we, and get rid of it? What shall we put in its place?

S: I will love my sister for who she is. I trust that she can take care of herself. It is not my job to change her; it is only my job to love and be kind to her. I can be detached from her issues and love her.

ME: Good, and you can take this message deep into your heart centre too so that you carry it with you at all times. Let the healing and the release begin. Now I want you to check and see if there were any negative beliefs that you had about yourself that you carried with you from that life.

S: Yes, I believed that I had to hide my abilities and my self.

ME: Okay, good. It is time to let that go now, so what would be a better belief for you to have?

S: That it is okay for me to be seen; that I can bring my talents out into the light and I can do my work openly.

ME: Wonderful. Now as you return back to your safe place there is going to be a guide there with a message for you. What do they say?

S: He says that I have done well and that I must be true to myself. He is saying that I am getting a lot of help and that I am not alone in this life. My guides are all watching out for me. I know that I have been called here to do this work, but it is up to me if I want to take up the challenge; I have free will. He says that all I have to do is allow myself to be courageous and I will get all the help that I need. I do have a choice but I have to trust that the work I have been assigned to do, on my healing path, is for the highest good – for everyone, not just for me.

The session came to an end. When Sara opened her eyes, she smiled and said, "Not much uncertainty there then about my life path or what I need to do to step up to my highest potential?"

I had to agree. When you find your path, there is little point in trying to fight it really. You just have to trust that it will all unfold perfectly. Sara left determined to focus her attention on making her alternative therapy practice work. I had no doubt that it would be a success.

So what about your life? How are you going to make sense of the patterns and the experiences that you have had so far? How can you begin to understand what your life lesson is this time around, and how can you discover your true life purpose? How can you ensure that nothing stops you from reaching your highest potential?

The best way for you to do this is to explore at the unconscious level, but before you do that it is really helpful for you to create a map of the journey of your life so far, the path that you have already walked. Then you can begin to understand who you are, the patterns that have appeared in your life, and the kinds of people that keep reappearing. Once you get a clear idea of what is working and what is not working, you will know what needs to change. Clearing away the people, and the habits, and the beliefs that no longer serve you means that you will be free to plan the rest of the journey and ensure that it is going to be the best that it can be.

This exercise can help you to start to see clearly who you have been and who you really are so that you are free to choose who you really want to be.

EXERCISE 10: *The Story of Your Life*

If you were going to create the film of your life, what genre would it be? A romance, a thriller, a drama, a comedy, an adventure, a tragedy, or perhaps a combination?

Having a new perspective and a different view of your life can help you to make sense of it all and help you to identify the patterns that were always there but were perhaps just a little too far out of conscious awareness for you to see them. It would be a good idea to take some time now to understand the story of your life, so that you know who you are, where you have come from, and who and what has influenced you so far.

It is so important for you to recall and remember the key things that have happened to you, the people and the challenges you have faced along the road of life that you have travelled so far, be it yellow bricks or not, and to make sure that the rest of your journey takes you where you want to go. Rumi, the Persian mystic, said that you should never be satisfied with listening to other people's stories and that you should unfold your own myth. I couldn't agree more.

THE STORY OF YOUR LIFE

Step One
Get yourself some large sheets of paper and some coloured pens.

Step Two
Get your lists of the key people and significant relationships that have appeared in your life and your list of the key experiences, good and bad.

Step Three
Get your lists of achievements and challenges.

Step Four
Draw a line that runs horizontally across the middle of the pages in yellow
pen if you have it; black will do fine if not. This is the time line, or the path
of your life.

Step Five
Mark the sheets out with the correct ages on them.
1. From birth to the time you were ten years old.
2. From 10 until 20.
3. From 21 until you were 30, and on in 10-year segments until you reach
   your current age.
The final sheets will be for your past lives and your future life.

   The past life sheet will enable you to mark out any other lives that you
have become aware of.

   The final sheet is to extend out until the date at which you estimate that
you may live until; just take a guess, the exact date doesn't really matter.
What you do with this sheet later will.

Step Six
Now begin to plot the details of your story along the path of life; add in
the peaks and the troughs, the highs and the lows. Good events above the
line and bad below. They will go as high or low as you feel is relevant to the
emotional impact you experienced at the time. If you have coloured pens
put:
1. Your childhood, family, and home life in red.
2. Your education and work life in orange.

3. Your achievements, successes, and failures in yellow.
4. Your relationships in green.
5. Your financial success in turquoise.
6. Your spiritual life in dark blue.
7. Moments of inspiration and epiphanies in purple.

Step Seven

Once you have charted your life, take some time to review it; perhaps you could allow a good and trusted friend to be a witness to it, to help you to identify the patterns, the good and bad, that you have repeated.

1. What are the main themes that appear?
2. What kind of a movie would this be?
3. If you were going to choose someone to play the part of your life, who would it be and why?
4. What types of people keep appearing?
5. What are the patterns contained within your life story?
6 What needs to change?
7. What could you do differently?
8. What kind of movie would you prefer to live?
9. What can you do to make positive changes happen?

When you are able to see the story of your life for what it really is, you get to be the master of your fate – not the victim of circumstance.

11

Can You Wish Your Way
to a Fabulous Future?

Dorothy, the Scarecrow, the Tin Man, the Cowardly Lion, my clients, and I learnt a huge amount about ourselves and our place in the world as a result of being brave enough to walk this path and see into the heart of who we really are. I invite you, as a result of reading this book, to really ask yourself questions, not just about your present life, but also about the other lives that you may have lived and to ponder on why you chose to be here now at this moment in time.

Often just pondering on these questions will allow insights to emerge, and you may wish to explore at a deeper level and find out for yourself what your past lives can teach you. You can use this information to help you to live the rest of your life in the most empowering way, because when you get a sense of who you really are and what you are really capable of there is nothing that can stop you. None of the old fears will hold you back, none of the old sabotaging behaviours, none of the old sabotaging inner voices, and none of the old negative beliefs. You will be free to choose the life you want to live, although sometimes the only difficult thing left is knowing which fabulous future to choose.

Often my clients come back for another session once they are clear because, although they now feel free to live the life they deserve, they are unsure of exactly what it is they want. The best answer for this is for them to explore their future lives, which they can do very easily once they are in the trance state.

How do future life sessions work?

About ten years ago I had a future life session with Anne Jirsch, one of the pioneers of future life progression. I subsequently trained with her and am now a director of her Past and Future Life Society. At the time I had just started working as a hypnotherapist, building up my practice and really enjoying the work that I was doing. I wanted to know if I was on the right path and where my work would lead me. In the session she took me 2 years, 5 years, and 10 years into the future, and then on to my next life.

In the two-year part of the session I saw myself teaching; I had many students who were all practicing hypnosis, the classroom was formal, and I was dressed in a suit – very unlike me.

In the five-year part I saw myself sat around a camp fire, with people singing and chanting; the energy was powerful and I felt a sense of real joy in this place. I was not sure of the exact location other than it was in the desert somewhere.

In the ten-year part of the session I saw myself on a stage, working with a large group, I was doing a workshop for Alternatives, one of the best Mind Body Spirit centres in London. I saw myself talking, sharing stories, and taking the group on a guided journey. At the end there was much hugging and smiling. I was very proud to be in this place. I saw myself with a book published and running retreats in various places around the world. Beyond that I saw a beautiful retreat centre where I worked with a team of incredible people; it was a place that inspired people to come from around the world to expand their awareness of themselves and to heal. This was a vision that was way beyond my wildest dreams.

In my next life, about 100 years into the future, I saw myself teaching energy work to young children. The world was a very different place; gone was the old order, and there was a return to a more natural way of life. Small communities that were self-sufficient – gone was the need for excess. Each had what they needed and no more, and the people were happy. I was teaching the children to utilize their own special gifts; they were each taught according to what they loved, and as a re-sult were able to excel in everything that they did. They were taught that they were all connected and that we were all a part of everything, that everything was energy. There was a big focus on harnessing the power of the elements – the sun, the wind, and water – to power homes and work spaces. As a result the environment was clean and the earth was able to provide, in abundance, all that was needed. It was a time of great peace and love.

The message that my future self gave me was that I should not wait until my next life to teach this work, that I should begin the journey at once; this way of sharing and educating was the right way and the message should be spread as soon as possible to a world that was in turmoil. I had not contemplated teaching at that time, but I awoke from the session with a determination to find a way; I didn't have to wait very long.

Within a few weeks of the session I received a call from Ursula James, one of my former lecturers. She had been teaching clinical hypnosis at medical schools around the country for some years and was in need of some new lecturers. She asked if I would be interested, and within a few months I began. It was extraordinary; the satisfaction of teaching hypnosis was immense but to be able to take it into the halls of Oxford and Cambridge, as well as many other universities was immense.

The students, who were sceptical at first, soon embraced the idea, especially when they found that their memories improved, they slept better, they were less stressed, and their exam results went up. Needless to say I went to work in a suit. I got very involved in the work I was doing and forgot about my session with Anne; a few years later I was invited on a Shamanic trip to Egypt, with a group of German NLP practitioners. We travelled from one energy site to the next practising different energy techniques and connecting with the wonders that Egypt has to offer. We travelled by jeep into the desert, where we camped for the night and it was only when darkness fell and the Bedouin began to sing and dance around the campfire that I remembered my session. It was exactly as I had seen it; it made dèjá-vu seem like an ordinary occurrence. I literally had shivers all over me when I realized that I had already experienced this scene. From there my focus on energy work continued, and I endeavoured to share it with the people that I came into contact with.

Ten years on, incredibly, I found myself presenting to Alternatives; I was running a past life workshop. There were indeed lots of hugs and much smiling at the end; particularly from me, still not quite believing that I was there – just as I had seen all those years ago. My first book is now in your hands, and my first retreats have already begun. I know that what I experienced that day has happened in my life exactly as I saw that it would happen. I am very excited about my future and the healing centre that I know is on its way, a place that will help people to learn more about the truth of who they really are and find the inner freedom they need to succeed.

Doing this work means that I have no fear for the safety of our planet as the future I saw was a very great improvement on where we are now. It was a world where people remembered to take care of themselves, but most importantly the planet and each other; it was such a powerful message. It was Joseph Campbell who said that when the people of the planet stopped thinking primarily about themselves and their own self-preservation, they would undergo a truly heroic transformation of consciousness, and he was right.

My future self spoke the truth, in the session, when she said, "Why wait?" I decided not to and my life changed within a very short space of time. Getting access to this information is like providing rocket fuel for your inner goals and desires, because once you have seen what wonderful things the future has in store, why would you wait? And once you are ready, the doors to opportunity open wide and you just step right on in. Future Life Progression is another incredible tool that can help you to decide where you want to go, but in the meantime you may just want to do the exercise at the end of the chapter. This is the one that I did when I needed to change my life, and it served me well.

How many people ever really take time out to stop and think about where their choices in life will lead them?

Not enough; as a result, they don't usually create a definite plan for their life or choose the goals that are important to them. Not doing this can be a dangerous thing. It means that they get caught up in the dreams and the goals of the people around them: family, peers, significant others. In my time teaching at medical schools all over the country, I spoke with many of the students about this and it was astounding just how many of them had no real interest in medicine; the dream of being a doctor belonged to their parents and, with no real thought of what they wanted for themselves, they went along with it for an easy life. Seven years' training is a long time to commit to something that you have no passion for. It is no wonder many in that field are not as enthusiastic about helping others as they might be – if their job was really their passion. So having a clear idea of who they are, what they want, what their passion is, and where their skills lie is hugely important.

How many people live their lives in quiet frustration, dreams of another life just below the surface?

Many of my clients come to see me at points in their lives where they feel the need for a change; where they are no longer happy or satisfied and they want to understand more about themselves and what is possible for them in the future.

I had one client who was struggling with her job; she was incredibly organized and conscientious, but she had great difficulty saying "no" to anyone, including her partner who gave her very little help around the home, even though they both worked the same long hours. She found that her work load was increasing by the day, she was exhausted, and she felt very overwhelmed by how much others expected of her. She knew that something had to change but was not sure how to go about it. It was time for her to explore her future life, five years on. As she floated into her most probable future she saw that she had married her partner, they had moved to the country, and she had two small children. He worked in the city and commuted every day, which meant only spending time with the children at weekends as they were already in bed by the time he got home and not yet up when he had to leave. They were living in a comfortable house and she was able to juggle her time around the children, running the home, and maintaining her part-time job. She was comfortable but felt a little stretched.

As I took her into her alternative future she found herself in the same house, same children, only this time she had more time on her hands. She had recognized her talents in the workplace and as a result had a much better job. This meant that she had more money and had employed someone to help with the house and the children. She felt much more empowered in this version, although she was not sure that she liked the idea of someone else spending so much time with her children. They did get to have nice holidays, and so there was more quality time as a family.

Then I took her into her most fabulous future. For my client it was a huge revelation; she saw herself in a much bigger house. This time she and her husband were working together, in all ways; keeping the house and running a business – something that she had often thought about but had never believed was possible. They worked from home most of the time and were able to schedule their hours around the children, meaning much more quality time as a family.

When I asked her what had changed in order for this to be a possibility she laughed and said, "I started saying no; I recognized how good I am at running things, whether my home or my job, and decided to use those skills to create my own business." Then she laughed and said, "The first thing that changed was that I told my partner in no uncertain terms that he was to start helping out – with the cooking and the cleaning and the ironing – and he said he only let me do it all because he was afraid that I would think he was not good enough at it. I see now that I am a bit of a perfectionist and would rather do things myself than them not be perfect; time to let that one go."

When she came out of the trance she was very excited, having stepped into that life for that short time she had experienced how good it felt to be in control of her life, to have her own business, a better relationship with her partner and her future children – all because she was able to see that her inability to say "no" at times was holding her back. She left determined to implement the changes.

I saw her a few months later and she looked and sounded like a different person, no longer stressed and exhausted. She had spoken with her boss and insisted that her work load be reduced; he agreed without question, not wanting to lose her. She spoke with her partner, who had turned out to be very willing to help out more; he had expressed surprise that she hadn't spoken up sooner. She was amazed to discover that he had been planning to speak to her about moving out of London, and he became really excited about the idea of getting married, starting a family, and setting up a business together. Within weeks of the session she had enrolled herself on a part-time business management course so that when they were ready to go she would have all the skills she needed to make her business a success. She told me that once she had experienced this version of the future there was nothing that would stop her from having it.

And of course the wonderful thing that we know about this work is that once clients see these events in the future, a seed gets planted, and the time frame shifts so that they find things happening far sooner than they ever imagined. I love seeing the excitement in a client's face as they understand just how amazing their life can be and knowing that they have the opportunity to make it happen.

Peter

In the chapter about soulmates I introduced you to my client, Peter, who was able to use his past life clearance to get rid of almost all of his anxiety around getting married, but there was a still a bit of a concern; his parents' marriage had been a disaster, and he really couldn't imagine what a healthy, happy marriage would look like. We decided it would be helpful for him to explore his future to see just what might be in store. He decided that five years in was enough.

The journey began:

ME: I want you to go to your most probable future if you stay on the same path you are on now; the one where you have doubts about the idea of getting married.

P: I am living alone, struggling to placate another girlfriend who is making demands about getting married and having a family. The anxiety is still there.

ME: I want you to explore an alternative version of the future where you release your anxiety and explore the idea of getting married.

P: I am married to my current girlfriend, who is looking radiant and beautiful; we have two small children, two boys who leapt at me lovingly as I get back from work. They have filled my home with joy and laughter.

ME: Good. Remember this good feeling; now I want you to meet with your higher self to see what advice it has for you.

P: He says that I have much love to share, and it is time for me to open my heart fully to all the joy that life can bring.

ME: I want you now to travel into your most optimal future, where you step up to your highest potential and really live your best life.

P: I am delighted to see the same wife and children, only this time my wife and I are in business together; the combination of our efforts has created a magnificent lifestyle for us both. I can see now how two minds can be so much better

234

than one, and all of the fears that I have been holding onto about not wanting to be "tied down," or restricted, by sharing my life with someone else, are dissolving.

ME: If you had any advice for "the you" in the present, what would it be?

P: As I look around at the wonderful life that is just out there waiting for me, I have to say, "What are you waiting for?"

His only worry from that point on was how he should propose.

EXERCISE 11: *Write Your Future*

Take a moment to close your eyes and imagine floating all the way out to the end of your life and imagine looking back.

1. What would you regret not having done?
2. What would you wish that you had done more of?
3. What or who was most important to you?
4. What would you like to leave behind as a legacy to the world?
5. If you were going to sum up what your life meant, what would it be?
6. How have you contributed or made a difference in the world?
7. What was the most important thing that you learnt along the way?
8. If the older and wiser you had some advice for the "You" now, what would it be?
9. What would you like your epitaph to be?

Write this information down on your final sheet. Once you have decided who you want to be, and the life that you desire, you can start to create a plan of action to get you there. By visualizing already having it, and imagining how good it will feel once you are there, you will activate the reticular activating system of your mind; this is the part of your mind that at the unconscious level is always looking for the things that you have labelled as important, and it can only know if things are important if you pay particular attention to them and be very clear about what you want.

One of the ways that you can do this is to create a vision board that has pictures of all the things that you want on it. You can spend a little time each day looking at it so that you give yourself a constant reminder of what you want and where it is that you are headed. A wise man once said, "If you don't know where you are going, you will end up somewhere else."

And if you find that you have too many choices, then you may want to explore each alternative one in more depth in a Future Life session.

In Conclusion

I hope that you have enjoyed the stories contained within this book and have begun to get a sense of just how powerful, amazing, and beautiful you and all the other billions of souls on this planet really are. At the beginning of this book I shared with you a lifetime I had in Atlantis, a time of beauty and peace and tranquility; it was an experience that has stayed with me, and I still think of it to this day. In that experience I was aware of the connection between the people and planet, the peace and the joy that existed for all. At that time there was, as there is now, a desire to expand the minds of people and their conscious awareness of who they really are. This had to be done without giving them too much too soon, for fear they would destroy themselves.

My subsequent journeys back to that life showed me that the end of that time was not all peace and joy. What I experienced, at the end, was a world where personal needs and desires had become more important than the needs of the greater good. Selfishness and greed had become a feature – not for all but for some. And because of the delicate nature of the system – a system that was powered by crystal energy, similar in some ways to atomic energy – an imbalance was started that meant that the society and the way it functioned could no longer survive. When a few chose to take, and take, and not respect the needs of the many, when they chose to abuse others and enslave them to do their will, they changed the energy and the vibrations of that energy. So much so that it could not be sustained as it was; the imbalance was so great that eventually the whole thing collapsed and everything was destroyed. It was a bit like mother earth having a major clutter clearing, an earthly cleanse, because she could no longer tolerate the abuse of her planet or the people who were such an integral part of the whole.

Some of the more enlightened souls knew that this would happen and escaped to other parts of the world, where they started to build smaller societies based on their superior knowledge. We see the signs of this in the monuments of the ancient Egyptians, the Mayans, the Aztecs, and many of the indigenous tribes who hold wisdom beyond that which we will ever know. In my work, and my research into past lives, I discovered that this was not the first time this had happened; my explorations revealed in great detail, from not just one but from many sources, that there was a time before this when another great civilization had emerged. This civilization suffered a very similar ending. It was called Lemuria. I believe that I was there too, alongside many of my colleagues, and curiously – or maybe not – many people I get to meet.

One girl in particular was sat next to me at a talk about hypnosis; there was no reference to past lives and yet as we sat working through an exercise she felt compelled to tell me that she and her family, who were from Siberia, communicated telepathically with one another and they believed that they had all been together in Lemuria. I was just working on this chapter when it happened, and so I am not sure which one of us was more surprised. Just another case of synchronicity for me, but what was strange about it was that I had been in two minds about whether to share my Lemurian story, thinking that for some readers it might seem a little far fetched – a little too "woo woo," and I didn't want to prevent people from taking this work seriously. After the conversation at the talk, my mind was made up; the experiences that I and my clients had had were going in.

The experiences of Lemuria were very similar to Atlantis: a beautiful and cultured civilization, with a wonderful community of people who were all connected, who worked together. There was no need for money; there was an abundance of food, water, and power, and electricity was freely available. Everyone who lived there had everything they needed and more; it was a time of great contentment, and there was a real sense of equality and freedom. Each person was connected via crystals to an energy grid; this grid was fed by the people who sent energy through it to a central source. This energy was then utilized for power and there was always enough – more than enough. My role, and the roles of several of my colleagues and clients at this time, was to be part of a team who monitored the energy and ensured that it was flowing properly – getting to the places it needed to be. It was a job I loved, as the energy had a powerful and delightful vibration.

The world at that time was sparsely populated so there was not a great need in the way of resources; each took just what they needed at the time, aware that there would always be enough. There was no need to store or take more than was needed; all flowed just as it should. However at this time things were not so rosy for beings from other planets, other dimensions. Some of these beings were suffering from great hardships and lack and, as a result, fear of annihilation. Many travelled to the earth, having heard of its bounties. They were welcomed and brought in to the communities but their fears and the mistrust, which had been generated through years and years of suffering, meant that they were prone to taking more from the grid than they needed. They would hoard and hide away foodstuffs, and even found ways to store the energy itself. On top of that their energy was very different to those on the earth plane; it was a different vibration and as a result it was not compatible with the energy of the grid. This meant they put nothing in. Instead of joining the communities that had welcomed them, they created communities of their own, separate and insular; this meant that the energy that had once flowed so beautifully and evenly got interrupted. Where one of their communities developed, the energy would be drained and not replenished. This started to cause problems for the maintenance of the grid; it started to become depleted and as a result the system was starting to fail. As monitors of this energy we noticed that this was happening, and we attempted to inform and warn the elders of the time, the ones who held the seats of government and power – albeit that it was not a government as we know it today, more a council. But this council was busy with its own affairs, a little like the church. These elders had been falsely led to believe by the leaders of these communities that they were contributing; they had not seen fit to question this, as we had, and believed it when they were told that all was well. It served these beings that had come from afar to charm and convince the elders that they were no threat and their charm was considerable.

The warnings from myself and the other members of the team were ignored. We were just "workers"; just some of the little people with jobs to do. Egos and a belief that they knew best got in the way and, in the end – frustrated and resigned to what would inevitably happen – we gave up. (This was surprisingly familiar to me with my challenge with the church in the current day.) The outsider communities continued to grow and the energy continued to be depleted until one day it just ran out; it was like someone had just pulled a plug and everything stopped. Knowing what the outcome of this would be, we all began searching for the people that mattered to us, our family and friends; we had tried to warn them, and some people had been able to leave to travel to other parts of the planet. But we never knew whether they survived or not because, as we were looking for our loved ones, a wave of energy – like that of an atom bomb – came towards us, in slow motion. We could see it as it approached, destroying everything in its path. We knew that if they had listened, if they had heeded the warnings, things could have been different; but now it was too late. The next thing we knew we were blasted into space and then it all went black.

In the healing part of the session we were able to go back and meet with the elders who apologized for not listening; they realized that it had been foolish pride, ego, and a desire to hold court, to have the power, to be seen as great and good providers, whatever the cost, that had led to the destruction of that world. They had allowed greed and selfishness to permeate and destroy what had once been so beautiful and so bountiful. It seems like such a powerful metaphor for these times. The people living on the earth right now have to be aware of the destructive power of greed and selfishness, which can be seen in so many cultures, where more is produced than is needed, more is consumed than is needed, and so much is destroyed in the process. People really have to start asking themselves, "Why? How did it come to this? Can the world really survive if things carry on the way they are?" At some point something will have to give.

In the Lemurian life people became resigned to the fact that we were heading for destruction and they gave up. They stopped trying to make a difference; they stopped taking proper care of themselves and their world – something that really mustn't happen again. Being here on this earth is such a privilege, such a gift, and I believe that it is up to each and every person here to do their bit. You did choose to be here, after all. You may ask what you can do to make a difference and the answer is easy: All you have to do is heal yourself; find ways to forgive those that have done you wrong, love unconditionally – both yourself and others, and restrain from the mass consumption and materialism that has swept over the world. If you can remember to live in the now, to have gratitude for all that you have, to share with your communities, and find ways to love others and your planet, then you will have done more than enough.

Someone said that if just one percent of the population shifted into a space of loving kindness we could shift the balance and get the world back on track; you can be part of that one percent, in your own way, shining a light, a beacon of love and respect that will shine out, and reach the many who have yet to see clearly what they are doing to themselves and to the world. If you just take responsibility for who you are and what you do while you are here, you will be helping to ensure that future generations live in a world that will sustain them, so that your children, if you have any, and your children's children will live happily and safely; so that they will have enough to eat and clean water to drink, to make sure that the oceans survive and the creatures that depend upon it for life. All it takes is for you to honour and respect your world in the way that the ancients did before you, where love and respect for everything was the way. If you want to contribute to the earth's healing, just follow the wise words of Gandhi; he said it perfectly when he asked people to be the change they wanted to see in the world.

Some people saw the end of 2012 as a time of fear and possible destruction, whilst others were waiting for the shift to come that would take us into the golden age that was foretold by Edgar Cayce, the Mayans, and the Hopi Indians, just to name a few. They believed that the golden age would provide people with every-thing they needed – if they made the choice to connect and work together in har-mony and in love – and I think they were right. There is still such a lot that can be learnt from your ancestors and the lives you lived before, particularly lives within the indigenous people of the world – the ones who treated and still treat the planet as a thing to be revered. I say, whatever the date is, you should clear your decks, clear out your mental, physical, and emotional clutter so that whatever happens, you are ready to live your life in the most optimal way; you are fully prepared for what great things may come. Just like the vestal virgins who waited for the lord, the wise ones who filled up their oil lamps so that when the time came they had all the light that they needed to bring the bridegroom home.

As I said before, you have to "Trust in God, but tie up your camel." As you move forward in your life, allow yourself to find a loving space within you and fo-cus on states of gratitude, joy, and abundance. As you focus on them, the universe and those that guide you know how to provide you with more of the same. I am sure that my disgruntled religion teachers would be delighted to know that the bible and its words of wisdom do have a place in my world today, only I choose to focus on the messages of love and empowerment, not just from that book but from all of the other books that I have read.

This book has been dedicated to all that are young in heart and in mind, and those who are ready and willing to take chances: to risk failing in order to learn, to risk being hurt so that they can know love, to embrace the changes life will bring, and to face their fears and their shadows head on. And, in the immortal words of Susan Jeffers, to feel the fear and do it anyway.

I have shared a lot of my favourite stories and sayings with you in this book, but my favourite saying of all time, the one I would like to share with you again, and the epitaph that I would like to have on my gravestone, if I have one, is this: Life gives you everything you need; you may not know you need it when you get it, but it will always become apparent later. I ask of you now:

- What is it that you need to do to be the best you can be?
- What are the gifts that you have been given, and what have you learnt along the way?
- What are you going to do with the time that you have left here on earth?
- In what small way can you contribute to the planet and the beings that live here?

Many of the past life journeys that I have shared with you in this book have a theme; either people connect with love, they share and evolve, or they feel separate and fearful and they destroy. The message is clear. You are free to choose the direction that your life and your future lives will follow. You can rewrite the stories. You can create a happier world for yourself and those around you, where dreams really do come true and where you can say, hand on heart: *There is no place like home.*

Earth is your home, for now; and just like Dorothy and her friends, be wise, be loving, and have courage in your convictions. Just be the best you that you can be – that's all it takes.

I would like to end as I began with a short Native American Indian story:

Once upon a time a wise man was speaking to his son.

"Son," he said, "inside of you there are two wolves. One is full of anger and hate, judgment and despair; the other is full of love and joy, acceptance and peace. These two wolves will wage a war within you that will sometimes tear you apart; but know this: only one of the wolves can win."

"Father," said the young boy, eyes wide open, "which of the wolves will be the winner?"

"Ah," said the man. "That all depends on which one you feed!"   Source unknown.

As I finish writing these pages I am taken all the way back to that "Why" question I was so fond of asking when I was a little girl, the one about why people were not being kinder and nicer to each other. As I ponder on it I am aware of just how important being kind really is. Because once you see that, there is no separation. We are all connected – all peoples, regardless of race or creed; all living creatures; the entire planet. We are all one and the same; it just makes sense. Jesus, who I believe was a very wise man and part of a very loving couple with his twin soul and wife Mary Magdalene, tried to teach this message through his stories all those years ago. Unfortunately, the message didn't really sink in. He said, "Love one another as you would be loved," and "As you do unto another, you do unto me." He didn't just mean himself; he meant the whole of humanity. His simple message was the truth; a truth that got buried under dogma and lies for a very long time. I am also aware of something very important that I would like to share with you before I go.

In the course of my travels I learnt that I didn't actually need an enlightened master to show me the way. Sure, the people I learnt from taught me a huge amount, and all the books that I read too, but the truth is that everything that you ever need to know about you and about life and about the universe is already inside you; all they do is remind you of what you already know. So I hope that you will take the time to be kind to yourself and the people around you, and to take the positive learnings and messages from this book and allow them to light up your journey through life, as you go forward on the path to Inner Freedom. The path may not always be smooth, but it will always be an adventure – if you choose for it to be so.

Will you follow the yellow brick road and see where it takes you?

I hope you will, and may your magic shoes take you to wherever it is that your heart desires.

With love and blessings,

Lorraine x

EXERCISE 12: *Personal Exploration*

You may be drawn to find a therapist to work with you as you start your journey to healing, or you can begin it by listening to the MP3 tracks that accompany this book. But know this: Just by reading this book your journey to change has already begun, and each time you access your unconscious – and the realms of infinite possibility – you will discover more and more about who you really are.

The answers you seek lie deep inside your mind. All you have to do is find a place and a time to discover them for yourself; you now have the key, and the treasure is right at your fingertips. And whatever you discover, always remember to be grateful for it all, no matter what.

There are two free MP3 tracks for you to listen to – these can be found on the media page on my website – *www.innerjourneys.co.uk*. The first track is designed to take you into deep relaxation and the second to take you into a positive past life.

If you want to explore lives where unfinished business or unresolved karma is present and needs to be cleared, then you may wish to consider seeing a practitioner. That way you can ensure that you clear away any unhelpful clutter and deal with any unfinished business of your own. There will be information about how to find a reputable practitioner at the end of this book.

As you start to build an idea of your other lives and the stories that emerge, you will begin to get a sense that they are all just stories, all just experiences that your soul has on its journey to wholeness. Each life lived is part of a learning process, and so in each moment of your life and in each experience that you have you must always take the time to wonder: "What can I learn from this?" This will apply especially to the challenging events and the challenging people that appear in your life; and as you learn to be the observer of the challenges rather than the victim of them, you will find that you reclaim your power and a real sense of inner freedom.

I would be delighted to hear from you
and hear about any of the experiences
that you have had as a result of your explorations.
You can send any information to me at
info@innerjourneys.co.uk.

About The Author
Lorraine Flaherty

Lorraine Flaherty is a international therapist and trainer, who has created the process called Inner Freedom Therapy, which incorporates the tools of hypnotherapy, NLP, Past Life Regression, Future Life Progression, the Life Between Lives, Inner Child Therapy, and Clearing Energy and Spirit Attachments to help people to reach their full potential. She teaches clinical hypnosis to medical students, doctors, dentists, and midwives in United Kingdom universities including Oxford and Cambridge.

She currently has a busy Central London practice, and runs workshops and retreats on a variety of topics, all connected to personal empowerment.

She is very passionate about helping people to change their lives, and her experience has taught her that the answers to most problems lie within the individual. Accessing the unconscious realms allow for this information to emerge and solutions to be found.

For more information, you can go to
www.innerjourneys.co.uk, www.empoweredlives.co.uk,
or you can email her at: *info@innerjourneys.co.uk.*

To find a Therapist or for Information on how to become a Therapist

LORRAINE FLAHERTY *www.innerjourneys.co.uk*
www.empoweredlives.co.uk.
To learn PAST LIFE REGRESSION THERAPY: *www.regressionacademy.com*
To learn LIFE BETWEEN LIVES: *www.regressionacademy.com*
To learn FUTURE LIFE PROGRESSION: *www.futurelifeprogression.co.uk*
For the PAST AND FUTURE LIFE SOCIETY: *www.pfls.com*
For PSYCHIC READINGS with Anne Jirsch: *www.annejirsch.com*
To learn CLINICAL HYPNOTHERAPY at Hypnova: *www.hypnova.com*
To learn NLP with Jessica Robbins: *www.jessicarobbins.com*
To learn NLP with Richard Bandler: *www.nlplifetraining.com*
For THE ANGELS OF ATLANTIS/ALCHEMY OF VOICE
with Stewart Pearce: *www.alchemyofvoice.com*
For ANGELIC REIKI with Alexandra Wenman:
www.angelic-intervention.co.uk
For ENVISION COACHING with Cathy Dixon: *www.empoweredlives.co.uk*
For PSYCHIC SURGERY with Brian Walsh (The Miracle Man):
www.brianwalsh.co.uk
For 5 DIMENSIONAL BODY MOVEMENT with Mark Chesters:
www.markchesters.com
For MEDITATION with Sandy Newbigging: *www.sandynewbigging.com*
For CRYSTALS AND BOOKS at Stepping Stones:
www.steppingstonesgreenwich.co.uk
For PROTECTION OILS from Divine Essence: *www.divineaspect.com*
For SPIRITUAL HEALING or SPIRITUAL EMERGENCIES
with Janet Treloar: *www.planet-therapies.com*
To find a PRACTITIONER in your area, go to:
www.regressionacademy.co.uk
www.plra.co.uk
www.pastliferegression.co.uk
For SPIRIT RELEASE, go to:
www.spiritual-regression-therapy-association.com
www.spiritrelease.com

Recommended Reading List

CLINICAL HYPNOSIS
Ursula James, *Clinical Hypnosis Handbook* (Radcliffe Publishing, 2005)
——, *You Can Be Amazing* (Century, 2007)
——, *The Source* (Preface Publishing, 2011)
Stephen Wolinsky, *Trances People Live* (The Bramble Company, 1991)

REINCARNATION
S. Rinpoche, *The Tibetan Book of the Living and Dying* (Rider, 1992)

COLLECTIVE UNCONSCIOUS
Carl Jung, *Archetypes and the Collective Unconscious* (Routledge, 1991)
——, *Synchronicity: An Acausal Connecting Principle* (Bollingen,1952,1993)

PAST LIVES
Edgar Cayce, *On Atlantis* (Paperback Library,1968)
Dr. Ian Stevenson, *Twenty Cases Suggestive of Reincarnation* (University Press of
    Virginia, 1974)
——, *Where Reincarnation and Biology Intersect* (Praeger Publishers, 1997)
Andy Tomlinson, *Healing the Eternal Soul* (O Books, 2006)
——, *Transforming the Eternal Soul* (From the Heart Press, 2011)
Dr. Brian Wiess, *Many Lives Many Master* (Piatkus, 1994)
——, *Through Time into Healing* (Piatkus, 1998)
——, *Only Love Is Real* (Piatkus, 1997)
——, *Messages from the Masters* (Piatkus, 2000)
——, *Same Soul, Many Bodies* (Piatkus, 2004)
——, *Mirrors of Time: Using Regression for Physical, Emotional
    and Spiritual Healing* (Hay House UK, 2004)
M. L. LaBay, *Past Life Regression: A Guide for Practitioners* (Trafford Publishing,
    2004)
Roger Woolger, *Other Lives, Other Selves* (Bantam Books, 1988)
——, *Healing Your Past Lives* (Sounds True Inc, 2004)
Winafred Lucas, *Regression Therapy: A Handbook for Professionals* (Deep Forest
    Press, 1996)
Andy Tomlinson, *Transforming the Eternal Soul* (From the Heart Press, 2011)
Ian Lawton, *The Book of the Soul* (RS Press, 2004)

——, *The Holographic Soul* (RS Press, 2010)
——, *The Little Book of the Soul* (RS Press, 2010)

FUTURE LIVES
Anne Jirsch, *The Future Is Yours* (Piatkus, 2008)
——, *Instant Intuition* (Piatkus, 2007)

LIFE BETWEEN LIVES
Dr. Michael Newton, *Journey of Souls* (Llewellyn Press, 1994)
——, *Destiny of Souls* (Llewellyn press, 2000)
——, *Life Between Lives: Hypnotherapy for Spiritual Regression* (Llewellyn, 2004)
Andy Tomlinson and Ian Lawton, *Exploring the Eternal Soul* (O Books, 2007)
——, *The Wisdom of the Soul* (RS Press, 2010)
——, *History of the Soul* (RS Press, 2010)
——, *The Big Book of the Soul* (RS Press, 2010)
R. Shwartz, *Your Soul's Plan* (Frog Books, 2007)

ANGELS OF ATLANTIS
Stewart Pearce, *The Angels of Atlantis: Twelve Mighty Forces to Transform Your Life Forever* (Findhorn Press, 2011)
——, *The Heart's Note: Sounding Love in Your Life from Your Heart's Secret Chamber* (Findhorn Press, 2010)
——, *The Alchemy of Voice: Transform and Enrich Your Life Through the Power of Your Voice* (Findhorn Press, 2010)

NLP AND HYPNOSIS
Paul McKenna, *I Can Make You Happy* (Bantam Press, 2011)
——, *Change Your Life in Seven Days* (Bantam Press, 2010)
——, *Instant Confidence* (Bantam Press, 2006)
Richard Bandler, *Get the Life You Want* (Harper Element, 2009)
——, *The Secrets of Being Happy* (IM Press, Incorporated, 2011)
——, *The Ultimate Introduction to NLP* (Harper Collins, 2011)
Robert Dilts, *Beliefs* (Metamorphous Press Oregon, 1993)

MEDITATION
Sandy Newbigging, *Thunk* (Findhorn Press, 2012)

SPIRIT RELEASEMENT
L. Ireland-Frey, *Freeing the Captives* (Hampton Roads Publishing, 1999)
Shakuntala Modi, MD, *Remarkable Healings* (Hampton Roads Publishing, 1997)
W. Baldwin, *Spirit Releasement Therapy* (Headline Books, 1995)
Sue Allen, *Spirit Release: A Practical Handbook* (O Books, 2007)

Dolores Cannon, *Between Death and Life: Conversations with a Spirit* (Gateway, 2003)

INNER CHILD
Brandon Bays, *The Journey* (Thorsons, 1999)
John Bradshaw, *The Homecoming* (Piatkus, 1991)
Debbie Ford, *Dark Side of the Light Chasers* (Hodder and Stoughton, 1998)
——, *Why Good People Do Bad Things* (Harper Collins, 2008)
P. Parks, *Rescuing the Inner Child* (Human Horizons series, 2002)

MAYAN AND HOPI PROPHECIES
Drunvalo Melchizedek, *Serpent of the Light: Beyond 2012 - The Movement of the Earth's Kundalini and the Rise of the Female Light, 1949 to 2013* (Weiser Books, 2008)
——, *Living in the Heart: How to Enter into the Sacred Space Within the Heart* (Light Technology Publishing, 2003)

MYTHOLOGY
Joseph Campbell, *The Hero's Journey: Joseph Campbell on His Life and Work* (Harper & Row, 1991)

COSMIC ORDERING
Barbell Mohr, *The Cosmic Ordering Service* (Hodder, 2006)
——, *Instant Cosmic Ordering* (Hodder, 2008)
——, *The 21 Golden Rules for Cosmic Ordering* (Hay House, 2011)

LAW OF ATTRACTION
Abraham Hicks, *Ask and It Is Given* (Hay House, 2008)
——, *The Law of Attraction* (Hay House, 2007)
Rhonda Byrne, *The Secret* (Simon & Schuster Ltd., 2006)

RELIGION
The Bible

OTHER SOURCES
Wikipedia, Google
The Akashic Records, The Collective Consciousness

Thank You

I would like to take this opportunity to say thank you to all the people who have helped me on my journey through life and to those who contributed to this book coming together. Firstly, to my parents, for the not so enviable task of raising me; I was not the easiest child, and I thank you for your love and support over the years. I would also like to thank my sister for always being there for me. I would like to thank the rest of my family – for all the times together good and bad. My friends, of whom there are too many to mention but you know who you are, I love you all. To my ex-partners, a big thank you for both the challenges and the love that we shared. My teachers: Thank you for being inspiring and sharing your wisdom. To my students, thank you for listening. To my clients, thank you for being ready to change. To my guides, thank you for helping me to find the right path. To the angels, thank you for keeping me safe, for your unconditional love, and the steady supply of parking spaces when I need them. Thank you to all the people at Findhorn Press for believing in me and my book. Finally, to all the people who bought the book – a very, very big thank you to you all.

FINDHORN PRESS

Life-Changing Books

For a complete catalogue,
please contact:

Findhorn Press Ltd
117-121 High Street,
Forres IV36 1AB,
Scotland, UK

t +44 (0)1309 690582
f +44 (0)131 777 2711
e info@findhornpress.com

or consult our catalogue online
(with secure order facility) on
www.findhornpress.com

For information on the Findhorn Foundation:
www.findhorn.org